On South Mountain

The Dark Secrets of
the Goler Clan

David Cruise &
Alison Griffiths

VIKING

VIKING
Published by the Penguin Group
Penguin Books Canada Ltd, 10 Alcorn Avenue, Toronto, Ontario, Canada M4V 3B2
Penguin Books Ltd, 27 Wrights Lane, London w8 5TZ, England
Viking Penguin, a division of Penguin Books USA Inc., 375 Hudson Street, New York, New York 10014, U.S.A.
Penguin Books Australia Ltd, Ringwood, Victoria, Australia
Penguin Books (NZ) Ltd, cnr Rosedale and Airborne Roads, Albany, Auckland 1310, New Zealand

Penguin Books Ltd, Registered Offices: Harmondsworth, Middlesex, England

10 9 8 7 6 5 4 3 2 1

Printed and bound in the U.S.A. on acid free paper. ∞

CANADIAN CATALOGUING IN PUBLICATION DATA

Cruise, David, 1950–
    On South Mountain: the dark secrets of the Goler clan

ISBN 0-670-87388-8

1. Goler family. 2. Incest – Nova Scotia – South Mountain Region (Annapolis and Kings). I. Griffiths, Alison, 1953– . II. Title.

HV 6570.9.C3C78 1997   364.15'36   C97-930392-3

Visit Penguin Canada's web site at www.penguin.ca

To Jellybean and the children of the Goler Clan
—both past and present

Contents

Note to Readers

IN THE COURSE OF RESEARCHING and writing this book we've made several decisions that we hope readers will understand and appreciate. The most difficult task we faced was tracking down the Goler children, then convincing them to talk. We were successful in finding them all. In two cases, the children had no recollection of their time on the Mountain. We chose not to disrupt their lives or spark unwanted recollections.

Several of the children have gone to considerable lengths to hide themselves and although they did talk to us, in the end they remained fearful of exposure. We have protected their anonymity by giving them all false names. We have also disguised the physical descriptions and location of any victims we felt could be discovered by reading this book. Regrettably, we felt obliged to disguise the names of three of the adult Clan members who were convicted because to identify them would have led to the children.

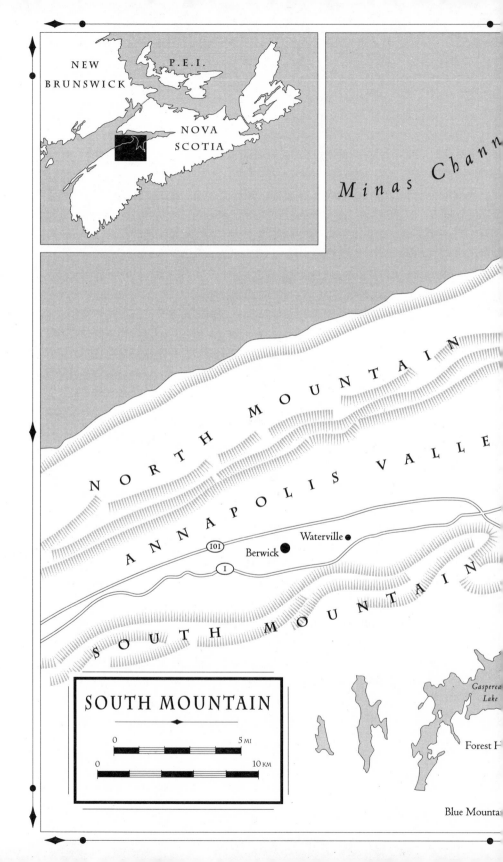

NEW
BRUNSWICK

P.E.I.

NOVA
SCOTIA

Minas Chann

NORTH MOUNTAIN

ANNAPOLIS VALLE

101

Waterville

Berwick

1

SOUTH MOUNTAIN

Gasperea
Lake

Forest H

SOUTH MOUNTAIN

0   5 MI

0   10 KM

Blue Mounta

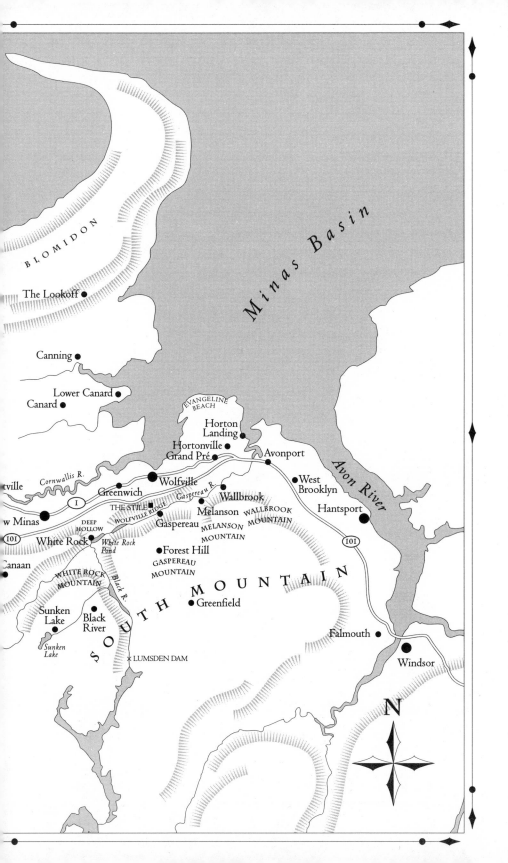

Goler Family Tree

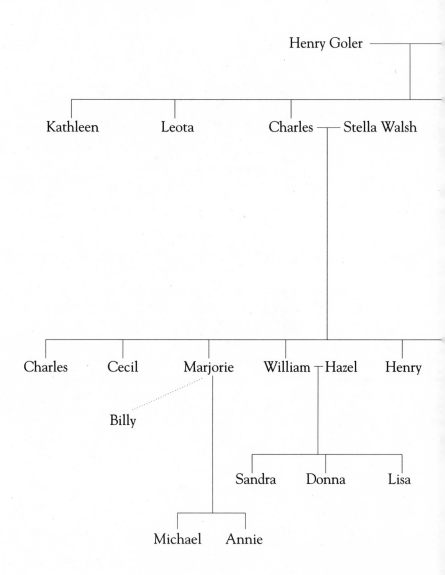

———— Mary Walsh

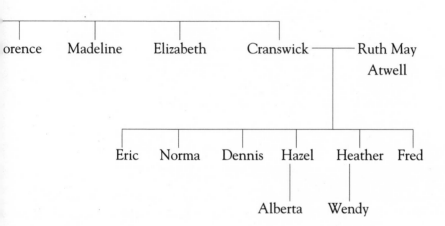

orence   Madeline   Elizabeth   Cranswick ———— Ruth May
                                                       Atwell

                    Eric   Norma   Dennis   Hazel   Heather   Fred

                                    Alberta   Wendy

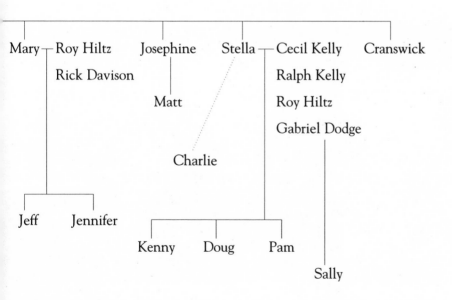

Mary ⊤ Roy Hiltz   Josephine   Stella ⊤ Cecil Kelly   Cranswick
        Rick Davison   Ralph Kelly
                        Matt   Roy Hiltz
                                             Gabriel Dodge
                            Charlie

Jeff   Jennifer

            Kenny   Doug   Pam

                                    Sally

PART ONE

Chapter One

The Mountain &
the Valley

◆ THE STILE IS QUIET. THE ACRES OF
coarse grass surrounding it are cut regularly, giving the illusion of use.
But, like a forgotten memorial to an obscure event or individual, a
mild long-term disinterest is evident. Even in the height of summer,
the browning stubble is barely trodden, save for a narrow path from
the small, gravel parking lot down to the Stile itself. Though the view
is still gratifying, the once unimpeded panorama to the south has been
partly obscured by bushes. A jungle of suckers, crowning the apple
trees that rim the lower section, reach to heaven from the cracked
and peeling arms of old branches. In early fall, when the ripe, juicy
lushness of the Annapolis Valley's famous apple crop tumbles joyously
from bins, barrels and barns, the Stile's meagre offerings drop to the
ground dull-skinned, shrivelled and diseased.

Half a century ago the Stile was an important place. Poised on a
gentle ridge, it separated two worlds—the picturesque university
town of Wolfville snugged in the Annapolis Valley on one side, and
on the other the Gaspereau Valley lying in the shadow of South
Mountain, a seventy-five-mile chain of ancient hills that form the
Valley's southern boundary. In those days the Stile was a destination.

Often friends would climb up the steps leading over the fence, find a comfortably worn spot and share a thermos of tea while ruminating, gossiping or confiding as they gazed over the gentle beauty of Gaspereau Valley tucked against the Mountain slopes to the south. "Over the brow of the hill, thousands have come," observed Esther Clark Wright, a Stile devotee, "laden with kettles and pots, with baskets and rugs, old Wolfville residents, summer visitors, lovers hand in hand, college classes, high school classes, boy scouts, girl guides, strangers and sojourners, their laughter echoing down the years, their songs listing in the memory."

The top step of the Stile was rubbed smooth and bent in the middle by hundreds of bottoms, young and old, which perched upon it. On the posts and along the rails, risers and steps, the initials and names of students, lovers, tourists and children were carved and recarved. Amid the rough letters a bit of artistry: flowers, hearts and flourishes punctuated by streaks of pipe soot and the round black brand of stubbed-out cigarettes. Farther down the Stile park, on the edge of a tangle of spruce trees that rose out of the village of Gaspereau to meet the Ridge, lay the charred remains of camp-fires, the odd bit of forgotten picnic silverware and the occasional illicit liquor bottle.

A Sunday picnicker once knocked together a table and bench seats for easier Sabbath munching, though students from Acadia University in Wolfville preferred to strew blankets on the grass and lounge with studied casualness as they flirted, smoked and imbibed while solving the ills of the world. The students were drawn mainly from dozens of communities sprinkled throughout the Annapolis Valley, from hard-working fishing villages on Nova Scotia's south shore or from farming hamlets in the province's Bible belt, where church was merely the weekly icing on a life lived contentedly and seriously according to the Word. To these wide-eyed youngsters the glamour, worldliness and sheer bustle of Acadia University was thrilling and the Stile epitomized what made the town of Wolfville different from any place they had ever known. Things happened there. A famous Irish poet might appear one afternoon to take in the view, or perhaps a British cabinet minister, a Nobel-prize-winning chemist or even a movie star might arrive, arm-in-arm with a child-hood friend who happened to be teaching at Acadia.

It was only a matter of weeks after their arrival before the students' home towns appeared hopelessly insular and intellectually frozen by comparison. Brookvale, for example, was a typical, though mythical, Valley community, created by writer Delacy Evans Foster to disguise his real birthplace, a tiny village too small to merit even a pinprick on most maps. In a place where "the Devil was as real as a note in the bank," his dry, jabbing observations about his neigh-bours might have caused them to mistake him for someone who dwelled in Hell's great, roiling cauldron of sin.

Life in Brookvale, concluded Foster, could best be summed up as "remote, dull, stupid, backward, and lonely." He emphasized that there were many similar communities from one end of the Annapo-lis Valley to the other. In 1948, just before Foster moved away, the spark of industry and progress had reached Brookvale, bringing with it flivvers, radios, telephones, electric lights and even daily mail—in short, "all the luxuries of life except a Lion's Club." But the per-sonality of the little cluster of houses was far too entrenched to be dislodged by any gadget dreamed up by Henry Ford, Thomas Edison or Alexander Graham Bell. "It was still drab, dull, stupid, and lonely," sighed Foster as he packed his bags for retirement in Middleton, a nearby Valley metropolis of five hundred people.

Out of the hay fields, apple orchards and market gardens of such hamlets came the young adults who made the pilgrimage to Wolfville and Acadia University. Most Valley parents considered Dalhousie, in the city of Halifax sixty-five miles away, to be too worldly for their children, not to mention too secular. These young men and women, at first hesitant and awkward with their freedom, soon gulped back university life as if fearing it would be snatched from them at any moment.

For most students the first real taste of their new existence came at the annual initiation-week corn boil held at the Stile. From that point on, the small park set on the Ridge dividing Wolfville from Gaspereau and the South Mountain became a regular fixture in their lives. The Stile also bade them adieu when their time at Acadia ended. Every spring, on a morning that virtually every student recalls as exquisitely fine, the graduating class hauled baskets of food up to the Stile for the annual Baccalaureate Sunday breakfast. The day of celebration never failed to rouse and rile Wolfville residents. The pious objected to the Sabbath's desecration and the fallen to having their sleep-in disrupted when the students returned to the town in cavalcade, horns honking and voices bellowing, supported by assorted musical instruments.

The Stile was such a central element in university and community life that when the town celebrated Acadia's one hundredth anniversary in 1938, it was the only place considered for the Sunday vesper service. "The weather co-operated, the preacher was excellent, and at the close of the service a trio of girls sang the prayer," recalled Esther Clark Wright fondly. "'God be in my head and in my understanding; God be in mine eyes, and in my looking...' We had been watching the shadow of Wolfville Ridge creep slowly up South Mountain as the sun sank lower and lower across the Basin, beyond the northern hills. It was a cold evening, and in the pink and purple sky above South Mountain, the full moon was already showing light. We had added another to the cluster of memories around the Stile."

The Stile also played host to celebrations of a different sort. Generations of hands, clammy with anticipation of a marriage proposal to be offered or received, rubbed the wood of the Stile to a high polish. The sweet agony of getting out just the right words in question or response filled spring and summer evenings with the tension of love. So many proposals were tendered and accepted at the Stile that a young woman had a difficult time, at a certain point in her courtship, suppressing her anticipation when a beau suggested an evening of sunset watching on the Ridge. After the question was popped, relief at having survived the moment settled into wonder, and couples happily indulged in hours of thrilling discussion about future homes, jobs and children.

The Stile's location, at the top of the hump rising from Wolfville's back, exacted a price out of city-softened legs and fine calf-hide footwear. The tart-tongued and vigorous Esther Clark Wright, first a student (class of '19) and then a lecturer at Acadia University, insisted that all her many visitors, unless they were missing a limb or bed-ridden, journey to the Stile. "It does not, we believe, show a due spirit of reverence for this valuable institution to approach it in any other way," she declared firmly as she marshalled group after group up Wolfville's Highland Avenue towards the Ridge and the Stile. Wright, a force of nature akin to an Atlantic hurricane, reeled off a running commentary of sights and oddities along the way. Her guests, who usually began to heave and blow long before the halfway mark, were grateful for the stream of historical footnotes that caused her to stop now and again to emphasize a point.

A sociologist by education, a social reformer by passion, a writer by inclination and an enthusiastic and caustic gossip by avocation, Wright let no aspect of the human condition pass without judgment. As they walked she pointed out certain houses along Highland Avenue that many praised for their quaint Victorian charm. To her they were an abomination of "fussiness." When a guest inquired about her preferred style of architecture, Wright pointed down the hill to the stone Baptist church and said with finality, "The pews in there suit me."

Wright had an opinion on everything and everyone. In this lumpy, awkward house a peculiar man lived who disgracefully refused to wear a hat during an age when headgear was as essential as footwear. He built a handful of row houses, dismissed by her as "stalls." Over there in another house a man had died, leaving behind his wife and daughter. The widow refused to budge from her property and soon died herself, leaving the place to the daughter, who turned every room into a cattery until the stench and cacophony galvanized the neighbours into forcing the Board of Health to clean the place out.

A pair of selfish old spinsters lived here, there dwelled a man rumoured to possess a secret and illicit fortune from darkest Africa. Farther on, just as Wright's companions were getting desperate for a rest, was the home of ancient I.B. Oakes, Wolfville's oldest man. Determined to show that age, as he neared the century mark, was no barrier to activity, Oakes tackled chores shunned by much younger men. The "old dear" once decided to set up a ladder and

remove the storm windows for the coming warm weather, but he top-
pled over, head first through the windows. "And it was such good
glass, too," bemoaned his long-suffering missus. Oakes emerged
unscathed and unchastened.

In yet another gabled house with requisite porch had lived a
daughter made tragic and half mad by her widowed mother's well-
meaning but impossible demands on her. The mother's fierce spirit,
which kept the family together after the father's early death, crushed
the girl, who perched on life like a restless bird, alighting but never
roosting. She died shortly after her mother, and Wright passed on a
local's observation: "Wouldn't her mother be disgusted with her for
dying so soon."

On Wright would forge, past a former tea-room and the old telephone exchange where many a love affair had been consummated
or broken, always with the curious operator listening in. Just before
orchards and fields replaced Wolfville's houses stretched the unpleas-
ant mud of Pleasant Street, the last road before the Ridge. And
beyond it the walkers, beginning to think seriously about rebellion,
would suddenly be stunned by what had been hidden until then—
a vista stretched out below them that instantly dispelled the unchar-
itable thoughts they'd been harbouring about their host. To the
north, across the Valley, Blomidon Mountain's chalky, regal nose jut-
ted out into the folded red siltstone of Minas Basin. To the east and
west the gentle landscape was seamed by the fences of neat farms
with long rows of apple orchards. Wright, after allowing her guests
to inhale the beauty, shooed them along the farm track at the top
of the Ridge until they reached the Stile.

In those days, the Stile was never merely a stopping place, a way-
side to stretch limbs and admire the view perfunctorily before moving on. It was a focus of many community lives—at certain times of
the year bird-watchers, at others students or ladies and their young
men, on Sundays family gatherings. It was a small star in all that
made the Valley exquisite, and its privileged location allowed anyone to drink in the soft diversity of a blessed land, its rises and hollows, tidal flats, dikes, rivers and tidy farmland. There was no other
spot that spoke of the Valley so completely.

Today, the Stile is a concrete edifice, listing slightly to one side. The fence it straddled has long since gone. Around it the orderly park waits patiently for the odd visitor. The houses on Highland Avenue are little changed, though asphalt has tamed Pleasant Street's mud and the farm track along the Wolfville Ridge is now paved and officially called Ridge Road. Few students bother to drive, much less walk, to the Stile any more, and many Wolfville residents don't even know it exists, let alone what it once meant. Houses have overtaken the apple orchards on the slopes above the university, and a modern highway has now amputated the shoulder of South Mountain just below the Stile. The students' short cut, a path directly from the Stile through the woods and down to the university, is overgrown and its twin, the path leading south to the miniature Gaspereau Valley and South Mountain, is only faintly visible in the brush. What does remain is the still breathtaking panorama. But it is a view that hides as much as it reveals. The eye takes in a picture of the land but receives no sense of its essence. Only the determined and curious will discover the disharmony and difference. The Valley and the Mountain are as unlike as any two species can be.

The section of valley, shore and mountain commanded by the Stile is no one thing; nothing binds its regions together like Saskatchewan's broad swath of short-grass prairie, the Rockies' peaks, northern Ontario's endless symphony of rock, tree and lake or the west coast's fjords. Its sections are arranged separate and distinct from one another, though often mere miles apart. It's a surprising discovery to outsiders who consider the Annapolis Valley a homogeneous entity comprising apple orchards and quaint towns. So much in the Valley is cheek-by-jowl yet worlds apart. Dikeland undulates faintly against traditional farmland but makes no connection with the fields and orchards, the prominence of Blomidon seems to disdain the pallid flatness of all it surveys, the scraggy brush of South Mountain carries nothing of itself into the towns strung along the Valley floor and, as the Annapolis Valley pushes west, dunes and heather erupt inexplicably and just as suddenly disappear thirty miles along.

The biggest surprise, if you venture from the Stile, is South Mountain itself. From the Ridge it appears as a façade of green, a monochromatic palette stretching across the horizon, gentle and yielding, broken only by the narrow Gaspereau Valley against its lower slopes. But the Mountain, as locals call it, serves up mysteries at every turn. So lush from a distance, the ancient, once towering hills are mostly granite, thinly covered with a dusting of coarse, grainy, infertile soil. The plant life creating the mirage of softness is the result of eons of desperate upward striving.

Even the most tentative foray onto the Mountain uncovers the unexpected. Streams cut deep chasms in the ground as if they were mighty rivers and time-scoured boulders appear as if dropped by a careless hand. In an area of stunted, third-growth scrub, a majestic three-hundred-year-old pine survives on the shore of a boggy lake. Deep in an ancient river-carved gorge, a sparkle catches the eye— a deposit of quartzite. In an abandoned gravel pit, a coffin-like hunk of granite sits, inexplicably singular in its massiveness, among broken scree.

Dense fog enshrouds one depression, while the next—to all appearances identical—is clear. Suddenly, like a miracle, a tiny perfect valley appears imbedded in the Mountain like a thumbprint, but its fertility ends abruptly as valley meets mountain and the soil depth once again shrinks to nothing.

Life has a hard struggle here, but once established it clings ferociously.

There is an eeriness about the succession of hills that make up the South Mountain chain. When alone among them you feel more solitary and isolated than in the Rockies or on the vast unpopulated stretches of the Prairies. Standing in contemplation one sometimes feels an invisible hand on the shoulder. There is a sense of hauntedness here—of beings offstage, of events unformed but waiting.

Human implements do not always work as advertised on the Mountain. Cellular phones are erratic—working one day and not the next, in the same spot. Radio and television reception are chancy at best, and machinery of all types seems to break down more often and wear out more quickly than elsewhere. Though people have logged, quarried and mined the Mountain, built power stations, rammed roads through and settled it after a fashion—unless one is in direct contact with these works there is no sense that humankind has ever set foot, ever had an impact on South Mountain.

Weather adds to the Mountain's mystery. The entire Valley sits in the midst of a notoriously fickle and unpredictable weather tract. Storms drive in from the south and west as three powerful natural phenomena vie for control—the frigid Labrador current, the warm Gulf Stream and the prevailing dry westerlies. The counterpunch of hurricanes pummels the area every few decades. On the Mountain every extreme of weather is intensified and no one who lives beyond the Ridge has much patience with those from the Valley who complain about the vagaries of the four seasons.

The separateness of the Mountain is enshrined in its geology, as if the continents collaborated a few hundred million years ago and decided to ostracize it. Precambrian volcanoes, three-quarters of a billion years ago, laid down a blueprint for what the Mountain was to become when molten magma poured into the folded arms of massive young mountains thrusting upward from the oceans. After 400 million years, erosion had smoothed the sharp relief and rubbed the mountains down to mere hills, shedding their layers into sandstone, shale and limestone, which muddied the seas and filled chasms and crevasses with deposits that time and pressure would turn into hard, resistant quartzite. For 80 million years the earth's land masses edged towards each other across the Iapetus Ocean. Nova Scotia was pushed along, riding the prow of the great continental drift towards its eventual embrace with Africa.

During this time, hot, dry winds scoured the sandy landscape of equatorial Annapolis Valley. Its rises and dips were gentle, the vista scorched and colourless, except when torrential rains washed across its broad plains, driving thousands of tons of silt into the narrow strait now separating North America from Africa. During this time also, the land that was to become South Mountain was already pulling itself away, establishing its uniqueness.

Life, eagerly taking hold around the planet, shunned the Mountain. Superficially, little distinguished the region from anywhere else. It shared the same weather as the rest of southern Nova Scotia but the great ocean, which receded as the continents marched together, deposited less of itself on the Mountain than elsewhere. The granite and quartzite rock making up much of South Mountain held more firmly against the wearing forces of wind and rain than elsewhere in the Valley.

Despite the massive geological upheaval that racked the globe for the next half a billion years, its character changed very little. It is borne out in the lakes, rivers, forests and rocky outcroppings of the Mountain—and in the people. They too are hard, unyielding, determined—altogether different.

The life-giving swamps in what was to become the Valley's lowlands were also found on the Mountain but the deposits of marine sediment, rich in the Valley, were thin in comparison. Warm shallow seas over much of Nova Scotia nurtured the early plant life. Sea lilies flourished in the Valley but their evidence ends in New Canaan, a tiny community on the lip of the Mountain. The fossilized signatures of fish scales, twigs, worm burrows and arthropods, insect-like creatures that had evolved sufficiently to have jointed appendages, are found in the Valley silt and sandstone, but nowhere on the Mountain.

The courtship of the great continents ended, as it was destined to do, with a cataclysmic union of tectonic plates colliding and bending to each other's will. At last the supercontinent of Pangaea was formed, trapping the tiny island of Nova Scotia at its heart. There it would remain for 200 million years until a massive tectonic clash flung the continents apart and Nova Scotia drifted north across the 40th parallel. The collision was stunning, touching off an epoch of jousting among the land masses that would create mountains to dwarf the Himalayas. Geologists coyly call it an "episode," a 10-million-year-long incident around the late morning of the planet's life. Volcanoes spewed out billions of tons of granite magma, building a chain of jagged peaks along the spine of Nova Scotia—the South Mountain Batholith.

Alexander Pope was not thinking of the Annapolis Valley when he borrowed the Greek word *bathos* and re-crafted it to mean a swift, ignominious come-down, a descent from the high and noble into the mire of the commonplace. And when geologists reborrowed the term for South Mountain, they were simply describing its peaks, which, over the ages, descended from their lofty heights into gently rising large hills that provided the southern boundary of the Annapolis Valley. But one might find grim amusement in the antecedents of the word in light of later events.

A serenity of colour and form marks the Minas Basin today. It is gentleness incarnate; even Blomidon's prominence can't interrupt the broad soothing expanse of tidal flats and adjacent dikeland. Standing a quarter of a mile out, but still only knee-deep in the womb-like temperature of the Basin's summer water, there is nothing to disturb the eye. The hardness of South Mountain is but a blur of green in the distance. But beneath the enveloping red mud lies a once powerful fault, one of the determinators of North America's recent history. Sleeping today, the Cobequid Fault helped spoil the marriage of the continents and push the dinosaurs towards extinction.

As Triassic gave way to Jurassic, rifting stretched and thinned the crustal surface like an old woman's skin. Lava, rich in basalt, erupted from the great cracks opening up as the continents reluctantly gave up their bond. More than 150 million years ago, layer upon layer of basalt flowed hotly across the Fundy landscape on the edge of the Cobequid Fault. North Mountain was born to create the northern boundary of the Annapolis Valley, ending in the thrust of Blomidon into Minas Basin and the Bay of Fundy.

North Mountain is as different from its southern sibling as any two individuals can be. Where the granite of South Mountain has resisted time, creature and man, only grudgingly revealing its secrets to the most determined, North Mountain is a treasure of accessible surprises. The Blomidon Peninsula whips out into the Bay of Fundy like a cowlick and hugs a wondrous array of time's tracks against the cliffs of the inner curve, called Scots Bay. Evidence of great lava floods, forests, tropical lakes, prehistoric life from lowly worms to dinosaurs are embedded in the gas bubbles of the volcanic basalt. Amethyst, agate, jasper and chalcedony yield themselves up to hammer and chisel along with dozens of other tongue-twisting minerals and gemstones.

Tectonic clashes, volcanic uprising and continental drift laid down the essential character of the Mountain and the Valley with spectacular episodes of conflict—a character still evident in the rocks, cliffs, shoreline and lakes of the two disparate kin. But it was left to the inexorable crawl of the glaciers to sculpt the face of both Mountain and Valley, to caress the uplands' sharp edges, patiently grind down its stark peaks and lie thick and heavy on the lowlands, pressing, pressing, forcing the land down to submit to the sea.

The ice came and retreated four times, scoring the granite mass of South Mountain, occasionally leaving its calling card in the form of a huge slab of rock sitting alone in a field, as if dropped from the sky. By the time of the last great glacier, ten thousand years ago, the peaks of the Mountain, twice risen higher than those of the Hindu Kush, were ground down like the teeth of an aged bear.

Though the impervious granite and quartzite bowed down somewhat to the force of wind, time, water and ice, not much else, including humankind, has been able to alter the essence of South Mountain. It is a place of power, of force—it dominates, transforms, mutilates. It is the Mountain. People have interfered with it, cut its trees and dammed its rivers, but they have never changed the Mountain. It remains what it is, remote, unassailable. It moulds people, places a stamp on them that survives generations.

Chapter Two

Man, God &
the Godless

✦ AS THE LAST FAT ICE-CAP TOPPING
South Mountain melted back into itself, life returned. The lowlands gradually welcomed animals well adapted to subarctic conditions—hares, foxes, ptarmigan, moose and caribou. Following
them came small bands of nomadic people who roamed parts of
Nova Scotia between nine and eleven thousand years ago. But the
fickle Maritime climate gave them a relatively brief tenure. The
weather warmed radically over the next four thousand years, the
seas rose again and the nomads moved on. With each millennium,
the land grew richer and more diverse as the landscape evolved
rapidly from tundra to boreal forest and then to thick woodlands
of pine, birch and spruce. The era has been labelled the Great Hia-
tus as if, because humankind no longer trod the region, neither did
anything else of note.

When the Micmac, a branch of the Algonquin-speaking people,
came to the Valley about eighteen hundred years ago, the lower
slopes of South Mountain protected and nurtured them. The Micmac set up camps for long months of fishing at the mouth of the
Gaspereau River, which poured off the Mountain offering up a rich

diet of rainbow smelt, Atlantic salmon, striped sea bass, eel and shad, supplemented by plentiful beaver, river otter, woodchuck and duck. In winter the Micmac moved into the Mountain's dense forest and bush, where they sheltered from the cruel westerlies while hunting their winter diet of moose and deer.

The Micmac, a peaceful people with unsophisticated tools made from slate and semiprecious stones, considered themselves blessed. Their benevolent god, Glooscap, lived in the Blomidon cliffs, where he comfortably surveyed his dominion. He had fashioned the Micmac out of an ash tree and promised never to let them go hungry as long as all in his domain remained exactly as he created it. If any dared defy him, Glooscap exacted quick revenge. When a zealous beaver dammed Minas Basin, he redug the channel in a fury and flung deity-sized handfuls of Fundy mud at its fleeing back. Five islands were created where the mud landed.

In 1524 Giovanni Verrazzano, an Italian commissioned by the King of France, was the first white explorer to sail up the Bay of Fundy. He gave the whole region, including all he could see of Nova Scotia, New Brunswick and parts of Maine, a hopeful name— Arcadie, "land of good and plenty." But eighty years later, it proved to be neither for Samuel de Champlain and his small group of settlers. They wintered in Port Royal at the far west end of the Valley and were routed during the punishing winter of 1604. Many returned to France with horrendous tales of privation and appalling weather.

A handful endured, joined by a few more hardy and stubborn souls from France, but by 1690, almost 170 years after the first white man's boat nosed its way into Glooscap's kingdom, there were fewer than eight hundred settlers in all of what is now Nova Scotia. They were clustered in three main villages: the original Port Royal, sitting on the Annapolis Basin; Minas, tucked against the southwest shore of the Minas Basin; and Beaubassin on the Cumberland Basin near the present-day border of Nova Scotia and New Brunswick.

The settlers at Minas, today Grand Pré, had immigrated from the low-lying Saintonge region around La Rochelle, France. On the long, difficult voyage to the New World, they carefully tended the seeds, cuttings and root divisions of the plants they intended to introduce to the land they knew as La Cadie or Acadie—choke-cherry, Lombardy poplar, honeysuckle, Bouncing Bet, wormwood, caraway, hops and many varieties of apple, plum and pear trees.

The Acadians were skilled, patient farmers who laboriously diked and drained the salt-soaked tidal marshland, turning it into fertile fields. The dikes were clever engineering feats made of marsh sod cut into rectangular chunks and piled twelve to thirteen feet wide and five feet high. At the base of each dike the Acadians buried a hollow log, which they later replaced with tunnels of squared planks when the first sawmill started operation. Inside the *aboiteaux* they fitted hinged doors, which acted like the valves in a vein, keeping out the salt-water as the massive Fundy tides rose but allowing the fresh rain-water to escape.

Typically, it took three or four years for rain to leach salt out of the soil, but once done, the dikeland readily grew wheat, peas, hemp, flax, rye, oats and vegetables in surplus enough to allow trade. While the Acadians waited for nature to purge their land, they fished and harvested the marsh grasses—"salt hay"—to feed their livestock. Once the marsh froze and no more work could be done, they drove teams of oxen to the lower slopes of South Mountain to cut wood for the endless winter. They trod carefully on the Mountain—it was not a place to tarry or dwell. Deep within its hills lay treacherous boulder-strewn gorges, furious rivers and dense forests that snatched away the sunlight and confused trespassers with miles of tangled brush.

By 1700 the Acadians, who had spread out over twenty-one hamlets surrounding Minas Basin, were selling their surplus food to the French forts at Louisbourg and Annapolis and buying livestock, millstones, forges and tools from the New England colonies.

Little is more serene to the eye today than the Acadians' section of the Valley, but it was a constant pawn during more than a century of conflict between England and France, bouncing back and forth between the two countries nine times between 1604 and 1710. The Acadians became as skilled at being flexibly neutral as they were at building dikes. Though they squabbled and scrapped fitfully among themselves, competing for control of key rivers or the rights to extend their settlement area, they carefully navigated the larger political waters. When Acadie was French, they traded illegally with the New England colonists and legally with the French fortress at Louisbourg. When it became English, legal and illegal reversed.

Finally, in 1713, the Treaty of Utrecht handed Acadie to the English. A succession of English governors encouraged the Acadians to swear an oath of allegiance to the Crown but most of them were in no hurry to make such a precipitous agreement when their land could just as easily become French once again. Then came the Seven Years War in 1744, the founding of Halifax five years later and the installation as governor of General Charles Lawrence, an ambitious, arrogant, bull-headed man with an intense dislike of anything Catholic or French and an almost hysterical suspicion of any who would not swear allegiance to the King.

The Acadians were aloof and distrusted outsiders of any religion or flag but they were also practical people. Though their various English and French overlords were necessary afflictions, they realized early on that the Micmac were essential to their survival, and they developed a peaceful, useful alliance with them. Like the French before him, Governor Lawrence considered the Micmac to be worthless as allies, but as enemies, particularly on the side of the Acadians, they could upset England's plans to settle the region with loyal Protestants.

In late August 1755, while Sir Thomas Robinson, the British Secretary of State, was penning a letter to Lawrence cautioning him to deal with the Acadians carefully and slowly, the governor had already set into play "the noble and great project of banishing the French Neutrals from the Province," an act, he crowed, that would prove to be "one of the greatest deeds the *English* in America have ever achieved." Without authority, let alone an order from England, Lawrence and his council in Halifax, comprising mainly New Englanders, sent Colonel John Winslow to Grand Pré to enact their plan. Winslow summoned all the men and boys capable of bearing arms to the church under the guise of delivering an important message from the King, then informed the 418 stunned Acadians that they were under arrest and their "lands and tenements, cattle of all kinds and livestock of all sorts" were forfeited to the Crown in preparation for their expulsion from Nova Scotia. "I am through his Majesty's goodness directed to allow you liberty to carry off your money and household goods as many as you can without discommoding the vessels you go in," Winslow added magnanimously.

After twenty-nine days locked in the church, the 418 men and boys, together with their families and most of the Acadians who had been imprisoned in nearby Fort Edward—2,182 people in all—trudged sadly onto English ships. By then they'd discovered that their fellow Acadians on the Cumberland Basin had already been deported. As the prison boats pulled away into the bay, the soldiers flung themselves into an orgy of destruction, torching houses, barns, smithies, mills and sheds and smashing anything they couldn't burn. The dikes, the only thing not destroyed utterly, continued to do their silent, efficient work as the Fundy winds bore the stench of char out to sea. The *Grand Dérangement* was complete.

The English took care to leave no critical mass of Acadians in any of their new homes, New England, Maryland, Pennsylvania, South Carolina and the West Indies. A number of families remained imprisoned in Fort Edward for nearly a decade, and three hundred of the deported managed to return when they commandeered a ship. Many of the escapees wandered aimlessly, half-starved, for years, others anglicized their names and tried to assimilate into the English culture. A few fugitives hid briefly on South Mountain, knowing the British would never penetrate its mysterious depths. And others fled into hiding elsewhere in the province. Occasionally the remaining Acadians joined forces with the Micmac, also dispossessed, to raid and worry at English settlements. Today there are two small reservations set aside for the Micmac on South Mountain, both classified as bog on the Government of Canada topographical maps.

The English quickly discovered that evicting the Acadians created a bigger problem than the one they had supposedly solved. Stripping the land of farmers meant that there was no one to provision the British garrisons in the province. As a result, food and fodder had to be imported at great cost from New England. On October 12, 1758, after the English captured Louisbourg and took

control of the entire province, Governor Lawrence issued a proclamation in the *Boston Gazette* to entice settlers to the land of good
and plenty. There was little response so he tried again in January
1759, desperate to get people onto the land in time for spring planting. The second time, by emphasizing generous land grants and
freedom to practise their religion, he got nibbles from Connecticut
and Rhode Island. Though anxious for new opportunities, particularly land, and eager to be free of religious persecution, the New
Englanders cautiously sent agents to Nova Scotia in May 1759 to
investigate.

It seemed almost too good to be true. One township, for the Rhode
Islanders, would be created in Falmouth at the eastern end of the
Valley. The Acadian land was to be split into two townships for
three hundred and fifty families, Cornwallis—all the land to the
north of the river—and Horton—all the land to the south. The
town of Wolfville would eventually be located in Horton Township.
The area had been surveyed and laid out for town sites, churches
and schools with forts to protect the settlers and their land. The
grants themselves were large, 500 acres per man in Horton and 667
in Cornwallis divided among farmland, timber plots on South Mountain and dikeland with fishing rights on the main rivers, the
Gaspereau, the Avon and the Cornwallis, with additional land for
some settlers on islands in the Minas Basin for access to ocean fishing.
Furthermore, the government agreed to transport every colonist, his
dependants, stock, equipment and personal belongings gratis.
Lawrence added the further enticement of free corn in the first year
as well as arms and ammunition.

They were called Planters, these inheritors of the Acadian land.
They were of old Puritan stock; their ancestors had been dissenters,
ultra-reformists within the Church of England who fled to the New
World in the seventeenth century seeking freedom for their ideas
and ideals. In New England, they called themselves Congregationalists, giving autonomy to individual churches, releasing them
from the oppression of a central authority like the hated Church
of England.

Although some of the Planters were middle class but landless, most who came to the Valley had been pushed to the bottom of a religious and social system that had been growing more rigid by the year. Originally Puritan property in New England was administered by a small group of men in trust for the whole community; newcomers got plots of land to work if they lived an unblemished life and brought their children up appropriately. But over several generations, the system crumbled as settlement increased, families multiplied and the demand for arable land safe from savages drove a once plentiful commodity into scarcity. Greedy administrators gradually assumed ownership of the land, forcing others to become labourers, farm-hands and servants. Paper money appeared, debt began to accumulate and grudges quickly followed.

A schism in the Congregationalist church developed, mirroring the divisions between owners and labourers. Called the Old Lights, the ownership élite gravitated towards a faith based on book learning while the New Lights, mostly commoners who laboured on the land or staffed businesses, believed in enlightenment provided by an inner light, visions and feelings. As the rift widened, the Old Light adherents passed laws quashing the basic rights of New Light followers and limiting their opportunities for advancement.

Just as the Old Lights were expelling New Light sons from colleges, declaring marriages and baptisms invalid, revoking citizenship and confiscating goods and property because the heretical fundamentalists refused to pay tithe to the Old Light ministers, Governor Lawrence's proclamation appeared in the Boston newspaper. Once again freedom beckoned. In their new home, inner knowledge would once again guide their lives, not the spirit-deadening book learning promoted by the wealthy Old Lights.

When the Planters' boats rounded Blomidon and sailed into the Minas Basin in June 1760, the Valley spread out before them like an open basket. Apple buds were just beginning to swell, the untended Acadian fields grew a riot of self-seeded plants, the gentle bays offered shelter for boats and in the background the thick green shoulders of South Mountain hugged the sky, promising many lifetimes of fuel. The first order of business was setting up a draw to allocate the land. Once that was accomplished, the real horse trading began. Some related families consolidated far-flung allotments while the few with capital amassed bigger or better holdings. A handful of settlers sold their farmland and their town plots in Horton or Cornwallis, reasoning that they'd be at least as well off on their South Mountain timber lots, rich with game and handy to well-stocked rivers, and they'd have cash in hand to tide them over any hard patches. Most thought they could establish farms on the forested vastness of the Mountain, unaware that ancient geological forces had already removed that option.

The colonists' first years were faith testers. The Valley threw every bit of its anomalous weather at the newcomers; furious westerly winter winds howled demonically for weeks on end, spring floods snatched away fishing weirs and overwhelmed the dikes, and the Valley's own particular brand of throbbing, airless humidity suffocated them during the summer. The Planters had been enticed to the area to replace the Acadian farmers but most knew little about the craft. Ironically, the name Planter signified not agricultural prowess, but the planting of people in new colonies. While the large land grants enticed the settlers, they had been mainly labourers or fishermen not farmers, employees not proprietors, and many were from the New England underclass with no experience running their own operations. What's more, they came from established New England communities and were unaccustomed to the deprivation inherent in founding a new colony.

Critically, the Planters had no idea what to make of the dikes. In their ignorance, they allowed the efficient mechanisms holding back the sea—already needing repair after years without the Acadians— to fail. It was only when the government released some imprisoned Acadians from Fort Edward to fix the dikes that the precious farmland was saved from the sea.

The 1762 census of Horton Township tallied 900 colonists in 150 families. The following year there were 154 families. In 1765, many of those with sufficient money, including most of the clergy, began to leave. Soon all but one man of the cloth had returned to New England. By 1770, Horton had shrunk to 117 families, approximately 600 people in all. In 1783, after the American Revolution, loyalists to the Crown swelled the population in the Valley, but many departed promptly when confronted by the staggering amount of work required to establish farms in the new land.

At first, the lives of the widely scattered South Mountain settlers differed little from those in the Valley. Most tried farming but, except for those fortunate enough to have plots in Gaspereau Valley on the edge of the Mountain, they found the land too stony and infertile for crops. Typically the settlers kept a few animals on a wood lot, tended a meagre garden patch and supplemented their larder with hunting and fishing. Self-reliance was a survival necessity on the Mountain. In most cases, the closest neighbour was at least a day's ride away across rough terrain riven by swift-flowing, rocky rivers and streams. Travel down the Mountain into the Valley was a treacherous undertaking along steep, indistinct trails. In winter those on the Mountain could be snowed in to the eaves for weeks.

Though conditions were harsher on the Mountain than in the Valley, there was some compensation in the ready supply of building materials, fuel and plentiful fish and game. And because the settlers were so spread out and had little to do with the Valley communities, there was less pressure to meet community standards. Houses were built for utility rather than to please the neighbours or to mimic the style of those left behind in New England.

The early South Mountain settlers were just as religious as those in the Valley, but distance, the shortage of horses and awful or non-existent roads meant that they could rarely travel into the Valley for community worship. Births and deaths were recorded in the family Bible, which was read on Sundays, if a family member was literate.

By the early 1800s, overall conditions were still little better than they had been in the horrendous first few decades of settlement. Even farmers on the best land, not to mention those trying to eke out subsistence on the Mountain, were still dependent on grain and seed hand-outs from Halifax. Few outsiders who visited the Valley could have predicted that the region would one day become synonymous with agricultural prosperity. One traveller observed that Valley farmers were not only "ignorant, indolent, bad managers" but "slovenly" and lazy to boot and the worst of them could be found in

Horton Township. Halifax residents were particularly contemptuous of the constant pleas from Horton and Cornwallis for support from the government. This "scum of the colonies," complained the news-papers, was soiling the future of the province and Nova Scotia could not go on being "inundated with persons who are not only useless but burdensome."

As outsiders denigrated the struggling Planters in the Valley, so too the Planters found an outlet for their own disapproval—South Mountain. From the beginning, those on the Mountain were marked because they sold their land instead of weathering the hardships to create viable farms. The Puritans, ever on the look-out for signs of degeneracy, considered the very act of leaving the community cause for suspicion about a man's character.

In the Valley, ever stricter religious adherence became the solace for many in their battle to establish themselves. By the early 1770s, all but one of the clergy had hightailed it out of "Nova Scarcity," as a departee called it, so there was no central body to oversee how the faith was kept. Piety remained a fairly individual matter defined by hard work and abstinence from drinking and frivolity. Those who erred, in the community's opinion, were shunned and ostracized. Sometimes this social censure became so extreme that the victims could escape only by selling off their holdings and moving, often to South Mountain.

In the first years of the Planters, Ebenezer Moulton, a Baptist from Massachusetts, tried to bring the faithful and fallen together in his journeys through Horton and Cornwallis. But the new church quickly foundered on disagreement, and enthusiasm for organized religion fizzled. The flame didn't die completely though, and in 1775, a fiery mystic by the name of Henry Alline fanned it into a power-ful evangelical flame.

The church formed by Alline was an odd collection of Moulton's converted Baptists, New Light Congregationalists, Methodists and a handful of the curious. He cared little about labels, desiring only to preach the gospel of repentance. Sin, his charismatic sermons emphasized, crossed all creeds, colours and religions. Casting off its heavy veil was the only worthwhile pursuit of God's children. But to Alline's intense frustration, his followers spent as much time arguing about methods of baptism as they did contemplating ways of repenting and matters of the spirit. "The Christians were sometimes blest with liberty in their souls," he wrote of his Cornwallis congregation, "but the work of conviction had been declining ever since the dispute began about water baptism." Soon after, he sadly noted that many of those who had flocked to be awakened by him had "gone back to sin and vanity" and the debate about water baptism—child or adult, sprinkle or immerse—was as contentious as ever.

Over the next fifty years there was continuous forming and reforming of religious boundaries as Congregationalism was overwhelmed by promoters of the Baptist, Methodist and Presbyterian churches. Initially, the magnetism of whatever itinerant preacher was in the neighbourhood determined which church was ascendant, but Baptists eventually took control. Even within that faith, however, parishes allied or separated according to their views on the water baptism rite. At times the sprinkle or dip argument split both families and friends. Church members on both sides of the debate insisted that the church lists clearly indicate who was immersed and who was not, so no mistake could be made. It was one more rift in what was to be a long history of rifts and divisions in the Valley.

Before churches were built, shunning was the preferred way to condemn those who strayed from the rigid puritanical code. But with the growth of churches, expulsion from the congregation became a more effective tool. Throughout the Valley, the faithful found sin lurking around every corner. Apples, a legacy of the Acadians, made a cheap, potent brew and anyone caught, or even suspected of, imbibing might turn up at a Sabbath meeting to find himself and his family roundly denounced from the pulpit with a strident demand for repentance. Sins of all sorts occupied the minds of the nineteenth-century Baptists, with profanity, merriment, dancing, smoking and card playing all weighing heavily on the scale of vice.

God-fearing church people, even in the twentieth century, had great difficulty finding entertainment that didn't contravene half a dozen strictures. Delacy Foster and his wife, Mary, both good Baptists, loved to play cards, those "paste-boards of Beelzebub." They searched out a deck called Nations, which the ecclesiastical authorities of the time had grudgingly passed as Christian, because the sinful numbers and faces had been replaced with continents. "But just to be sure on this point, one of our Brookvale deacons had asked Doctor McNeil for his opinion on this great moral issue. The deacon naturally didn't want to take any chances, and wasn't going to order a deck from T. Eaton's without his minister's full approval. Well, the Reverend okayed them, and so we didn't feel we had to pull down the blinds when we played Nations. Not even Doctor McNeil would object to a game of this sort. All the teeth had been drawn. But we did speak of the ten and the eight of the various suits, and so retained a trace of Satan's terminology."

The town of Wolfville didn't exist until the 1830s, so the first Baptist church in the Valley was built in Horton Township near Grand Pré. There, on Sunday, the names of the fallen, who hadn't taken such precautions as the Fosters later did, were read solemnly from the pulpit and excluded from church membership unless they repented publicly, loudly and convincingly. The congregation came mainly from the lowland farms in the Valley with a scattering from the small settlement in Gaspereau and even fewer from the first Mountain communities of Greenfield and Black River. With little more than cart tracks leading down from the Mountain, almost no one risked their wagons or legs for the Sabbath trek into the Valley, particularly during the winter months. It didn't take long for the Valley citizens, already suspicious of those on the Mountain simply for being there, to brand them faithless.

By the 1840s the focus of the Valley had shifted from Horton to Wolfville, and the number of churches, mostly Baptist, had multiplied from one to eight. There were none on the Mountain. In truth, the religious and behavioural differences between the Mountain and the Valley were negligible at first, but as the years wore on they widened incrementally. In some cases the isolation on the Mountain hardened and strengthened faith. Some travelled miles through the hills to share their worship with their nearest neighbours and diligently schooled their children in the ways of the Bible. But others took the path of least resistance; religious observance on the Mountain declined as those who could read died out, Bibles gathered dust, and the Sabbath became a day for socializing rather than worship.

The Mountain population slowly increased from the original failed Planters as a few from each successive group who immigrated to Nova Scotia ended up there. Some, unaware of the difficulties, were diligent settlers eager to carve out a life, but others sought out the Mountain as a refuge. Many bought land, primarily sections of the wood lots granted to the original settlers, but others simply squatted—there was plenty of land, and who was there to tell someone that it didn't belong to them?

———————————◆———————————

The isolation and primitive conditions forced Mountain dwellers into a day-to-day existence of hunting, fishing, gathering and growing whatever crops would survive in thin soil, usually potatoes and turnips. Most on the Mountain lived in crude one-room houses. As families inevitably increased in size, a lean-to might be added, depending on the industriousness of the family. Hygiene was often one of the first things to go and, given the slow, muddy ten- or fifteen-mile ride into Wolfville or the nearest Valley town, medical care was non-existent. As literacy decreased, births, deaths and marriages were often not recorded. Lineage became a matter of oral history.

Valley people denigrated those on the Mountain as sinners having low moral fibre, cleanliness being a primary test. They came to conclude that "the Mountain people were born bad." It was a convenient theory, which, coupled with their theology stressing man's helplessness in the face of predestination, relieved them from any responsibility for the fate of those who had gone to the Mountain. In turn, Mountain folk came to see Valley people as money-grubbing, disapproving despots. Eventually, the Mountain people armoured themselves against Valley opinion by becoming even less inclined to conform to their expectations of behaviour, dress, education and faith. Slowly but surely, eccentricities increased without the regulating social influence of schools or churches.

It all became a self-fulfilling prophecy: the people of the Mountain were denigrated first by the Valley farmers and then, as towns developed, by the townsfolk, and as their social isolation increased and lifestyle differences took hold and became the norm, their lives reinforced the Valley's original opinion of any who lived on the Mountain.

Occasionally, a minister with true Baptist missionary zeal in his blood would take it upon himself to reach out to the communities without churches. In 1814, Reverend Edward Manning made a foray into Gaspereau, which the Valley residents at the time considered Mountain, much to the annoyance of those who lived there. He preached in a barn as there was no church. "O Lord, when will apostolic purity in practice revive in this land of infidelity," wrote the dismayed reverend. "The aged are stupified and irreligious, the rising generation who have been neglected by their irreligious parents are profane, ignorant, heady, high-minded, Sabbath-breakers, debauched, gay and dissolute and are, in fact, unfit for civil or decent society."

Gaspereau, a tiny farming village tucked into a narrow valley between the Ridge and the slopes of South Mountain, and only five miles from Wolfville, is a perfect example of the divisions between the Valley and the Mountain. When the community built its first church in 1841, the congregation worked just as enthusiastically to separate themselves from the Mountain dwellers as Wolfville and the Valley were toiling to exclude the Gaspereau brethren and the rest of the degenerate stock "back there." Once a ministry was established in the Gaspereau Valley the churchgoers, in order to protect the faithful from contamination, created a taboo against marrying outside the church membership.

Since many on the Mountain considered the Gaspereau farmers to be no better than the grasping, narrow-minded citizens of the Valley and refused to attend their church, there was never any shortage of the lost or fallen to hold up as examples of all that was bad. It wasn't sufficient to attend church and live by God's word—members were expected to patrol their own vigorously and never shirk their duty if a family member strayed. One Gaspereau farmer discovered his married daughter had claimed as her own a child born to his unmarried daughter. In a frenzy of righteousness, he put forth both their names for exclusion.

Between 1841 and 1876, fifty poor souls accused of the core sins—blasphemy, lawlessness and atheism—were condemned to eternal damnation and ordered never to darken the church's doors. Another 137 were admonished for the more delicate sins of envy, pride and bitterness, but not excluded. Since many were Mountain dwellers who didn't attend church anyway, the punishment had little impact.

Churchgoers in the marginal Mountain farm hamlets of Greenfield and Black River agitated for their own parishes, which the church eagerly agreed to because it further discouraged Mountain people from travelling down into the Valley. Eventually, the Wolfville Baptists built a small meeting house on the Ridge behind the town, ostensibly to reach out to those living "back there." Conveniently, it acted more as a blockade keeping the undesirables from crossing the Ridge and coming down into the Valley. By the mid-nineteenth century the Mountain communities, including Gaspereau, had earned a reputation for "poor giving," and since Baptist ministers were paid by the church membership few were eager to stay for long.

In 1899 and 1900 alone, five ministers trooped into Gaspereau in succession and quickly left; the turnover at the Ridge church with its motley congregation was even higher. Wolfville and the growing villages in the Valley came to be preferred parishes; the rest were left to itinerants and divinity students. But thanks to the Methodists, the Mountain wasn't left entirely to its own devices. Those vigorous converters had already established a beach-head in the small black community of Falmouth at the west end of the Valley, as well as in Grand Pré and a few surrounding hamlets. Not only did they encourage mixing among classes but they tolerated black and white together—even in the same bed.

As the Valley grew and eventually prospered in the mid-1800s, undesirables inevitably came into the town churches from time to time—poor whites, farm workers, travelling salesmen, "coloureds" and people from South Mountain, working as charwomen and part-time labourers. In response to this influx, the Wolfville Baptist

church created a separate non-denominational mission in 1890. Services were held in the back of a store until the Tabernacle was erected
on the edge of town in 1903 to serve the disparate congregation.
Many generations of college students were sent down to the building near Wolfville Creek to sing in the choir and add their bit of
testimony to the meetings.

In 1910, a pastorate headed up by students was formed in two of
the "better" and more affluent Mountain communities, Greenfield
and Black River. In the early 1920s, the "worst" mountain communities, Melanson Mountain, West Brooklyn and Rogers Settlement,
by then called Forest Hill, were joined into one mission. The pastor sent to administer it was so obviously unqualified and reluctant
that he even provoked criticism from within the Baptist community.
Branding him untrained, negativistic and disparaging, an Acadia
divinity student later concluded that the only thing the pastor had
in common with his flock was that "he has had as much antagonism
and suspicion toward the valley and the town elite as have the mountain people themselves."

The student saw through the hypocrisy of the mission and the
practice of sending students to the Mountain to preach. It was segregation pure and simple, he concluded, a way to keep the Valley
churches pure. After intensive research, he discovered that Valley
people, uneducated and educated alike, considered such segregation
necessary and appropriate and had felt that way for generations.

"While some of the people living on the long range south of the
town [Wolfville] are respectable farmers," sociologist Edith White
observed in her 1923 thesis, "many are ignorant, shiftless and
immoral. So long as there are neighboring areas populated by illiterate people with low moral standards, they will be a menace to the
town." White advocated a separate poor farm and an insane asylum
to deal with Mountain problems. She did believe that social services
should be provided on the Mountain but only to keep the recipients
out of Wolfville.

At least one outsider noticed how hard the Valley towns worked
to separate themselves from the Mountain. "Within five miles of
Wolfville, on the slope of South Mountain, lies an unsavory district,

where scattered families live in poverty and ignorance," observed a Dr. Thompson in his letters home. "Few of the inhabitants can read or write, shiftlessness and immorality are common, and the region is all but neglected by adjacent communities."

The Maginot Line originally drawn by the Planters between the good Valley people and the irredeemable sinners on the Mountain was fostered by the Baptist Church, then entrenched by the schools. Initially, the Planters viewed education with intense suspicion. Book learning and other materialistic pursuits were precisely the foundation on which the oppressive class structure in New England had been built. It was more important to *feel* one's faith than know it through words on a page. Though some of the settlers were educated and did come from a tradition of literacy, most saw education as yet another tool used by the self-proclaimed upper class to whipsaw them.

A tiny school in Horton Township had served the handful of Planters with an interest in educating their offspring, though attendance was sporadic and mostly by girls. But as more settlers from different backgrounds came to the Valley, the demand for schooling increased. The Baptists formed Horton Academy in 1828 and Acadia College ten years later (it became Acadia University in 1891). Weather, distance, tuition and the demands of farming, fishing or hunting meant the two schools basically served only the Valley population, which was fine by the families who sent their children there. The Free School Act of 1864 made education affordable but by then it was too late; the rift between the Mountain and the Valley was as deep as any glacial crevasse.

A school didn't appear on the Mountain until the 1920s and its single-room successors were small, poorly equipped and staffed by teachers who often didn't have high school education themselves. Long after university degrees were common among teachers in the province, even in rural areas, the underqualified continued to teach in the Mountain schools. They saw their mission as providing instruction in washing, dressing and speaking—with heavy emphasis on washing—rather than reading and writing.

Any Mountain children who made the trek into the Valley for

high school invariably found themselves the targets of vicious ridicule. Most just quit. As late as 1955, Esther Clark Wright couldn't find a single person from South Mountain, outside the village of Gaspereau, who had finished high school. "In the schools, the children sit two years in each grade, and are then pushed on, to expose them to a different set of lessons. Before they reach high school, they are old enough to leave school. In recent years, any attempt to give them additional training in handicrafts has not brought much success, for their dullness of comprehension prevents them from benefitting very much from this or any other kind of instruction."

The *Grand Dérangement* of the Acadians was the beginning of a tradition of expulsions and ostracism in a beautiful land where "them" and "us" was defined first by geological and then by human history. Just as the granite mass of South Mountain is forever separate from the fertile red clay of the Valley and the volcanic basalt of North Mountain, so the people who inhabited the area erected barrier after barrier against intruders while embracing religions that discouraged mingling among classes and cultures. In time, what began as a simple division between the morally industrious and the slothful reprobates was mirrored in the divisions between town people and Valley farmers, university and non-university, the Baptists and all other faiths. But one thing everyone could agree on regardless of church affiliation, employment or residence—there was no one lower than those who lived on the Mountain.

Chapter Three

The Clans

✦ A HUNDRED YEARS AFTER THE FIRST
Planters escaped their intolerant, restrictive New England communities, the very society they had fled was flourishing in the new land.
The gulf between Them and Us, the Mountain and the Valley, had
become an uncrossable ocean. Morality, prosperity, industry, intelligence all descended as one ascended the Mountain. Names became
vital in distinguishing the good families from the bad.

Ironically, many of the "worst" Mountain names originated with
dedicated, hard-working settlers. Rolen Rogers of Connecticut was
one of the Planters with farming experience. He arrived in the Valley with the first settlers and his name is enshrined in the original
Horton Township land grant list. An ambitious man, he quickly
doubled his five-hundred-acre share by purchasing another grantee's
allotment in 1761 for £100. Over the next ten years, he acquired
more farmland, salt-marsh and dikeland while building up his livestock herd.

Rolen Rogers was becoming a wealthy man—not on the scale of
Colonel Henry Denny Denson or Colonel Joseph Frederick Wallet
DesBarres, Rhode Islanders who had created baronial estates of

several thousand acres in Falmouth Township at the east end of the Valley, complete with plantation-style mansions grandly called Mount Denson and Castle Frederick—but a man of substance nonetheless. In addition to two homes on his farm plot near Wolfville, he had a small orchard, a mill and an assortment of horses, swine, cattle, bulls and sheep and sufficient money to buy expensive goods like tea, spices, molasses and glass. Within fifteen years of arrival, Rogers had a net worth of over £1,000, a sizable sum for the time. Three times Rogers served as a member of the Petit Jury, and in 1775 the governor of Nova Scotia appointed him as one of eight provincial highway surveyors. He also petitioned the government for better local roads in Horton, particularly leading up to Gaspereau Mountain, where he had his timber lot. Nor did Rogers shirk his responsibility for maintaining community morals. He and several other men signed a petition condemning a couple who were living together "without the benefit of clergy."

It seemed that in every way Rolen was striving to make his family's name prominent—socially, economically and spiritually. But he was also trying to cast off a dark shadow that followed him to the new land. His great-grandfather, James, an astute businessman and devout Puritan, had once been the wealthiest man in Connecticut. At a point when he and his wife, Elizabeth, appeared to have all that anyone could possibly desire, they were persuaded by two of their sons to convert to a new faith, a blend of Quaker and Baptist beliefs. John Rogers led the group, called Rogerenes, which attracted a small number of other well-to-do Puritans. It wasn't enough for the Rogerenes to fly in the face of the established Congregationalist church by publishing pamphlets outlining their beliefs. They also barged into Sunday services and disrupted the worship by loudly proclaiming their new gospel. John Rogers married three times over forty-four years, once having two wives at the same time. He was rigid and unwavering in his insistence that all Rogerenes follow to the letter the new doctrine. When anyone strayed, as his brother Jonathan did by taking medicine instead of relying on faith healing and by not stating publicly that he worked on the Sabbath, John personally oversaw their excommunication.

Reaction to the Rogerenes came swiftly and harshly. For several decades they were alternately jailed, flogged and shunned. John Rogers spent fifteen years in prison, which only added to the Rogerenes' zeal. Not even the confiscation of their property kept them from promoting their heretical faith.

By the time Rolen Rogers left New England for Nova Scotia in 1760, the outlaw sect had dwindled to a few dozen people, mostly related. The Rogers name was thoroughly blackened and very little remained of James's hard-won fortune. His fellow Planters were well aware of Rolen's connection to the Rogerenes, and those strongest in their Congregationalist faith kept their distance lest they be tainted by the heretical family.

Rolen and his wife, Lucretia, his first cousin, brought their five children to Nova Scotia. Three more were born in the Valley. Rolen may not have shared the religious extremism of his family but he did inherit the business sense of his grandfather. Not all of Rolen's offspring proved as energetic as he. Moses was a sickly child and, though listed as a labourer, he wasn't able to work for much of his eighty years. John had little ambition, didn't marry and died at thirty-one. But Rolen Jr., the oldest son, was cut from the same cloth as his father. He was literate, a skilled farmer, an expert at animal husbandry and most important, he seemed to have inherited his father's knack of buying and selling land at a profit. It looked as if the family was on the road to re-establishing the position they'd once held.

Then, in 1777, the Rogers' lives fell apart, suddenly and catastrophically. Early that year, an aggrieved Cyrus Martin visited one of the Horton justices of the peace, Nathan Dewolf, complaining that Rolen and his son had stolen two of his large barrow swine from the common pasture and slaughtered them both. The very accusation was a devastating blow, once again bringing the family name into question. In a society where an inattentive man could be fined a shilling for letting a sheep wander and five for a horse that strayed, theft was a very serious matter. One of the first things the Planters did when they arrived was to erect a pillory and a whipping post—both of which were quickly broken in. A forger had his ear cut off before enduring an hour of public humiliation in the pillory and a thief caught red-handed with three yards of stolen cloth was whipped into unconsciousness.

Father and son were found guilty. Solemn-faced escorts delivered them to the whipping post, set prominently in Horton's tiny town centre. There they shackled first the father and then the son to the wooden pillar and lashed each of them thirty-nine times with a leather bullwhip. When they were released, bleeding and shamed, Rolen Rogers's tenure as one of Horton's leading citizens was over.

Disgraced, the Rogers family felt the full force of Puritan revulsion. They were shunned. Neighbours crossed the road to avoid them and former friends wouldn't converse with them. Rolen Sr. abruptly withdrew from public service. After seventeen years of building and acquisition, he began shedding his holdings. Eighteen months after the trial, he divided 500 acres between two of his sons, Moses and John, selling a further 120 acres to Rolen Jr. Shortly after that he moved from the Valley to his wood plot on the Mountain above present-day Gaspereau.

Rogers's outcast status didn't prevent the "good" citizens from doing business with him, as long as it was to their profit. Elisha Dewolf, whose family bestowed its name on Wolfville, had been buying up land from the moment he set foot in Horton Landing. He eagerly snapped up a big chunk of Rolen Sr.'s farmland. His brother Daniel bought another fifty acres. Rolen Sr. also sold off a chunk of his property to Prince Brown, a black man who had won his freedom by fighting with the British forces during the American Revolution. That land too ended up in Dewolf hands.

Moses Rogers could do little with his allotment on the Mountain, and his sister Alice was forced to sell it to support him. This parcel of land was also eventually absorbed into the growing Dewolf family estate. When Rolen Sr. died in 1805, all that was left of his substantial holdings were a handful of acres on the Mountain, by then called Rogers Mountain or Rogers Settlement.

In 1783, Rolen Jr. married Hannah Jeffers, the feisty daughter of John and Elizabeth, Rhode Islanders who took up grants in Falmouth Township. Their marriage was such a coup for the disgraced Rolen that many concluded there was something wrong with Hannah for her father to give his consent. Others considered she got what she deserved since her own family was disgraced because her parents had one child out of wedlock. Their opinion of the marriage was confirmed at the death of Hannah's mother, Elizabeth, when her will revealed an extraordinary codicil—she had left her property to a black man, James Amy, to use until his death.

The union of Rolen Jr. and Hannah Rogers, followed quickly by their decision to settle on one of the family's South Mountain wood lots, was a fateful one, for they and their progeny came to personify the evil that Valley people saw on the Mountain. The first three of Rolen Jr.'s seven children, born two years apart, were Catherine, Jonathan and Joseph, healthy and apparently normal. What happened next, or why, is lost in the minds and bodies of Rolen Jr. and Hannah. The fourth child, Isaac, was born in 1791 and three more children followed. All were branded "feeble-minded." Though there isn't a shred of evidence, it has been widely assumed to this day that Hannah was the source of their affliction because she too was "feeble-minded."

But the good Valley citizens knew the real cause: the sins of the father and grandfather were being visited in this curse on the third generation. In the thick and solemn Horton Township Book, a record of births, deaths and marriages, a black X beside the names of the four bleeds into the page. The mark denotes those born "foolish." It might as well have been scored into the granite of the Mountain itself.

The moral code of the staunch New Light Planters was unwavering. In their minds, it was a short trip from deficient to criminal to evil. By the early 1800s, Rogers Settlement had grown into a couple of dozen dilapidated, one-room shacks. Rolen had given his three "right-minded" children six-acre lots on the Mountain to raise their families. The plots were too small to farm, even if there had been any topsoil among the rock and scrub, and they survived by fishing, hunting, cutting wood and labouring on the roads and farms of Valley farmers and landowners. Though conditions were harsh, the Rogers clan multiplied rapidly. Rolen Jr. and Hannah's grandchildren and great-grandchildren produced large broods of their own, often

ten or more—most of whom stayed on the Mountain in the vicinity of the original settlement. By that point, the lots had been cut and cut again, some smaller than half an acre—just enough for a little house with space for a pig or two and a few chickens. A single one-room shack frequently housed several generations as properties became too small to subdivide further and subsequent children could not afford to buy their own parcels.

While the Rogers clan was the most extreme example of descent in the social order, there were others. John Atwell, a literate carpenter, was one of the original grantees in Horton Township. Like Rolen Rogers Sr., he bought and sold property and served the community in several capacities. But a series of "moral" problems, starting with a charge of carrying grain to the mill on a Sunday and culminating with a fight during which he knocked out another man's tooth, pushed him to the fringes of society. Eventually he also moved to the Mountain, founding the large Atwell clan.

In the mid-1800s, when villages and farms were growing and prospering along the Valley from Grand Pré to Kentville, the term "rogersy" came to describe anything dirty, dishevelled or poorly kept—or any kind of indolent or immoral behaviour. The attitude was so firmly entrenched that it became increasingly difficult for members of the Rogers clan to break out of the deepening abyss of poverty, ill health and unemployment that their name and location had consigned them to. Marriage was one possible escape route but the better citizens on the Mountain, in the slightly more prosperous communities of Gaspereau, Greenfield and Black River, let alone the good Baptists of the Valley, abhorred the idea of marriage to anyone known to be a descendant of the dreadful Rogerses.

Though Gaspereau was considered Mountain by the Valley, the proud, industrious Coldwells from the small hamlet would never, for example, marry into the Atwell, Scovill or Kinnie clans on the Mountain if they wanted to maintain their social standing. For the Rogers, marrying up, which was the only direction, became almost impossible after Hannah and Rolen produced their last four unfortunate children. That these children's infirmities were as likely the result of disease or birth-related problems as genetic "foolishness," no one understood or cared. Theirs was tainted blood. The only escape was to leave the Mountain, and preferably the Valley, to take up residence someplace where one's name didn't immediately reduce the marriageable population by 90 percent.

And that is precisely what Elisha Rogers, Rolen Jr.'s grandson, did. Like Rolen Jr., Elisha managed to marry off the Mountain when Deborah Dimock of Shubenacadie agreed to be his wife. But unlike Rolen Jr., he eventually took the next step and left the Mountain. Elisha was a shy man who didn't like to thrust himself forward, but his strong-minded wife had no such inhibitions, especially when it came to their nine children. Deborah's grandfather had been a respected Baptist minister, and she had grown up believing in the Good Book and the benefits of education. Though they lived much of their married life on the Mountain, she ensured that her children could read and write, unlike the majority of Elisha's relatives on the Rogers side.

In 1869, Deborah convinced Elisha to leave the Mountain for Windham Hill in the province's Cumberland County. There, she reasoned, the family could make something of itself, away from the Mountain's stigma. Three of their sons became successful farmers, and a fourth became a high school principal. Benjamin Rogers, a prosperous grocery merchant and later mayor of Stellarton, was a stalwart in the temperance movement. And, though her two daughters didn't marry brilliantly, they brought no disgrace to the family with their unions. Four generations later, two famous Windham Hill descendants were born, the late Stan Rogers, a singer and songwriter who chronicled the agonies and glories of Nova Scotia's history in his wonderful ballads, and his brother Garnet. When Stan died in an airplane fire, Garnet, who had been his accompanist, launched his own successful solo career. Oddly, none of the brothers' hundreds of songs about Nova Scotia are set on South Mountain.

When Elisha and Deborah moved to Windham Hill, they established the "good" branch of the Rogers clan. The "bad" remained in the progressively more squalid Rogers Settlement. Other clans, such as the Welches, also split when one of the family members left the Mountain. The prosperous twentieth-century Welches, who boasted

merchants, apple farmers and even a senator in the family, got a little help from Mountain accents and illiteracy which, in time, had
corrupted the Mountain name to Walsh. It was much easier to deny
kinship when names were spelled differently on the Mountain.

Rachel, one of Rolen Jr.'s twenty-two grandchildren, married
Jonathan Welch, known on the Mountain as Old Jaunt, and lived
at Rogers Settlement with their nine children. On his half-acre lot,
Old Jaunt built a small log cabin for his bride, which contained, for
the Mountain, a few surprising luxuries—a fine stone fireplace large
enough to take four-foot logs and a grand four-poster bed complete
with drapes. One of their sons, Jonathan—Young Jaunt—fell in love
with Hannah Butler, from a respectable family. The Butlers were
descended from a good line begun when artisan Henry Butler came
to Nova Scotia. Hannah's mother, a MacInnis, could also claim qual-
ity in her background, people who lived by the Book and accomplished things. Solid Baptists and good citizens, the Butlers weren't
happy to have their family name tied to the lowest class on the
Mountain.

Young Jaunt and Hannah Welch settled on the Mountain behind
Gaspereau Valley. Jonathan had been a farmer, seaman and, finally,
day labourer. Jonathan and Hannah produced two sons and three
daughters.

One of the girls, Ada, was sharp-tongued, quick and afraid of very
little in life. She could nail just about anyone to the wall with a look
and though locals freely derided her four hefty female cousins known
as the "Durham Heifers," they were careful to launch jibes at Ada
only from a distance. "Ada," the rumours went, "walks the road"—
the local euphemism for prostitution. She never married, as far as
anyone could determine, but she had four children. Bill Schofield,
a descendant of one of the Planters "gone to the Mountain" and originally called Scovill, fathered the first of her children. The next
three, Stella, Freda and Josie, were sired by her own father—or so
the story went and so all the decent people of both Mountain and
Valley firmly believed. No amount of good, God-fearing Butler blood
would shake that conviction.

One day, in the early years of social services payments, a man employed by the county to determine who on the Mountain was eligible for support knocked on Ada's door. Canvassing the Mountain was a disagreeable chore. One had to wade through mud and debris to get to the tumbledown shacks and then be greeted by the viper's brand of hostility that Mountain residents saved for interfering types from town, but there were occasional perks. A social services payment, or government hand-out, was a powerful lever a man could use to exercise his option on the women of the Mountain hamlets—a tradition continued to this day. When Ada admitted the man to her home, he noticed a new addition to her family. "Now then, Ada," he said familiarly, "who's the father of *this* one?" Ada caught him with a stare, then sent him scurrying. "You are," she snarled. No one ever saw him in that neighbourhood again.

The separation of Mountain and Valley was complete by now. Even the best citizens who owned mills on the Mountain or farms in Gaspereau Valley found it difficult to overcome the stigma of location. A family could try to protect itself from infection with bad blood from the clans through careful marriage into respectable families but, in the end, it didn't matter who you were, what you owned or who you married—all that counted was where you lived.

Since the first Planters came to Gaspereau in the eighteenth century, the residents of the community convinced themselves that, though Gaspereau Valley was situated "back of the ridge" behind Wolfville, they had nothing in common with the clans pockmarked over the Mountain rising at their back. Then, in 1852, a careless remark by the Acadia College president made it all too clear how wrong they were—as far as the Valley was concerned Gaspereau occupied the same social depths as the rest of South Mountain.

It all started when Reverend E.D. Very, pastor of the Portland, New Brunswick, Baptist church and amateur geologist, and his friend Professor Isaac Chipman took a group of students on a prospecting trip to Blomidon. As they made their way to the Wolfville wharf, they could just make out the swelling tide line in the distance and smell the whiff of salt in the air layered with that particular earthy smell that rises from the red Minas Basin mud when the wind is just so and the nose is undistracted.

Isaac Chipman was that rare individual who combined a brilliant academic mind with the ability to get things done. During Acadia's early days, he was instrumental in creating a solid financial and educational base for the young college. When Acadia needed a new building for its growing student body, Chipman, to the amazement of his fellow board members, built it by cajoling free materials and labour out of the notoriously thrifty Valley people.

Their sailboat left the Wolfville wharf as the sun warmed the turbid Basin waters, turning them from ink black to reddish brown. Two hired hands, Perez Coldwell and George Benjamin of Gaspereau, worked the rudder and sails, pointing the boat towards Blomidon, one of the finest locations for specimen hunting in the world. No lover is as fickle nor child as capricious as the winds that chase each other up the Bay of Fundy, into the Minas Basin and over the dikes. Nova Scotia is a maritime land and every coastal sailor lays claim to braving the most pernicious blows that have ever licked their way across a sea-girt shore. But the trick to a Fundy wind is that it never fools the same way twice. Like the Valley itself, it lulls even the wary into believing it is gentleness incarnate.

Shortly after they set sail for home, a frisky westerly scooped into their sails not far off the shore and quickly worked up to a stiff blow. Then out of nowhere, the seas surged, striking the boat hard, lifting it high and as it subsided, pouring over the men, sending them scrambling for bailing implements. The stern dipped low and the swell flipped the boat over, bottom up. One of the students disappeared before the others had even oriented themselves. Gasping and shouting to one another, they floundered towards the upended boat.

The onslaught continued tearing the mainsail from the mast and left Isaac Chipman clinging frantically to it, trying to stay afloat. Their woollen clothes dragged at them as they fought against the sea. Reverend Very made one last attempt to swim to safety but the fatal malaise of exhaustion paralysed him and he sank below the surface. Isaac Chipman uttered a few faint cries before he too succumbed. George Benjamin, the only survivor, was left hanging onto the boat.

Gone was the entire graduating class of 1853 and all but one of the class of '54. Gone too was the most determined and effective man the college had ever known. "Thus were lost," lamented Acadia's president, completing a long and impassioned eulogy at Chipman's funeral, "six precious souls and the man from Gaspereau." It's a phrase that still reverberates on the Mountain.

The people in Gaspereau have never forgotten just who were the precious souls and who was the other. Though few today are aware of the details of the incident, the implications of the comment are indelibly written into the collective consciousness of any who make their home on the granite basolith of South Mountain. "As a password the phrase is hard to beat," observed Esther Clark Wright a century later. "If in any part of the world one murmurs, 'six precious souls,' and some hearer responds, 'and the man from Gaspereau,' liaison is at once established. He too has at some time dwelt on the hillsides looking across the Basin of Minas toward Blomidon."

The inadvertent stab by Acadia's president found a tender target in the residents of Gaspereau. Already annoyed by then at being lumped in with the rest of the Mountain, citizens of the lovely village caught between the heart and the hind end of the Valley—as most considered the Mountain to be—were particularly outraged because the maligned dead man from Gaspereau was in fact a member of the village's leading family, the Coldwells. From the time of its founding until 1940, five of thirteen young men and women from Gaspereau who attended Acadia were Coldwells. Family historians concede that the first Coldwell in the area had been a teen-age deserter from the British navy. But "Captain" William, as he later styled himself, acquired land, began the eighteenth-century version of a real estate agency while siring a large brood of children, most of whom settled in Gaspereau.

The Coldwells were law-abiding, reliable Baptists who took life seriously. No one would dare suggest that there was anything rogersy about them. They didn't sell their land to outsiders and, more important, took care who their sons and daughters married. Between 1760 and 1950, none of the 613 descendants of Captain William ever married a Rogers, Welch, Atwell or Morine, widely derided as the lowest-class families on the Mountain. One particularly shining light, Albert Coldwell, not only graduated from Acadia in 1869 but went on to teach at the college and become mayor of the town. Around him one was careful about casting aspersions on Gaspereau.

The insensitivity of the Valley, particularly the university, towards the Mountain didn't end with "the man from Gaspereau." A few years after the sailing tragedy in Minas Basin, Dr. Sawyer, a professor at Acadia, accompanied the minister of the Kentville Baptist Church to Gaspereau to solicit funds from the church members. Their pitch was obvious from the title of their sermon—"Giving as an act of worship." If you don't start emptying your pockets, you tight-fisted, unappreciative Mountain folk, the underlying theme went, then all hopes of an ordained minister attached permanently to Gaspereau would disappear. Then Dr. Sawyer, totally oblivious to local feeling, punctuated his speech by enumerating "What we owe to Acadia College." If the congregation had pulled their attention away from his words for a moment, no doubt they would have heard the faint but outraged reply by the ghost of the man from Gaspereau—"Nothing!"

In the late nineteenth century, the dominant Baptist church began to take a slight interest in the Mountain. In the 1890s the Gaspereau Women's Missionary Society, made up of the better people in that community, adopted the increasingly decrepit Rogers Settlement as a project, holding a tea to raise funds for a mission house to bring the clan there closer to God—and teach them how to wash. Not to be outdone, other church organizations in the Valley sponsored good works on the Mountain; again the priority was upgrading the Mountain people's hygiene. Little of any substance was accomplished but at least the Valley Baptists could claim they were concerned about conditions on the Mountain.

One individual endlessly fascinated by the Mountain clans was the superintendent of the Tabernacle, the non-denominational church established by the Wolfville Baptists at the far end of town to serve the poorer classes. An odd little fellow with a beaming smile and endless optimism, Charles Patriquin had a string of business disasters before he took charge of the Tabernacle and its raggle-taggle congregation of cast-offs and misfits. Born in Wolfville, Patriquin had supported his family since the age of fourteen when illness invalided his father. From a harness maker's apprentice and barber shop partner, he moved into building, promoting developments in town and summer cottages on Evangeline Beach near Grand Pré, bringing the first merry-go-round to the beach in 1897 in his efforts to tempt visitors into buying cottages.

Patriquin tried apple farming on the resistant clay near the Wolfville dikes and quickly gave it up, though his onions were said to be the finest and juiciest found anywhere. He moved into fox and racoon farming before landing a government position as a temperance inspector and re-election worker for Sir Robert Borden's campaign. Finally he ended up where he was happiest, as secretary of the Children's Aid Society, where he was adored by the waifs and strays cared for by the organization. It was a natural fit for, along with his many schemes and occupations, Patriquin was a tireless community worker. He had become a town councillor at the turn of the century and promoted local good works, such as the construction of a lovely green common around the duck pond on the edge of town that today is still a focal point in Wolfville.

Charles Patriquin may have been an optimist with boundless energy, but when he took on the unwanted job of overseeing the Tabernacle its problems nearly overwhelmed even his good cheer. An assortment of drifters and itinerant workers, leavened by some of the Mountain's poorest citizens, made their way to the Tabernacle every week. Patriquin spent most of his time trying to teach literacy and encouraging those living in sin to regularize their relationships. He started a Sunday school program but was horrified to discover that few of the children had any grasp of the written word and standard lessons were a complete waste of time. He also worried and fretted that far too many of the children were obviously mentally deficient and had hearing and sight problems, as well as minor physical afflictions such as club feet.

Patriquin begged his friends and acquaintances who operated businesses in town or farms in the Valley to give odd jobs to the men of his Tabernacle flock. In the first two decades of the twentieth century, times were good in the Valley and employment easy to come by, so initially he received lots of offers and happily placed men in positions that would, at the very least, give them a few months of steady work. But he was soon inundated by complaints of equipment broken through neglect, tardiness, men who showed up one day then disappeared for a week and ignored instructions. It wasn't long before the sight of Patriquin approaching sent prospective employers ducking for cover.

Patriquin was one of the few Valley people who visited the Mountain in his attempts to encourage backsliders to return to the Tabernacle. He was stunned by the conditions he met in the tiny hamlets and wondered how children could survive with so little to eat. Many girls had babies at thirteen and fourteen and they usually remained at home, adding to the family sprawl. The Valley considered the Mountain to be one single, sinful entity but Patriquin realized that the clans were territorial, each hunkering down on its own small patch of land. Single names dominated on each one of the hills that made up the Mountain. Greenfield belonged to the Browns, Forest Hill to the Rogers, Black River to the Schofields, Morine Mountain to the Morines, Wallbrook Mountain to the Atwells, Pinch Mountain to the Pinches, and West Brooklyn to the Golers. Other families and groupings moved in and out of these areas, but the clans' solidarity coupled with their sheer numbers made them dominant.

Like many in the Valley, Charles Patriquin had heard of the Rogers clan and the stories that blamed Hannah and Rolen Jr. for much of the "defect" on the Mountain. After each foray onto the Mountain, his fascination with the clan grew. With the popularization of Charles Darwin's radical theories, genetics had become a fashionable parlour-room topic. Looked at in the right way, genetics helped explain what the Valley had known for over a century— the Mountain was born bad—literally. After a conversation with an Acadia sociologist, Patriquin decided to trace the Rogers' descendants and determine, once and for all, if the faulty genes of Rolen Jr. and Hannah had infected the Mountain. Though he started with the wrong generation, mistakenly believing that Rolen Sr. had married Hannah, he carefully traced 570 descendants of the fateful union, meticulously noting the foibles of the Rogers clan, shading, colour-coding and cross-hatching each generation to denote feeble-mindedness, jail sentences and unions between close family members.

Patriquin's Genealogy, as it came to be known, of 1921 was quickly followed up in 1923 by Edith White, a former Acadia student researching her graduate thesis at Columbia University. She too was fascinated by the Mountain clans and she used Patriquin's work to develop theories about how to deal with "degenerate stock in the community." Although she discussed issues of poverty, unemployment and hygiene, her greater concern was not how conditions came· to be on the Mountain but how the Valley could "be protected from the immigration which at the present time is augmenting its social problems." It was as if the Mountain people lived in the slums of Calcutta on the other side of the world, not in the hills just a few miles from the town.

Edith White chose six clans as her peep-hole into the Mountain communities, kindly giving them all pseudonyms, not to protect their privacy, but to shield Valley families who, through no fault of their own, shared the same last name. The Andrews, she noted, were a classic case of good gone bad, thanks to drink. Their notable characteristics included intermarriage with degenerate stock, poverty and mental defect. "Enough vitality remains in the stock, however," White concluded, "so that marriage with good stock results sometimes in healthy normal offspring."

The Williams clan distinguished itself to White through illegitimacy and dullness, but she did find some good among them. "Many of the girls are excellent cleaners, however, under proper supervision, and one of the boys is a skilled and dependable mechanic, though illiterate." Shiftlessness among the men and child truancy set the Denby clan apart, while the Fitzpatrick girls "are constantly hanging about the streets and are considered a social menace but the lack of any institution to which they could be committed prevents legal action." She found the Vining clan to be largely intelligent and ambitious but their low morals hampered their advancement in the world and prevented their escape from South Mountain. And finally there were the Carpenters, "whose most conspicuous characteristic is filth," declared White. "Two families live in hovels which the Visiting Nurse declares should be burned. In one of them, the nurse found a feeble-minded girl of fifteen sleeping in the same room with her father who was in the last stages of pulmonary tuberculosis and who was taking no precautions against the spread of the disease."

White attributed blame for the "Mountain Problem" directly to the flawed union between Rolen Jr. and Hannah Rogers and all the bad genetic couplings that followed. Prompted in part by her work, a royal commission investigated "mentally deficient persons" in Nova Scotia and concluded, as White did, that South Mountain had far more than its fair share with nearly 10 percent defective in certain generations, triple the provincial average.

Oddly, the more evidence academics, the church and the medical profession dug up to reinforce the Valley opinion of the Mountain, the more fascination with all things over the Ridge grew. Homilies developed centred on South Mountain. The better the view up there the more dissolute the viewer, was a favourite saying. South Mountain supplanted the bogeyman as a traditional warning to children. Many a bedtime parable ended with a Valley parent sombrely cautioning his or her child to walk the straight and narrow or "you'll surely end up on the Mountain."

Chapter Four

Esther &
the Mountain

◆ ESTHER CLARK WRIGHT WAS A FOR-
midable woman. Born in Fredericton, New Brunswick, in 1895 of
solid Loyalist stock, she was educated around the world at Acadia,
Stanford, Oxford, Radcliffe and the University of Toronto. A
lantern-jawed social activist from the old school, there was no rock
she was afraid to look under, no path she was prepared to leave
untrod, no man she deferred to and no individual she would let
escape without a tongue lashing if they raised her ire—usually by
uttering what she considered a stupid remark. Wright was a feminist
at a time when being one was defined by doing. But even in the
emancipated 1920s, Esther Clark Wright was a breed apart.

She thought nothing of tramping with a lone woman companion
through the heart of South Mountain just to satisfy her curiosity
about what was over the next rise. At the time many people were
leery of travelling through South Mountain in a car. She canoed its
rivers and in winter snow-shoed its fields and woods, as often as not
by herself. On one adventure in the 1930s, Esther and a woman
friend from Boston set out to walk the forty-two rugged miles from
Windsor over South Mountain to Chester, a popular seaside summer

place on the south shore. At the start they happily accepted a lift from a truck driver who entranced her companion with his accent— a Nova Scotia blend of Yankee and German—and regaled them with titbits about church silver recently discovered in the vicinity by hydro workers and rumoured to have been buried there by fleeing Acadians. They regretfully bade him goodbye when he turned off to New Ross and continued their journey on foot.

Early evening, with the sun bright, the air sweet and cool, shadow lengthening and all the landscape at its loveliest, is not time to stop walking. We went on. We had been warned of a stretch of woods in which it would not be well to be caught at nightfall.

We inquired how long the stretch of woods was and were told two or three miles. Walked on. The evening was still bright when we reached the beginning of the woods and we kept on. So did the woods.

The sun set, the light faded, three cars passed them going the other way then they were alone. There is nothing so endless as the woods of South Mountain when you are in the middle of them. Stretching blackly out in all directions, the trees seemed to close in on the women with every step. For miles they trudged along, passing only a couple of deserted houses and sawdust piles left behind by a portable mill, set up for a few weeks' work on the edge of the road. The two women considered breaking into the next house or barn and, if none appeared, returning to sleep in the sawdust. The mud on the road sucked at their feet and a damp, foresty smell, delightfully fragrant earlier, oppressed them. As they walked, immense rocks on either side towered gloomily; even the sight of a ghostly church at a crossroads didn't raise their spirits much.

Finally we came to a house in which people were living. It was exactly eight miles from the last dwelling houses which had been occupied.

As we approached the house, we saw a car. The girl who

answered our knock said she might have been able to let us have a bed had her brother not come home. There was, however, a house a mile down the road, where she was sure we could be accommodated.

There were already seven people and a scythe in the old sedan but we squeezed in too, and were deposited at a gate, further down the road. We stumbled up a long path to a little house on the hill. A man and a girl, whose relationship seemed a little vague, were in possession and agreed to let us have a room. The bed was not comfortable but by that time we were past caring.

The man and the girl with the vague relationship caught and held Esther Wright's attention. They and their kind were at the crux of the South Mountain enigma Wright spent fifty years trying to solve. In her long life there was little Wright couldn't mould to her will, pick apart to determine its core elements and illuminate under the powerful beam of her intellect—except the Mountain. It fascinated and defied her, its people in particular teased her with their elusiveness. Though she loved the Mountain, she scented dark and secret vices hidden within its depths.

Wright went again and again to the Mountain, intrigued by the inhabitants, the tiny hamlets, miniature churches and clusters of houses sprawled over clearings where the same one or two surnames were shared by everyone. Unlike so many who lived in the Valley towns, she never hesitated to mingle with those who lived "back there." She even had her own personal specimen.

There was a strange creature with a shock of sandy hair who used to appear down the path, generally in spring or summer. He was one of those not too bright individuals from somewhere back on the mountain, a chap who could never be relied upon to come at stated intervals, who could never be entrusted with any task requiring any degree of intelligence, and who had an uncanny flair for placing both his clumsy feet on any plant I had been nourishing with great care.

Nevertheless, his appearance was always welcome. He could saw and split wood, he could mow the lawn, and he could dig. I have forgotten his first name. His surname showed that he belonged to the well-known breed resulting from the marriage, many generations ago, of two members of good families, one of whom was of feeble intellect.

"Sonny from the Mountain" was my usual designation for him, and many a time, when I was tugging at some particularly heavy stone or groaning at the thought of all the work to be done, his tread upon the path, or his rough voice announcing his presence, was music to my ears.

Wright left the Valley to marry an Englishman and teach sociology at Stanford and Harvard. Her husband, Conrad Payling Wright, was a colourless man most forgot quickly, but he was probably the only kind of person who could have survived beside the furnace of Esther Clark Wright. Some suggest it was a marriage of convenience, and in truth she rarely mentions poor Conrad in her letters and writings. In her later years, Esther confined her infirm husband to the basement of her Wolfville house like an old, incontinent dog.

When Esther returned to teach at Acadia in 1943, she immediately refocused her attention on the Mountain. To most people in the Valley, particularly the educated professionals, everything beyond the Stile and the Ridge Road was dark and mysterious. Some ventured back to fish, hunt or picnic on the rocks at one of the spectacular gorges where the water battled its way furiously over immense granite obstacles. Young men from the avowedly dry Baptist Valley towns were known to drive the twisting Deep Hollow Road up the Mountain towards White Rock under cover of twilight, stop at a tumbledown house and, with hearts thudding sickeningly, ask whoever was inside about the cost of "refreshments."

The numerous bootleggers along the road amused themselves with stories about these nervous youngsters. Mary, from one of the Mountain's most populous clans, loved to invite the hooch-seekers in. When they inquired about the price of her husband's moonshine, she'd play with her blouse buttons coquettishly, smile toothlessly, stare pointedly at their crotches and demand what they had to trade. Their faces blanched as the implication sank home and she'd shriek with laughter at their consternation.

There was a limited sex trade on the Mountain, centred mostly on Deep Hollow Road where the moonshiners sold their wares. Dotted among the various research studies are references to women who "walked the road" to bring cash into families where none of the men worked. And there was at least one clan leader who "rented out" his nine- and ten-year-old daughters—no questions asked. Customers were Valley men from all walks of life—teachers, businessmen, the odd politician and a doctor.

In 1944, Wright suggested to a colleague—badgered is probably closer to the mark—that she use her class to conduct a field study in Gaspereau. Just to make sure they got it right, Wright went along. She was amused when the students, who had never been farther than the Stile, were surprised to discover that the village, neither Mountain nor Valley, appeared, on the surface, to be a suburb of Wolfville full of ordinary citizens, many of whom worked in town.

A generation ago, they had the reputation of being a tight little community, as restricted in their spiritual outlook as they were limited in their geographical range. They were God-fearing tight-fisted, house-proud, farm-proud people. They looked down on the less fortunate possessors of the poor land on the mountain areas above them, and, so it was said, reached out no helping hand. When they were compelled to call in for themselves services from outside, educational, religious, medical, they paid grudgingly the compensation asked.

Many times, as I have looked down on the narrow, self-contained, complete, miniature valley from the vantage point of the stile, I have wondered how much effect the narrowness of the valley had on the alleged narrowness of the outlook of the people.

Homes in Gaspereau, bisected by a lovely river and surrounded by dairy farms, were largely well-kept. But as the students explored further, they spotted a few crude-looking structures on the outskirts of the village. "Two of the girls chanced upon indescribable conditions of dirt and poverty in a household which could not give any satisfactory account of the relationship of the various persons who apparently live there," Wright noted.

The students, Wright and her colleague went from house to house in the Gaspereau area, probing lineage, church affiliation, education, employment, marriage and children. Wright encouraged the students to venture up the slopes of Gaspereau Mountain. The residents there were far more hostile; several set their dogs on the researchers.

The students found scores of exotic and intriguing relationships. In one situation, children were being raised by a grandmother but called her "mother." They called their real mother "sister." In another, two women living together said their husbands, who were brothers, lived together across the road. They had married the men, but when they didn't get along decided to switch husbands. That didn't improve things much so they moved in with each other. To confuse matters, they claimed to be aunt and niece but a family farther down the road maintained they were very definitely mother and daughter. Another family just as firmly maintained they were sisters.

In one home, Ethel Pinch introduced them to her eight children and to Curtis Pinch, at least a decade her junior, who lived with her. She had just delivered her fifteen-year-old daughter's baby and proudly boasted that she'd delivered all of her own as well. "2 room shack," the students jotted down in their field notes, "wind blow[s] in through cracks anywhere upstairs. Very poor but clean." At the home of Mr. and Mrs. Harold Kelly, they found eight children in the three-room structure—"Very poor, very little to eat + wear—children all have something wrong with eyes." In the corner of the notes one student scrawled, "Father does not know how many children he has! 14 by now?" When they came across Mrs. Rafuse and her five children, the woman insisted she had never been married although Eldon Atwell, living with her, had sired three of the children, "all children mentally deficient. 3 youngest unable to speak. living in shack—very poor and dirty."

Sorting out clan lines was a completely foreign experience to students whose own lives and families were neatly laid out. To add to their confusion, a number of the people they interviewed claimed not to be from the Mountain at all, only to reveal upon further questioning that they had in fact been born on a mountain, just not the one they'd been asked about. It was then the students realized that, though the Valley considered South Mountain a single entity, those who lived on it saw it as a series of mountains or hills, each with its own identity and clan affiliation. People talked about moving from Wallbrook Mountain to Gaspereau Mountain, about ten miles' distance, in the same way another person might explain that they'd immigrated from Switzerland to Canada.

The students were revolted by the poverty and filth, stunned that ten or twelve people could live in a few drafty rooms, aghast at the obviously sexual relationships between close family members, puzzled by the thick Mountain accents and amused that many of the women smoked pipes. In spite of their discomfort with what they found, the students' unpublished Gaspereau Study was the first suggestion that the genesis of the Mountain problem might be the "over industrious, over-moraled, farm-, house-, money-proud, clean, tidy upper class" of the Valley, rather than some evil inherent in "the indolent, laissez-fair, 'eat, drink and be merry' dirty, untidy lower class" Mountain folk.

A few years after Wright's field trip, the church again took a passing interest in the Mountain problem. Reverend Harry Renfree from Halifax shocked a Baptist youth group by denouncing "deplorable social, moral and economic conditions" on South Mountain. "Missionaries are not only needed in far-off places like India, with such a situation virtually in our own back yard," he emphasized. "It's hard to believe that in this Canada of ours such horrible conditions can be permitted to exist." Renfree punctuated his talk by relating the opinion of a visiting missionary that conditions on South Mountain were far worse than those he'd found in Bolivia.

Then Mrs. Paul Crawford, a home missionary, spoke of her time on the Mountain. "I don't know what they eat," she sighed. "I seldom see anything more than a few crusts of bread in their homes." She described decrepit beds covered only with rags, filth everywhere and sinful liaisons so common no one gave them a second thought. "The only time we ever see any outsiders in the area is when election time rolls around. Then politicians flock in with fistfuls of two-dollar bills and buy their votes. They think it's the government's duty to pay them to vote," she exclaimed.

Reaction came swiftly. W.O. Parker, a Valley politician, called Renfree and Crawford liars, declaring that their statements were "grossly exaggerated and a libel on the communities." Parker took particular umbrage at Mrs. Crawford's revelations about the children—"shockingly inaccurate and irresponsible," he huffed. "Mr. Renfree's statement unfavourably comparing South Mountain to Bolivia could only mean that conditions were pretty good in Bolivia," he fired back before indulging in a little fiction of his own. "There are 70 or 80 families in the areas mentioned. Practically every house has electric lights and modern electrical appliances. Nearly every man is employed at regular wages and certainly all those who are employable are working." For a time there was much harrumphing back and forth, with little result.

Esther Clark Wright monitored all developments on the Mountain. She pored over related research, maintained a voluminous correspondence with various experts and in addition to her own numerous visits, she grilled those few medical people, missionaries and social workers who had dealings on the Mountain. In the end, Wright never solved the puzzle of South Mountain, the hows and the whys of a "man and a girl whose relationship seemed a little vague."

It is a play ground and a poor farm; a source of power and a drag on the wheels of progress; a preserver of past ways of living and of old prejudice and nursery for the future; the last refuge of the unsuccessful born and the first rung on the ladder for the ambitious newcomer; a place where piety abounds and the scent of orgies of drunkenness, immorality, or hatred.

The mountain brings out the best and the worst of men. There are communities on South Mountain which have an enviable record of men and women who have added to the sum of human achievement. There are communities which have been a byword for ignorance, shiftlessness, and vice.

The Mountain had defeated everyone who had tried to change it but that didn't stop Esther Clark Wright from advocating the immediate airlift of an assault troop of professionals onto the Mountain.

The usual practice of having either the very recent graduates or the oldest, least successful ministers and teachers drifting around from one community to another, is of little value.

A real sense of mission on the part of those who would seek to serve rural communities, and an appreciation on the part of church and governmental authorities of the value of their work, with provision for adequate training and remuneration, for special recognition and compensation for the sacrifices involved, would be necessary to the success of any such undertaking.

But such a programme could result in the South Mountain becoming, in a new sense, the back bone of Nova Scotia.

In 1955, a group of the leading professionals in the Valley created a unique entity, the Acadia University Institute. Esther Clark Wright's name appears nowhere in its official papers but her fingerprints are everywhere in pestering memos, nudging letters and most particularly in the Institute's eventual activities. Its goals were extraordinarily ambitious—"to expand the contribution of Acadia University to its surrounding community... to conduct research in any field and implement the results of such research in the processes and patterns and problems of the area."

But it shortly became clear that the main, if unwritten, purpose of the Institute's existence was to probe South Mountain and replace nearly two centuries of rumour, folklore and myth with statistics and objective analysis. "The persistence and magnitude of these problems over a long period [on South Mountain]," Norman H. Morse, the institute's secretary, wrote in an unsuccessful attempt to solicit research funds from the provincial minister of welfare, "were important factors leading to the incorporation of the Acadia University

Institute which is now promoting this research in the hope that something will eventually be accomplished by way of improving the lot of people in several of the rural slum areas."

The Institute sponsored ten studies, of which six small ones covered a range of topics from ethnic history, farming practices and the lumber industry to sunken ships around the French fortress at Louisbourg and a Minas Basin ferry. But the other four, major studies specifically targeted the "mountain problems" of deaf mutism, mental retardation, inbreeding, illiteracy and crime.

In 1957, a geneticist from McGill University, Dr. F.C. Fraser, once again examined the marriage of Rolen Rogers Jr. and Hannah Jeffers. He wasn't as willing as Edith White had been thirty years earlier to lay the blame for the Mountain's problems on the "mentally defective" products of their union and on the subsequent close family matings common within "the clan." He painstakingly re-drew Charles Patriquin's genealogy, filling it with his own genetic symbols, before enumerating some shocking findings. While he agreed that the overall incidence of "mental deficiency" on South Mountain was far higher than normal—9.5 percent compared with the provincial average of 3 percent—he found an even higher percentage in some specific groups. The frequency of "defective" offspring rose to 13 percent when one of the parents was defective, and 50 percent when both were defective. Interestingly, Fraser found no increase in the "defective" rate in unions between close relatives.

Fraser felt his work was preliminary and flawed because of the small sample and the fact that he didn't "gain at first hand the 'feel' of the situation" by speaking directly to or even seeing a single person on the Mountain, because "members of The Clan should not be approached directly, as they are said to be timid, hostile people, who might become very uncooperative if they felt their affairs were being pried into." Fraser's finding that there was no increase in "defectives" in offspring from close relatives may have been the result of an inability to identify who was in fact related to whom. Instead, Fraser relied on informants, largely from the church and medical community, who identified "a group of 'ignorant, shiftless and immoral' (or perhaps more precisely 'amoral') people" on the

Mountain. The informants spoke of the very occasional clan member who broke out and finished high school, got a job and even became a respectable citizen. "Like," he was told, "a pumpkin-blossom growing on a dung-hill."

Fraser's admittedly preliminary results concerned the Institute enough that it funded a study to determine if the problem of mental deficiency on the Mountain and in nearby rural areas was bad enough to warrant special classes for the afflicted. The study tested 280 children, approximately 30 percent of the population in selected schools, who had repeated a grade and discovered that 81 percent had IQs lower than 89, the "dull normal" point, and 37 percent were at or below 50, the "retarded" or "defective" point, with some so low they couldn't be accurately measured. Once all the figures were churned through the statistical mill, the end result was another confirmation of the Mountain problem: children living there had more than three times the rate of mental "defectiveness" of those living elsewhere.

On the Mountain, most families know someone who is deaf or hard of hearing—it's unremarkable. The descendants of Rolen and Hannah have been raising deaf children for seven generations. In some families, as many as four offspring as well as an assortment of cousins, aunts and uncles are also deaf or hard of hearing. The incidence is so high that in the nineteenth century they developed their own sign language, an expressive mix of gestures, mouthing and body language comprehensible only among themselves. Few in the Valley were aware of how much deafness was a part of life on the Mountain because, until recently, those children didn't go to school, rarely found jobs and never married off the Mountain.

Hubert Soltan, studying "Deaf-mutism among the Clan" for the Institute, had free access to their medical files—in 1960, few bothered with niceties like permission. But he found a meagre pile: "In most of the families studied, medical attention was sought only in a dire emergency, such as at the time of death, and sometimes not even then."

Searching for clues to explain the high incidence of deafness, Soltan ruled out syphilis as a cause, a disease the Valley assumed was rampant among those who lived "back on the Mountain." Though there appeared to be at least twice the number of cases on the Mountain as in the population as a whole, generally there didn't appear to be a strong link to those with hearing problems. He raised the old genetic issue again when he found an "autosomal recessive mechanism" imported to the Mountain in the early nineteenth century by a mariner, Reginald Lake, who may have been mentally handicapped as well as deaf. Soltan concluded that Lake's genes combined with generations of inbreeding likely gave genetically linked deafness a place to flower.

Forgetting his own conclusion that those on the Mountain would have to be nearly dead before going to a doctor, Soltan suggested that his finding was useful should any of them seek genetic counselling or be "contemplating a consanguineous marriage." In that event, the physician could provide the prospective couple with a mathematical prediction on the odds of having a deaf child, as well as other genetic difficulties that might arise. Had he offered this service to any of the clans, they no doubt would have fixed him with that particular Mountain stare reserved for outsiders, especially those who smell like Valley. The stare, a mixture of contempt and suspicion, pasted on a face so blank it could be carved from stone, radiates a powerful message: "Why? Who cares? Go away." The Valley people don't like that stare; it unsettles them.

In truth, observable and anecdotal evidence suggests, even to a layperson, that an unusual incidence of medical problems on the Mountain isn't limited to deafness. Among Mountain people there seems to be a much higher rate of epilepsy, bad teeth, near-sightedness, heart problems and birth defects. Stories abound of so-and-so's child, born horribly deformed to a mother not yet a teenager, concluding with a quiet burial by the family, no doctor, no funeral, no record.

The scanty medical records made available to the Institute of six individuals, ranging in age from four months to twenty-six years, from one branch of a well-known Mountain clan provide a hint of the extent of the problem. Five out of the six children were deaf, three of whom were unable to communicate through writing or through a sign-language interpreter. One deaf boy, either thirteen or fourteen, no one remembering exactly when he was born, had never been to school and could not speak, read or write. Though no one could communicate with him, the family assured the doctor that he never complained. A thirteen-year-old deaf girl who was similarly unable to communicate with anyone also had no complaints, the doctor noted. She had gone no further than primary school. She had a heart murmur and a "double thumb right hand," a thumb twice as large as the one on the left. A twenty-six-year-old man appeared normal though deaf, but the examination wasn't completed because his medical records weren't available due to unexplained "sexual" difficulties. Similarly, the youngest, a four-month-old girl, was to all appearances normal. A boy, approximately ten years old, though deaf appeared normal if "fearful" during his examination. But a young girl, approximately age ten, had a number of problems. She was deaf and unable to communicate with anyone. As well, she suffered from "clubbing of the fingers" and unexplained but "frequent sudden jerking movements of the head to the right."

The fourth and most interesting study to come out of the Institute's dissection of the Mountain wasn't genealogical, genetic or medical but social, and it was done not by an academic but by a minister, Reverend George Hillis, in 1960. Hillis was part of a long line of Acadia divinity student ministers who had served in a Mountain parish. He conducted 673 interviews, visited 217 homes and frequently returned to re-question some of his "key informants." He talked to everyone in every family who would let him in the door, including the children.

According to his Valley interviewees, crime was a way of life "back there," with people from the Mountain slipping into the towns and farms to steal anything they could lay their hands on, from gasoline to chickens and clotheslines. "Any stealing in the valley is automatically assumed to have been the work of 'someone from the mountain.' Noteworthy is the reason valley farmers give for wanting to catch their thieves, not to have them imprisoned, but have them shamed and humiliated."

The reverend found a Valley farmer who had enlisted the RCMP to retrieve his stolen chickens. The thief, from the Mountain, was caught and the poultry returned but the farmer refused to lay charges, claiming he was satisfied with administering an admonishment. When the annoyed police officers pressed him, the farmer claimed it was well known that members of the thief's clan would retaliate by setting fire to his buildings. The reverend, suspicious of the farmer's fear, tried to find other instances of similar vengeance and could come up with only one or two fires that might be linked to retaliation. He concluded that the farmer, and others like him, were simply cheap; they didn't want to go to court and lose money because of time spent away from work. "[T]he valley folk find certain satisfaction in grumbling about their 'no-good' mountain neighbors and in 'being persecuted' by them. This state of affairs increases the valley superiority, righteousness and conviction that the mountain folk are 'a different class of people,' obviously a much lower class."

The more forthcoming of his Mountain subjects told him that their main form of recreation was "having a time," which usually meant a visit to the local bootlegger, loading up with illicit farm gas and then ignoring the speed limit in cars missing key parts and finally, if one was lucky, ending up the evening with someone else's wife or husband. A particularly favoured entertainment was getting young children drunk, then watching their antics.

Reverend Hillis's thesis, and its related papers, remain to this day the only extensive first-hand study of South Mountain and its people. He came up with some very un-Baptist-like observations—and not just about the Mountain.

The valley people have been ardent (almost merciless) crusaders of the temperance (total abstinence) cause. The present generation exhibits a good deal of confusion and disorganization regarding this value, although the occasional "prodigal" can be noted in every generation and in every family.

As strong as the alcohol attitude, has been an unyielding attitude toward premarital and extramarital sexual "affairs." Again, each generation, each family has its offenders. However, here particularly regarding premarital pregnancy, the offenders have threatened to outnumber the conformers.

Both these moral values are linked to the attempt to protect the valley from the mountain. Not only would drinking
or moral relaxation be "like the mountain," they would provide the atmosphere where "mixing" might take place.

Hillis laid considerable blame on his own chosen faith, as well as
the Valley in general, for the Mountain's poverty and isolation. The
early Baptist doctrine that all are brothers and all are sinners together
had been lost generations ago in the belief that "mountain folk were
born 'bad,' there was no hope of changing them and no sense
of responsibility toward them.... Salvation became identified with
material prosperity, and the poverty of the mountain was only proof
of their inevitable damnation."

Hillis's advisers were taken aback. "There are some rather strong
words of criticisms of clergy and aspersions toward other people," fretted Professor Fred Hockey, "which limit the possible circulation of
this thesis." Another professor, G.C. Baker, liked Hillis's provoca-
tive study but felt the work was better kept under lock and key. "On
page 16 a minister who is not named, but is nevertheless identifiable
by the context, is described as untrained, negativistic, disparaging.
This language, used of a professional person, might possibly be
actionable." Though he allowed that Valley professionals might
deserve reproach when it came to South Mountain, it shouldn't be
published as "the criticism is pretty well bound to stir up, rather
than abate, inter-regional antagonism."

Each of the Institute's four South Mountain studies, together
with their field notes, references and correspondence, was stamped
secret and confidential and buried in the university archives. They
were never seen by the academic community, much less by the public. Today few historians, sociologists, psychologists or medical professionals are aware that the studies even exist. Still, there was an
impact. While the studies were underway, the Institute's influential
board members touched off a flurry of activity aimed at the Mountain. They threw their weight behind the creation of the Fundy
Mental Health Centre, appointing four of its ten-member board to
it, and spearheaded, in 1959, the formation of the Horton Services

Council, with representatives from the Institute, the Fundy Mental Health Centre, the Valley Medical Society, the Public Health Services, the School of Theology of Acadia University and the Maritime School of Social Work. Both the Fundy Mental Health Centre and the Horton Services Council were directed to focus their efforts on the Mountain. Nowhere in its documents is there any explanation for the sudden interest in this wave of social services, but the Institute's purpose was clear, to clean up the mess on South Mountain.

Esther Clark Wright had, at last, her airlift of professionals, which was gearing up even as the Valley people continued on in their untroubled sleep. The Acadia University Institute disbanded in 1961. Though the prominent professionals behind the Institute had intended their creation to have a longer tenure, they were content in knowing that their research had diagnosed the problem and that they'd set into motion the necessary medical and social structures needed to fix the ills on the Mountain. They were wrong.

PART TWO

Chapter Five

White Rock

December 1983

✦ IT HAD BEEN AN UNCERTAIN MONTH ON South Mountain. Winter had closed in, released its grip, then closed in again several times. Men who made a good piece of their winter cash ploughing driveways on the Mountain wondered if there would be fat months ahead or lean ones. Mostly the Mountain was dependable and by mid-December winter had settled in. This year was different; there weren't as many calls from customers asking to be released from drifts banking up and over their driveways. People on the Mountain were careful with their money; if a thaw was around the corner, then maybe they could ram the car out to the road one more time and save a few bucks. After all, Christmas was coming.

You had to be cautious on Mountain roads. A flurry or two at the Stile could easily be a blizzard deeper into the myriad roads, many of them still dirt or gravel, that criss-crossed South Mountain. Valley people could be stupid about the Mountain. Occasionally, university students liked to drive up from Wolfville for some skating on one of the frozen ponds. They'd pick a day when a good westerly had cleared the ice for them—the kind of day when the blue sparkle in the air told you the ice would be good and solid. Then a few hours later they'd be stuck, desperately trying to rock the car free of the snow that had whipped in from nowhere. More than a few such explorers had to be helped back to civilization by someone from the Mountain who understood that tread and clearance had a special meaning away from the protection of the Valley towns. Freed, the students would escape back to the Valley, where they'd stop for burgers and lemon meringue pie at the White Spot in New Minas or coffee in Wolfville and laugh about their misadventure "back there" with "them."

What geography began in the separation of Valley and Mountain, humankind has elevated to an art form—nowhere is that more evident than in Wolfville, a town of about 3,500 where the sharp divisions between not only Mountain and Valley but also town and university are thinly papered over by manners, but evident nonetheless. Main Street, Wolfville, the only place where the four disparate groups—Mountain, Valley, town and university—meet, is an odd place to walk on a Saturday afternoon. The groupings would not be more obvious if they were colour-coded.

People from the Mountain often congregate in front of the supermarket in the centre of town, their clothing, accents and rough congeniality setting them apart. University professors, instructors and graduate students go about their weekend errands, their studied nonchalance and adopted small-town ease belied by their tight walk and educated conversation. University undergraduates, a different species entirely in every country on earth, dress very much like the people chatting easily outside the grocery. But they radiate an aura of difference: they are perching, not permanent, and they want it known. Assimilation with the residents of the town, let alone with the odd people of the little hamlets pockmarking the hills of the Mountain, is not part of the program. Valley farmers, looking typically rural, purposefully carry out their business, rarely lingering. They come to Wolfville to take care of affairs, then return home. Town dwellers make up the final group. For the most part, they dress casually and comfortably, business suits and dresses the exception rather than the rule. They greet one another cheerily, though they stop to talk less often than the Mountain folk, and when they do they don't tarry as

long. They have work to do, there is a purpose to them also, a destination. Theirs, they seem to be saying with every movement, is
not the easy life of Mountain or university where people seem to
have endless hours to gab and lounge.

There are several routes to the Gaspereau Valley from Wolfville,
but most who want to penetrate its higher regions drive a few miles
west to Deep Hollow Road. All Mountain roads can be treacherous,
none more so than the whippy snake of Deep Hollow running south
up and over White Rock Mountain. It starts out innocuously enough
at Horton District High School, which sits on a little rise just west
of the community of Greenwich, between Wolfville and Kentville.
It's a busy spot during the week, school buses coming and going, kids
playing on the broad fields spread out beside the school and shop-
pers hurrying to and from the malls of New Minas. In the summer,
the fruit stands draw thousands of visitors and a regular stream of
golfers head to the rolling KenWo golf course nearby.

Deep Hollow Road pulls away from this cheerful bustle and begins
its ascent of the Mountain, shedding the Valley as it goes. At first it
is an ordinary road bracketed by neat, modest bungalows, but when
it scoops below the highway overpass, the Mountain begins. Here
and there among the thick evergreens is a section of granite exposed
by blasting for the road. In one clearing two little houses share a half
acre of rough grass. Behind the homes solid grey rock rises—in the
spring it pours with melt-water, often flooding the cellars and turning the yards into quagmires. Farther along there used to be another
house wedged between the road and the rock on a small bit of flat
land the granite had given up. Now the site looks as if someone had
just stepped on the house and walked away. All that's left is a refrigerator, rubble from the chimney, piles of rotting lumber, assorted
belongings and heaps of garbage circling the remaining foundation—
the Mountain version of an Indian midden.

The road initially swings back and forth widely, then coils in
tighter loops, searching for the path of least resistance. Hancock
Brook accompanies Deep Hollow Road like a faithful pilot fish.
Inconspicuous today, it was once part of a substantial water course,
Black River, which poured off the Mountain and tailed out in a

dozen fingerling streams across the lowland delta before emptying into the Cornwallis River. The Gaspereau River, doggedly eroding its way west and creating its own little valley on the Mountain, eventually met up with Black River, captured its waters and consigned its lower half to brook status.

After a tortuous four-mile journey up from the Valley, the appearance of the village of White Rock is a surprise. It looks as if it has a past, some history, some substance to it. Unlike many hamlets on the Mountain, which usually consist of little more than a cluster of houses, White Rock shows the bones of industry in years gone by. The village, named for the unusual vein of white rock running through the quartzite here, has had its ups and downs—most Mountain settlements have had only downs. Even going back to the middle of the nineteenth century, White Rock had its "bubbles" as one resident put it; times of prosperity or at least the heartening promise of something about to happen.

Until the turn of the century, no one considered the Mountain useful for anything except fuel, fish and a hunting weekend or two. On weekends, even on Sundays, much to the disgust of White Rock residents, Valley fishermen came up the Mountain to catch some of the Gaspereau River's bounty or try for trout in one of the many lakes surrounding the community. In May and June, the more ambitious from Mountain and Valley alike set up a dip-netting system to snare a load of Gaspereau as the fish came up the river to spawn. The Gaspereau, a type of herring, were more of a challenge to eat than to catch, with their dozens of fine bones that defied the tongue's desperate attempts to keep them from sliding down the throat.

For a brief time, at the turn of the century, White Rock's modest fame as a fine spot for fishing drew a diverse array of visitors. These weren't common or garden variety tourists, who always stayed safely in the Valley, cosseted by apple trees and quaintness. These were visitors of a more adventurous sort and the wilds of the Mountain appealed to them. The brother of Sir Garnet Wolseley, commander at Khartoum, came for salmon, as did Lord William Seymour, commander of all Canadian forces, and a string of high admirals of the British fleet.

In the 1920s and early '30s, the village—then called White Rock Mills—was booming, not on the scale of the Valley, but well enough for the Mountain. There'd been sawmills and grist mills built and abandoned, each supplying a spark of hope for the future of the community and employment for the men. In those days, S.P. Benjamin's mill annually shipped out seven million feet of Mountain lumber to South America. Then a big-talking New Yorker named Thomas Kneeland excited the village when he proposed a pulp mill on the Gaspereau. It took three years to build and to produce its first load of pulp, after which it promptly went under. Kneeland, owing more than $80,000 to his employees, crept off the Mountain one night and was never seen again—but there were whispers that he never left at all, that he's buried in an unmarked grave somewhere on the Mountain.

Staves, barrel heads, shingles, carded wool and flour all provided employment "bubbles" for White Rock. By the 1920s, White Rock's hundred or so citizens considered themselves much more elevated than their neighbours in nearby Mountain communities. Decades earlier they had built their own church and temperance hall and had been the first, after the Free School Act passed in 1864, to petition the government for funds to build a school. Education had never been a priority on the Mountain, or so the government assumed— surely any who felt the need could go into the Valley for the purpose. But the route down from White Rock was deadly in winter, and after considerable agitation the community was given a paltry sum, just about enough to build a stoop. The residents took matters into their own hands and up went a small, grey school at the village crossroads.

Even as the Depression advanced, driving down lumber prices, White Rock's bubbles continued to form. There was Deep Hollow Road itself to be built, a concrete hydro dam to be constructed and a river to be diverted to increase the volume of water through the hydro power plant. After each bubble burst, the men would idle the seasons away, hoping and waiting for the next opportunity. Unlike the rest of the Mountain, they were accustomed to something always happening—eventually.

At one point in the 1930s, eight different mills were churning out lumber from dawn to twilight along the rivers leading out of White Rock. During the week, trucks, laden and empty, stirred the mud and dust on Deep Hollow as they lumbered in and out of White Rock. Women of the village claimed dust rags and brooms as their constant companions in the battle to keep dirt at bay. By 1937, the forty-three homes in the tiny village and surrounding community boasted, in addition to a school, a church, temperance hall, general store, meat market and smoke shop, twenty-five cars and four privately owned trucks.

With the advent of hydroelectric power it seemed as if White Rock's fortunes were assured. Eventually eight dams and five power stations were spread out on the Black and Gaspereau rivers near White Rock, creating lakes where none existed before and diverting the rivers in order to tap into the might of the water as it coursed down the Mountain.

Harvesting power on the Mountain around White Rock brought extraordinary wealth to the Valley. Hantsport's Roy Jodrey built his fortune, once rumoured to be the largest in the province, on the power supplied by impounded lakes, dams and canals of the Gaspereau watershed. And many smaller fortunes took seed in the opportunities presented by the Mountain's power. But by 1937, most of White Rock's bubbles had burst for good: the mills were closing one by one, the hydroelectric power work was largely completed, future construction would be minor and sporadic and continuing work would be done by technicians imported from town. "We now wait for something else to spring up that will give lots of work to the laborers," Charles O'Leary wrote hopefully that year. Forty-six years later White Rock was still waiting.

Clifford Long and Sons Lumber Mill, one of only two left on the entire Mountain, dominates the northeast corner of White Rock's crossroads. At the northwest corner is a ramshackle two-storey building, its parking lot used by mill workers. On the southwest corner the R.A. Ells supply company, which once sold a marvellous array of goods from bolts to brooms, stands empty. Set back slightly from the crossroads, on the fourth corner, the White Rock Baptist

Church, open from ten to twelve Sunday morning, and still shar-ing student ministers with the other Mountain communities, sits in a tidy clearing.

Leaving the crossroads at the centre of White Rock, Deep Hol-low Road veers over a small bridge. Hellgate Power Station, where the Gaspereau and Black rivers meet, lies below. It is quiet now, the falls long since tamed and the dam pools and ponds a testament to the works of humankind. But the Mountain crowds the power plant; a hundred feet away the forest is deep, dank and primitive—almost impenetrable.

The road climbs on past a sprinkling of picturesque, well-main-tained houses, a legacy of prosperous times. Higher up the hill from Hellgate, there is a cemetery. The graves date from 1770 to the pres-ent but there is no sign marking the cemetery, no hint it exists except on topographic maps, and the only access is through the property of a long-time White Rock resident who happily waves anyone through the gate and up the driveable path, which bends sharply, revealing a gravel- and boulder-strewn plateau. In the cemetery the names of White Rock's settlers and builders are carved and chiselled into wood and granite.

Deep Hollow Road continues on past the cemetery and up South Mountain. Suddenly one of the Mountain's surprises captures the unwary. At the crest of a hill, broad fields stretch out on both sides of the road. Even in December the gentle expanse is a lovely, pas-toral sight. But the real surprise lies behind as the Valley opens up its treasures in a stunning panorama. Nowhere else—not even at the Stile—does the entire land offer itself up so grandly. From the dikes to the Minas mud, Blomidon's cliffs and the orchards, everything that makes the Valley what it is can be seen from here.

Deep Hollow, unmindful of the splendour, continues up the long hill, curving around a stand of evergreens. Just past the trees three small houses, a woodshed and an outhouse sit in a clearing. Sur-rounding them the uncut hip-high grass and wild bush are frozen and blown into snow-topped tufts. One house is like a bombed-out hulk, windows gaping glassless, a piece of sheet—perhaps once a curtain—dangling from a second-storey window, cobwebs and debris decorating every corner of its crude interior. Clearly, it has not been lived in for many years and only Mountain tenacity keeps it standing.

Another house rises one and a half storeys. A few of its greyed boards faintly show a streak or two of white from some long-ago burst of painting energy. Its front porch is mostly gone and plastic flaps from the windows. Clusters of shingles cling to the roof. It looks as if someone once decided to renew or repair it, then gave up. A few shingles lie scattered on the ground or embedded in the frozen mud. Off to one side a miniature structure—like a card house but made from shingles—shows the mark of a child at play. A few bits of kindling form a pretend fence and clumps of feathers and down give the illusion of sheep huddling together against the wind.

From the outside, there is no discernible movement within the bigger house, though the faint light of a bare bulb comes from a back room. The windows are blank, unadorned by curtains. In the fading afternoon light, the flicker and glow of a black and white television reflect on the dirty glass. No shutters relieve the façade. It is a house of determined utility, where decades of hard use have stripped away any sense of hominess. It is also a house that claims the spot where it sits, inviting no intruders. There are many such houses on South Mountain, some tidy, some dishevelled, perched on patches of land but looking as if they might get up and move on any time. This house, though, is hunkered down and permanent; it has the look of generations.

Several cars are parked at various angles in the clearing, big-engined, nondescript, their days of glory long past. They are streaked with the mud and dust of the Mountain, and wind has blown a patchwork of paper and garbage up against them. One sits with its hood up, a few tools scattered around. There's no way to tell if they were dropped yesterday or last year. A couple of rusty bicycles lie in the long grass. In the side yard a refrigerator lies on its back, door askew, bird droppings covering the rim. Electrical wires snake away from it like innards. A rusted wood stove is nearby; a few feet of its pipe still poke straight up, the rest is scattered on the ground next to a bloated mattress. In the background, an outhouse tilts towards a shed crammed with firewood. Chickens scrabble in the bare dirt and rummage among the wood chips. The only other sign of life is a brown lump of fur curled tightly against the shed. The large dog, pure mongrel with shepherd and collie somewhere in its background, is secured to a tree by a thick chain and the ground around it is deeply rutted by paw prints from the animal's manic charges to the end of its tether.

There is a third building in the compound. A casual viewer might think it a large chicken coop. Ancient tar-paper sticks out between the wood and dangles from the haphazardly framed windows. The single panes of glass are dense with the film of decades. In a few places, the windows have been carelessly wiped by a bare hand leaving the inside of the house dimly visible. When the sun hits the windows at an angle, light refracts as if seen through an old Coke bottle. One missing pane is stuffed with the remains of a pillow.

The small one-storey house is basically a single room divided into a common living area and makeshift kitchen with two adjoining bedrooms, each separated from the main area by a sheet or a plastic shower curtain. The three rooms total 369 square feet, the larger bedroom ten feet by ten feet, the smaller ten by eight and the living room/kitchen/dining room twenty-one feet by nine. The floors are bare wood, and in the main living areas the wall studs and exterior planks are visible. Here and there light from the outside glints through a crack. The kitchen furniture consists of a battered chrome and vinyl table and chair set and a rough cupboard. In the living area, the only seating is two car seats bolted to a two-inch by ten-inch piece of board. The bedrooms each contain a three-quarter-sized iron bed.

A power pole connects the main house to electricity. An extra-long extension cord runs from it, over the ground, and into the smaller house to power the few lights and refrigerator, which is plugged in only when there is perishable food around. When those in the bigger house want the attention of those in the smaller house, they simply jiggle the plug of the extension cord, causing the lights to go on and off. There is no running water in either house.

This is the domain of the Goler Clan and has been since the mid-1940s, when they moved onto White Rock Mountain from West

Brooklyn on the lower slopes of the Mountain to the east, about twenty miles as the crow flies. In December 1983, sixty-five-year-old Stella Marie Goler, Clan matriarch, presides over the main house. Of average height for her age, with over-dyed black hair, Stella is thin to the point of gauntness; her legs are sticks with no inner thighs to give her any softness. Her slightly stooped back makes it seem as if she has spent her life with her shoulders hunched and arms wrapped tightly around her. The only hint of fleshiness is the round, smooth hump of her belly, so at odds with the rest of her, and the deep folds in the skin of her face.

Stella's eyes bear the mark of her mother, Ada Walsh, whose ancestors, named Welch, moved to the Mountain two hundred years ago. It was Ada with the sharp tongue who routed social assistance canvassers at the turn of the century. Stella's eyes are small and round, yet even encased in the wrinkles and lines of her six decades they are strikingly direct. Though there's a furtiveness in her body movements, there's no hint of it in her eyes, which fix upon you and search you out. Her voice is also her mother's, edgy and sharp, with less of the Mountain burr to soften it. The stamp of her father may be upon Stella, but no one, perhaps not even Ada—Ada "who walks the roads"—knows who that was. On the mother's side there's no doubt.

Stella Goler is a direct descendant of Rolen Rogers, the unfortunate founder of Rogers Settlement, later known as Forest Hill. In the Valley, Planter forebears are a source of pride. Proof that one is connected to the original settlers is evidence of belonging, a badge of status, and those who can trace their lineage to the eighteenth-century inheritors of the Acadian lands are proud of their families' long tenure. On the Mountain few know or care. Though the Mountain people's oral tradition is rich and colourful, far more so than the dry and sanitized archival records that document many of the Valley families, a sense of place is achieved not so much by ancestry but by the fact they've survived on the Mountain. Stella knows that cousins of hers, who go by the original name Welch, are rich and successful people in the Valley. But she wants "nuthin' to do with none of them." Like her mother, she is intensely suspicious of outsiders, who include anyone, related or not, outside the extended Goler Clan.

Stella's husband is seventy-eight-year-old Charles Edward Walton Goler. Owners of sawmills on the Mountain and orchards in the Valley remember him in his prime as a slow-moving though powerful man whose brawn, when he chose to use it, was a useful tool. "That man never got tired," his occasional employers marvel, citing examples of him easily manhandling a massive log off one of the lumber trucks or shouldering a huge sack of apples as easily as if it were a bag of feathers. But Charles's days as a worker were long ago. No one in the family can remember when he last held a job. A research survey done in 1959, when Charles was only fifty-three, described his occupation as "idle."

In his youth, Charles worked his father's farm in West Brooklyn with his younger brother, Cranswick. They were luckier than most who tried to farm the Mountain. The Goler homestead, located on the lower slopes, had slightly superior soil and drainage, allowing them to raise a few cattle and some market crops, making them more self-sufficient than most of their neighbours and relatives. They were also a little different in their faith, which various generations followed sporadically. They were Methodists, rare on the predominantly Baptist Mountain.

The Goler Clan on South Mountain originated with Munday Goler, a black man who bought his way to freedom by fighting for the British against the Americans in the War of 1812. En route by sea to Lower Horton, Nova Scotia, and the first land Munday would ever own himself, his son William was born. William Goler married a white woman, Maria, and their four children, listed in the 1871 census as "African," began the line that would move across the Mountain and find its way, through marriage, into the notorious Rogers family.

Today Munday Goler's black genes are so diluted they're all but invisible in the faces of the Clan he founded. But every now and then, his legacy shows up in the richer skin colour or the thick, wiry hair of his descendants.

In early winter 1983, Stella Goler is puttering around her tiny kitchen, ineffectively moving about the dirty dishes piled high beside the sink. Though her house is unbelievably filthy and squalid, she's particular about the washing up, pestering her grandchildren until they do the dishes for her. As for the rest of the cleaning, she has long ago given up, blaming, in a proud sort of way, her many children, especially the boys, for the grime that is a constant in her life.

Stella's husband, Charles, is nodding off in a ratty chair pulled up close to the stove. There is ice on the inside of the windows in the small room, but a semi-circle of warmth envelops him. His large belly rises and falls with every breath and an occasional phlegmy wheeze disturbs the dozen or so flies investigating his face.

In the back room the oldest of Charles and Stella's eight living children, forty-four-year-old Cecil, dozes on a fetid single bed. His three-inch fingernails curl out like yellow claws, and as he sleeps his fingers twitch and fret against each other. His face is almost invisible beneath a tangle of black beard and the stringy dark hair falling to his shoulders. Cecil spends most of his time in the bedroom or propped up in an old wheelchair. The family claims not to be sure what's wrong with him and when asked usually say he's "cripple" or he "went funny when he were a kid." In 1956, a doctor in the Valley examined seventeen-year-old Cecil. He made no comment about a physical infirmity but wrote, "Can't talk, has tantrums." Three years later, a research study described no physical infirmities either, simply, "cannot talk plain, 'feebleminded'." Just another Mountain mystery.

Two more of Charles and Stella's sons, Henry, thirty-seven, and Cranswick, twenty-nine, live in the main house. Henry has been gone for several hours. Cranswick is lumbering about readying himself for his regular chore, fetching water from the well. An older son, Charles, is long dead, but four daughters, Marjorie (forty-three), Mary (thirty-five), Stella (forty) and Josephine (thirty-two), live either on the Mountain or nearby. They, their current mates and their dozen children are frequent visitors, often staying for weeks in the summer, crammed into the main house or camped out in an old trailer Mary brings up to handle the overflow. As well, an assortment of family friends, most of them men, with some current or previous connection to one or more of the sisters, comes and goes.

Upstairs in one of the two bedrooms, a pair of young men, Billy Goler, eighteen, and Charlie Goler, twenty, stare fixedly at a poorly focused television screen. They are comfortable with each other, in the way of brothers, careless of each other's feelings though united in the face of outsiders. They are the sons of two of Stella's daughters, Marjorie and Stella.

The Goler compound is a place of lulls and furious activity. Visiting is almost a full-time occupation. Preparing for the trek to White Rock, for the Clan members who don't live there, can absorb hours. There are often other people to pick up, depending on whose cars are working, and supplies to be purchased in town. Once at the Goler compound, the arrivals behave as if they've never left. They spend more hours bringing each other up to date though the last visit may have been only a day or two ago. Old arguments and complaints are easily rekindled, jokes repeated and stories finished.

The third house is the domain of the third Goler son, William, thirty-eight, his girlfriend Wanda Whiston, twenty-five, and William's three children from his ex-wife Hazel: Sandra, fourteen, Donna (called Poochie by the family), eleven, and Lisa, seven.

William Goler is the Clan leader. Charles, his father, is no longer capable of butting heads with anyone. His brothers Cranswick and Henry are bigger and stronger but they defer to William. Stella, his mother, as is the way of the Clan, bows to the dominant male. William's sisters, though slightly less docile, also quickly fall into line when William cracks the whip. Outsiders know William as a "pleasant, co-operative, well-spoken fellow," but his violent rages are much feared within the Clan. He's of average height and not particularly imposing, but his thick body is wiry and strong. Alone among his generation of males, there isn't an overwhelming look of the Mountain about William. His unkempt hair is shaggy but his face is even-featured, almost handsome, in a rugged sort of way; with a shave, haircut, bath and a new set of clothes he could pass for someone from the Valley.

William makes all the important decisions and most of the minor ones in the family. He determines which outsiders become part of the Clan's extended circle. He establishes the rules, the initiations.

He dictates if and when the children go to school, whether they're allowed out of the house, and even at times what games they play. In times of crisis, William takes total command, much like a battlefield general. His anger and propensity for physical outbursts intimidate, but it is William's intellect that commands the Clan.

In 1961, a psychologist studying mental retardation for the Acadia Institute conducted intelligence tests on many children of the Mountain clans—including the Golers. William and his siblings scored far below average: Henry—47, Josephine—79, Mary—62, Stella—63, William—58. Superficially, William's score seems accurate: he is functionally illiterate and quit school in Grade 5 after a series of teachers categorized him as dull-witted and slow. But, just as ghetto blacks in the United States had low scores on standard IQ tests because they weren't familiar with the white cultural context of the questions, the Mountain children were hampered by their lack of exposure to the larger society. In fact, William is articulate and slyly intelligent. It is largely he who has steered the family through the reefs and shoals of collecting social assistance, which, in its various forms, has been integral to the Golers' subsistence for decades. Cranswick and Henry have worked seasonally at Long's Lumber Mill, just enough to qualify for assistance, and several sisters have low-paid service jobs. Employers unfailingly describe the Goler men and women as "pleasant" and "hard working." William, like his father, Charles, hasn't worked for years. To the untrained eye he appears healthy, but he claims to suffer from "fibrocytis," causing his hands and arms to shake.

It is a cool, calm December day, a welcome pause between winter's onslaughts. The smoke drifting out of the rust-stained chimney in the main house swirls and twirls listlessly in the flows and eddies of unseen wind currents. Standing against the side of William's house is a short section of rickety ladder.

A door opens in the main house. A bulky dishevelled man clad in a dingy lumberjack shirt walks heavily out carrying a metal pail. Cranswick Goler, a hulking Li'l Abner, is shy in the intellect department—the tests were right here—but adept at snaring small animals and a particularly patient fisherman. He is powerfully built and, though his meaty body looks lumpy and soft, there are few on the Mountain who can out-heave, out-lift or out-fight him. Cranswick kicks a partly shredded piece of plywood off the top of the well, attaches a piece of rope to his pail, retrieves a bucket of water and returns to the house. All is silent again.

Sometime later a slender girl slips out of the main house—eleven-year-old Donna Goler. Her shoulder-length brown hair is weeks overdue for a wash and her pants are grimy. Donna is a tiny child. Waif-like and pretty, with large hazel eyes, she is so delicate she looks as if a strong wind would carry her to the tree-tops. Her individual parts aren't memorable but taken as a whole she is a striking young girl.

She makes her way stealthily to the smaller house and quietly tries the knob on the front door, the only entrance to the house. It is locked. She glances back at the main house. Satisfied that no one is coming, she walks to the ladder at the side of the house and steps tentatively onto the first rung. It's solid, so she climbs up far enough to peer through the window of the bedroom, four feet above the ground.

The plastic and accumulated dirt make it difficult to see but she's helped by the illumination from the bare light bulb hanging from the ceiling. She rubs her sleeve over the plastic and presses her face close enough to make out two figures inside. William, her father, is roughly guiding Donna's sister Sandra into the room by a firm grip on her upper right arm. As she nears the bed, Sandra struggles. Her father shoves her down.

Sandra, at fourteen, is more conventionally attractive than Donna but she is slightly overweight. Her hair and clothing are just as filthy as her sister's. Donna can see but not hear William barking a command. Sandra's brief protest melts into resignation. Rising slightly she shoves her pants and underwear down to her ankles. She backs up onto the bed, not looking at her father. He pushes her to one side and she rolls over awkwardly on her stomach as her shoes catch in the fabric of her pants.

William Goler yanks down his zipper, spits copiously on his hand, wipes it over his erect penis, then grabs his daughter by the hips before driving himself deeply into her anus.

For several minutes the only sound is the rhythmic thudding of the bed hitting the wall, punctuated by Sandra's inadvertent grunts and squeaks of pain, as her father forces the full length of his penis into her again and again. Finally William's head snaps back and his mouth stretches wide in a silent scream of satisfaction. Seconds later he collapses on the bed, trapping Sandra beneath him. After a moment she wiggles out from underneath his weight and lies still.

Time passes and William reaches for his daughter again. He roughly cups her head with his hand, guiding it to his groin. Tears roll out of Sandra's eyes and down the sides of her open mouth.

On the ladder, Donna Goler shudders. It is a scene she has personally experienced, times without number, since her father introduced her to his pleasures four years earlier, when she was seven. Lately William has been showing increasing interest in Lisa, her younger sister, just turned seven. Another shudder racks Donna's thin body at the thought.

Chapter Six

Sandra Comes in from the Cold

January 1984

◆ SANDRA GOLER SITS SLUMPED AT HER
desk, disconnected from the class around her. This isn't unusual.
Some days there is a worn look about the girl, inconsistent with her
fourteen years. Those days, she just isn't there, and classroom activities go on without much involvement from her.

Wolfville High School is a nondescript, low-rise brick building
entirely at odds with the Victorian row houses and stately period
homes on the same street. Originally, an imposing two-storey building, typical of schools in the late nineteenth century, had been built
to house students from all grades, primarily from the Wolfville area.
As demand grew, the new school appeared and the old building handled the elementary grades.

Wolfville is a place where town kids rarely mix with those from
the rural areas, much less the Mountain. Teenagers from the hundreds of rural Valley hamlets and villages, together with the very few
from the Mountain who made it past Grade 8, usually attended one
of three large district high schools. But there have always been some
from the poorer element who attended Wolfville High, mostly kids
who lived across the tracks in the little enclave of shabby houses,

now prettily gentrified, together with a sprinkling from Gaspereau Valley and occasionally from Mountain communities like White Rock. But most of the Wolfville student population has always come from the middle-class and well-to-do families of town.

As a matter of course, the kids bussed in from the Mountain sat at the back, buffered by a row or two of empty seats. "They smelled so bad, no one wanted to get near them," reflects a Greenwich woman who rode the bus to school in the mid-1970s. "I kind of felt sorry for them. No one would be caught dead sitting with them— including me."

Though Sandra Goler is a young girl of at least average attractiveness, everything is against her when it comes to fitting in. She arrives at school week after week, wearing the same sour-smelling clothes or dressed completely inappropriately for the weather. If you get close you can catch the rank odour of wood smoke. Her attractiveness isn't enhanced by Mountain teeth, Mountain hygiene and Mountain grammar. Surrounded by the latest brand-name jeans, Lycra tights and over-size designer sweatshirts, she looks like a visiting alien. As a result, Sandra Goler has no friends from the Wolfville crowd, but when she is in the mood, she affects a brassy air and acts as if she doesn't care.

Sandra is often absent because of "colds" or "flu," which makes it all the more difficult to blend in as she misses so many assignments and classroom projects. She doesn't take part in any sports or clubs and never attends any after-school events. But then again, when Mountain children have tried to participate in extra-curricular functions in the Valley, the result hasn't always been pleasant.

———————◆———————

In April 1968, Wolfville's own Love Street Disc Band—L.S.D.— drew a huge crowd for a school dance. Next to the Lincolns, a fabled group from Truro whose keyboard man, John Gray, went on to write and perform award-winning musicals like *Billy Bishop Goes to War*, the L.S.D. was the most popular regional band of the day. It was the first warm night of spring, and the gym doors were wide open with students wandering in and out, trolling for partners or clustered in tight knots and regularly erupting with the over-loud laughter that is the teen-age mating call.

A grimy pick-up truck pulled into the curb disgorging three teenagers, two boys and a girl, before quickly pulling away. The teenagers walked over to the open gym doors, where they paused self-consciously for a couple of minutes as if trying to decide whether to enter. The girl gave one of the boys a shove and they all went in. Thirty minutes passed, and they hadn't moved from their spot against the wall in the gym. The music was suffocating and exhilarating and the three of them bobbed imperceptibly to it.

Eventually, chivvied by the boys, who wanted a smoke, the girl left the gym for the open space beside the school. Someone whispered, "Mountain cunt." The girl scowled and quickened her step. "I hear her pussy's so well-used she could fuck a horse with room left over." The anger on her face changed to embarrassment. A group of boys followed her chanting, "Do me, do me, do me like your daddy." As the tension grew, her companions stopped, instinctively standing back to back. Like sharks drawn by blood, several dozen more students joined the crowd around the three teenagers. The girl swore ferociously, her voice rising in volume against the taunting laughter. The boys said nothing, knowing that a word was all it would take to start a fight. "How much? How much for the bitch?"

The final electrical swell of "Light My Fire" ended the first set and students poured out of the gym. The taunters melted away, and as quickly as it had started, the confrontation was over. The girl and two boys quickly headed for Highland Avenue, half a block from the school, to hitch a ride back to the Mountain.

Two hours later the dance was over. Within seconds of the good-byes and see-you-laters, disgusted shouts punched through the night. In the parking lot, and up and down the streets around the school, vehicles listed on flattened rubber. Dozens of tires had been slashed.

———————◆———————

Sandra Goler has never attended a dance at Wolfville High. She'd have loved to, but her father would never allow it. The teacher glances at her from time to time, thinking she is more inattentive than usual. In fact, Sandra is wrestling with an idea. Fed up, the teacher sends her out of the room until she is ready to pay attention.

Sandra walks to the door and the tears come. Unaccustomed to displays of emotion from Sandra, the teacher follows her out. After a little gentle prodding, she blurts out that her father has been "doing her." Dumbfounded, the teacher hesitantly asks what she means by "doing." Sandra, recovering her equilibrium, is now a little impatient with the teacher's slowness. "You know... using me... like his wife." The teacher stares blankly. "Fucking me," Sandra adds matter-of-factly. Sandra's words send the teacher scuttling to find the principal. After a whispered exchange, the principal dials Family and Children's Services in Kentville. As luck would have it, he gets the only one of the three child protection workers who is an outsider—from away.

Dale Germaine moved to the Valley from Vancouver in 1982, almost as big a cultural leap as going from New York to Cajun country. Holding a master's degree in political economy and having some experience with the problems of a booming port city, she had a broader exposure to life's underbelly than most of the people she worked with. Though only twenty-eight when she arrived, she had a professional personality that had already been honed on social service stories; some true, some not, some so painfully bleak even the hardest heart would feel pain in the retelling. Germaine had refined a cool, slightly stand-offish professional exterior, underlined by the impatience—sometimes anger—of the very bright, which she managed to keep in check. Careful and detached, when she warmed to a person she occasionally shared the satisfactions, dark humours and ironies of her job. And most important, Dale Germaine hadn't grown up in this place, where the schism between Mountain and Valley was a fact of life.

From the moment she arrived, Germaine pushed up against the Valley biases about the Mountain, the belief that dirty deeds were taking place up there coupled with the equally firm assurance that nothing could be done about it. "We don't know anything about it and nobody wants to know anything about it," another worker in the area reluctantly admitted. The social workers, health professionals, educators were like everyone else in the Valley; they took a see-no-evil, hear-no-evil approach. They might know something but were content not to *really* know—at least to the point of doing anything, unless it was forced on them.

It is hard for outsiders to understand the yawning divide that, to this day, separates the Mountain and the Valley. It's difficult to distil two hundred years into a sentence or two, though most people in the Valley couldn't explain it if they were given all day. The divide is woven into the social fabric—it just is. Had Germaine known the history, she might have understood the attitude towards the Mountain among the various layers of health, education and legal professionals. "People were just looking the other way," she recalls with a mild astonishment a decade and a half later. "They'd react in a crisis but other than that . . . And the people were quite happy to be left alone. It wasn't popular at the time that anybody did anything."

On January 21, 1984, Germaine drove from her office in Kentville to Wolfville High, talked briefly to the teacher, then sat down with Sandra, who was now nervous and upset. She would alternately babble for a minute, then fall silent or become sullen and uncomprehending at Germaine's gentle questioning. Her words had an oddly mutinous undertone, not, as one would expect, the relief associated with confession. It all focused on Sandra's father, William Goler. She told of William "doin'," "fuckin'," "screwin'" her since she was nine or ten, she couldn't remember, fifteen or twenty times a month, she didn't know, it was too many times to remember—too many years.

Sandra graphically described sexual intercourse, buggery, fellatio and cunnilingus on beds, in sheds and in the cellar of the Goler compound. She'd been "done" so many times in so many ways it was impossible to remember exact times or dates—details blended into each other. But one thing Sandra Goler was certain of. "I don't want to be used as his wife no more," she told her stunned listener.

Germaine had never personally handled an incest case before but this one fit all the profiles. Incest was a burgeoning topic. The U.S. Department of Justice was planning a national symposium on child molestation for later in 1984 and a Canadian report to be entitled *Sexual Offences against Children in Canada* was ready for release. There was more literature available every day and, sadly, many more cases to study. If there was ever a textbook victim of incest it appeared to be Sandra Goler. Victims were most commonly between the ages of eight and twelve and though Sandra was fourteen, socially and intellectually she was years younger. Her impoverished background radiated from her, and girls from lower socio-economic classes were over 60 percent more likely to be victimized than middle-class children, the profiles of the time explained.

Social isolation was also a key factor. Children on isolated farms were more vulnerable to incest, as were those without friends and neighbours nearby. "Presumably, the physical presence of friends and neighbors acts as a deterrent to potential abusers," concluded one of the most influential studies of the day. "But even more than that, lonely children may be more susceptible to offers of attention and affection in exchange for sexual activities." Sandra's family, like many Mountain clans, "kept to itself."

Stepfathers also figured prominently in child sexual abuse, but an even more important factor was the absence of the mother. Sandra's mother, Hazel, had married twenty-four-year-old William Goler in 1969 when she was just sixteen. Born to a family marked with one of the lowest-class names on the Mountain, Hazel's pool of potential mates was limited. Though Goler was far from a "good" name, to her William was a catch. He was different from his brothers and the other young Mountain men of his generation, whom she considered lazy and stupid. There was a nervous energy about William Goler and he had ideas, he didn't take no for an answer and no one could push him around. He got angry a lot and often railed about people putting him down, or keeping him from what was rightly his, but at least he had spunk.

William also had a roving eye and a powerful belief in a man's prerogative. By 1979 Hazel had three children, Sandra, Donna and Lisa. They were enough for her. Hazel went down to the Kentville hospital to have her "tubes done." Tubal ligations were popular with Mountain women unwilling to be like their mothers, raising nine or ten children and getting pregnant every time a man felt like "stickin'" them. Such women sometimes went into hospital for an unexplained "women's" problem, had their operation and returned with no one the wiser.

Other forms of birth control were largely non-existent on the Mountain. There had always been whispers in the Valley that unwanted or stillborn babies of Mountain girls—some sired by Valley boys—ended up in unmarked graves. Some who live there, and a few who admit they bore such children, say it's more than mere rumour, that the slopes and hollows of the hills making up South Mountain shelter generations of baby bones.

During Hazel's stay in hospital, another young woman from the Mountain, twenty-year-old Wanda Whiston, moved in to "housekeep" for William. "Dad's girlfriend," Sandra spat out, contempt and hatred lacing her voice. Hazel returned from surgery to find her bed occupied. She was welcome to join in, William told her, but Wanda wasn't going anywhere. "You can take it or leave it. It don't matter to me." She left, walking miles down White Rock Mountain and ending up at a small general store where she called a friend to pick her up.

Girls living without their natural mothers, the literature claimed, were three times as vulnerable to their father's advances as those with both biological parents living in the same house. Mothers are important emotional and physical protectors of their daughters. Those who are distant, frequently ill or unaffectionate place their daughters at higher risk. As well, families dominated by powerful males who oppress their wives leave children more exposed to incest. If there ever was a male-dominated society it was the Goler Clan. Hazel, coming from outside the family, had always been at the bottom of the pecking order—little better off than the children. She was surrounded by Golers—Stella, Charles, William, Cecil, Henry, Cranswick, Billy—all of whom lived steps away. Added to them were William's sisters, Marjorie, Stella, Mary and Josephine, and their children, who were such frequent visitors they virtually lived in the small compound. For Hazel, survival meant keeping her head down and not making trouble.

———————◆———————

As Dale Germaine listened to Sandra Goler, Canada was taking its first faltering steps towards acknowledging and then dealing with the problem of incest. "She was 9 years old when it started," revealed a *Toronto Star* story. "He would grab her, fondle her. Playful little caresses. She didn't know it was wrong. She had a sense it wasn't right. She told no one. By 14 he was raping her whenever he could get her alone. 'It was rape with my permission,' the victim said, 'I couldn't fight him. He did whatever he wanted.'" Voices, tentative at first, joined a growing chorus.

"My mother was away on business a lot," explained a Campbell River, British Columbia, woman who was first raped by her father at age six and later by her grandfather. "My father was respected in the community. All four of us girls slept in the same room, and when we heard my father get up in the night, we knew he was coming for one of us. I learned to snore real good, but then I would feel guilty because I knew he was abusing my older sister. On the other hand when I submitted I hated my sister for not appreciating what I was doing for her. We never talked about it, and as long as we didn't talk, we didn't believe it was happening."

Hard on the heels of these revelations were indications that the problem was far more widespread than generally believed and the paucity of reported cases, let alone charges and convictions, had its roots in the supposed lack of credibility of children. In 1980, an eleven-year-old girl had told her child care worker that her father was forcing her to have sexual intercourse with her. "This is not a nice conversation," the worker responded primly, then changed the subject. That same year a mother confided to a psychiatrist that she thought her husband was fondling her five-year-old daughter. "There's no problem with your child, it's you who is crazy," diagnosed the psychiatrist.

Nineteen eighty-four was a gentler time—at least according to public perception. Front-line workers such as teachers and policemen had no special training in spotting and handling incest cases, and court officials, judges, and defence and prosecuting attorneys were often as naïve as the general public. But Dale Germaine had heard enough, and knew enough, to decide that there was no way she was sending Sandra Goler home that night. She decided to place her under the temporary protection of Family and Children's Services, then phoned the RCMP. Again fate had a hand. The two officers assigned to handle the call were Corporal Baxter Upshall and Constable Ted Corkum from the detachment in New Minas, a strip-mall village between Kentville and Wolfville. Upshall, who did the initial questioning and headed up the investigation, was one of the few policemen in the Valley who had experience investigating an incest case.

At a previous posting, a few years earlier, a young girl walked into the station and complained to Upshall about her father—a virtually unprecedented act, even today. "She was now scared that her sister had a baby and that the baby was going to be victimized by the father, or grandfather. So she came in," Upshall explained. "I had done that one and that went with all of his daughters; all five daughters plus a friend of the family had been victimized by him as well. That was one where the mother said I don't know what's all the fuss, we all did it anyway so what was the difference."

By the time Germaine had fully briefed Upshall, it was late afternoon. As Sandra was growing more anxious, they took her to an emergency home, leaving further questioning until the next day. Mid-morning on January 22, Sandra, accompanied by Dale Germaine and a second social worker, came to Upshall's office. Whether it was the chastening effects of the police station or a day away from the family, it was a subdued Sandra Goler who told her story again. The details were essentially the same but this time with an undercurrent of violence—shoves, grabs, threats and severe physical punishment. Almost as an aside, Sandra revealed that her father forbade her to use birth control because he wanted her to have a son by him.

As they questioned Sandra, something niggled at Upshall. Assuming she was telling the truth, which he did, he knew there had to be a specific reason she had come forward after enduring five years of sex with her father. On top of that, the Golers were notoriously close-mouthed and suspicious of outsiders—so something must be motivating her to break away from this entrenched pattern. No matter how dreadful their lives are, children have an extraordinary ability to inure themselves to abuse, to build themselves a cocoon and hide away from events as if they weren't happening. He was sure Sandra had done just that for most of her life.

Upshall weighed the possibility that the presence of Wanda Whiston was the catalyst. Sandra obviously loathed her for usurping her mother. But Wanda had been with William for four years. In the absence of a specific current provocation, that event seemed too far in the past to cause Sandra to come forward now. Sandra's age coupled with a few off-hand comments about boys gave Upshall a clue. He came to the conclusion that, Mountain or not, Sandra wanted what most teen-age girls want—to get out from under the controls of home and have a boyfriend, not necessarily in that order. She had already told Upshall that her father was very strict and controlling and when she occasionally visited her mother, living in a trailer in the Valley, she was given much more freedom. When Upshall gently questioned her about boyfriends, Sandra coyly told him that she liked the looks of a boy in a nearby family. When her father found out she'd been visiting them, he'd flown into a rage.

Upshall's working theory was that Sandra wanted out and William had no intention of letting her go. He guessed that Sandra's thinking was straightforward and probably based on the family's familiarity with social services. After she told her story, Upshall reasoned, she expected that her father would be questioned by the police, possibly reprimanded, then she would be sent to live with her mother and, finally, the greater world would be available to her. But she didn't reckon on Baxter Upshall.

Upshall's façade is that of an average policeman whose every action is dictated by the book. He's diligent and thorough enough to have earned the nickname Bulldog. Like most of his ilk, he speaks police English—a particular stilted version of the language that acts as a foil to outsiders. It's a useful camouflage that gives no hint of the feints and dodges his mind is capable of. He follows instinct, intuition and his gut more than he would like you to believe. There's also a hint of tension in the man, of something suppressed that he has harnessed and turned to do his bidding.

While Upshall believed Sandra Goler, he was also certain there was something more to her story, though he didn't know exactly what. "It was just a gut feeling you get when you're talking to somebody about something," Upshall relates. "It was probably more the things she didn't say at certain times and what she did say at others; the answers didn't come across the way they should have. So you start saying, what am I not hearing here? Her answers were too narrow, too precise about some things and went on in too much detail about other things that were insignificant." Upshall knew that the police would have to question Sandra's sisters, even if he was not completely confident of the basics of her story—it was procedure.

Upshall and the social workers discussed the mechanics of bringing in Donna and Lisa, deciding to waylay the school bus en route to their home in White Rock that afternoon. They didn't want to march into the Goler home and snatch the children away, risking, at best, fury and distress and, at worst, a confrontation that might put everyone in danger. After all, from what Sandra had said, there could be six or more adult males in the Goler compound and at least three deer rifles. But when the police tried to intercept the school bus, they discovered Donna and Lisa had already been dropped off. They would have to wait until the next day. This time they'd get the children directly from school.

It had been a bad two nights for Donna Goler. She was grateful for school because it kept her and Lisa away from home and away from her father. She knew from bitter experience that there would be consequences over Sandra's disappearance. Once William had slammed Sandra's fingers in the car trunk when the police returned her after an attempt to run away. While she stood there screaming, he dared her to try it again. Another time a teacher from Sandra's school brought her home and told William she had been saying bad things about him.

Donna had hated Sandra that day with a white-hot passion. While the teacher was still talking she grabbed Lisa, slipped out of the house and hid behind the woodshed, praying her father would take his anger out on Sandra alone.

Yet another time Sandra ran away to Hazel, her mother. William phoned to demand she return, and his ex-wife hung up on him. Then he ordered Donna to call, and in a rare, foolhardy display of resistance she refused. Infuriated, William stuffed her in the narrow, blazing hot space behind the wood stove where the heat singed her hair and blistered her skin.

The first night of Sandra's absence William raged, the second night he was strangely quiet and distracted, which terrified Donna even more. She didn't know that William had learned via the Mountain telegraph that there were police in the area. He didn't like the coincidence of a rare police excursion coming the day after Sandra had gone missing. Concerned by her father's unusual behaviour, Donna warned Lisa to keep her mouth shut because something big was happening. Dinner time came and went. Wanda "the housekeeper" just sneered at her when she said she and Lisa were hungry. Donna rummaged around, finally finding some crackers and a package of Tang. Better than nothing and better than potatoes. Donna once counted eight days in a row with just potatoes for dinner. She hated potatoes. Even so, on one of those nights, when Sandra stole a potato from her plate, Donna was so hungry she stabbed her sister with a fork.

✦

Later the second night, William told Lisa and Donna that Sandra was stirring up trouble. In a flat, grim voice he told them what would happen if they ever talked to the police or anyone from town— they'd be taken away from the family, they would never see their grandparents ever again, or their cousins. They'd be separated from each other, locked up in terrible places and beaten every day. There would be no Christmas, birthdays or Easter. "All they wanna do is put me in jail! They wanna lock me up. They been after me for years. You want me to go to jail?" he railed at his children. "You don't say nuthin' to no one. Understand? I ain't goin' to jail!"

Donna lay awake that night beside Lisa unable to shut the pictures out of her mind of a dreadful, lonely life cut off from the family and imprisoned by terrible people from the Valley. She didn't know how she would live if she didn't have Lisa. She looked after her little sister like a mother, worried about her, cuddled and protected her.

Some of the cloud around Donna lifted the next morning when she thought about the day ahead. Her class was going on a trip to the Acadia University pool. She could hardly wait. She didn't have a bathing suit of her own, but her favourite teacher found one for her. As the class was readying to leave, the principal called her into the office and said he would like her to stay behind because they had a special job for her. Donna was torn between bitter disappointment at missing the trip and pride that she had been singled out. She was alone in the classroom diligently cleaning the blackboards when the principal walked in, followed by a policeman, a woman from Family and Children's Services and Lisa.

Getting the children into the car was an unpleasant task. They didn't resist but were so plainly terrified it was almost worse than if they had run away. When they tried to separate them in the New Minas police station, Donna wrapped her arms around her sister and screamed at them. "I hate you!" she sobbed. "Get away from me! Don't touch my sister! You just want to put my father in jail. I hate you!"

After some gentle persuasion and promises that the girls would be apart for only a short while, they managed to pry Lisa out of Donna's iron grasp. Baxter Upshall was astonished at the strength of the small, slender child.

The social workers were surprised at the sensitivity of the policemen—who they felt certain would be ham-handed and clumsy in their handling of the children. Upshall, with children of his own, felt a special affinity for them right from the start. In the end he was the only official to be with the children from beginning to end. Constable Ted Corkum, nicknamed Blunt Jack in the detachment, was the biggest surprise. Forbidding in voice and manner, he could be gruff and peremptory in his dealings with adults. "If you're smart, you don't piss off Ted," a fellow officer cautions. But Blunt Jack proved to have an angel's touch with children. "Our interviews with the children went on for hours and hours, and we had to keep taking them out to Burger King or taking them here or taking them there," Dale Germaine recalls. "They were just so good with the kids. Every time they looked like they were starting to get tired, the men were the ones who told us to take them."

Questioning Lisa was very difficult. She was only seven and clearly a slow child who didn't have a full understanding of what they were asking her. Donna, on the other hand, was frightened but as defiant as a cornered wolverine. Moreover, she showed flashes of a penetrating intelligence; she immediately sensed Upshall's slightest evasion or duplicity—both of which are important tactics during police interrogation. He'd have to be very careful with this one. Upshall eventually got Donna talking by asking simple, seemingly harmless, questions about school and then the other children in the Clan before steering the conversation to the adults. He carefully avoided any mention of her father. Cautiously at first, then more readily, Donna talked about her grandparents, aunts, uncles, sisters and cousins.

Alarm bells went off in Upshall's and Germaine's minds when Donna detailed the social dynamics of the Goler Clan—the endless comings and goings of family members, friends and strangers and her and the other children's difficulty identifying who was whose father and mother and their confusion over cousins, half-brothers and -sisters. Living in two small houses with paper-thin walls, little more than sheds really, without indoor plumbing, it seemed impossible that others in the family would not have discovered William's secret.

Donna answered questions for an hour before abruptly falling silent. She sat like that for a minute, looking intently first at the policeman and then at the social worker. "He done me too," she announced calmly. "I don't want him doing Lisa no more."

Chapter Seven

The Clan

✦ DONNA'S "HE DONE ME TOO" WAS THE first in a series of grudging admissions. Nothing came out of her mouth without thought and often there seemed to be a battle, somewhere behind her fierce eyes, before she answered a question or confirmed a fact. And she frequently asked questions of her own— what ifs, what happens if I tell you such and such?—pausing to digest the answers before she gave up more information.

During two days of questioning, a horrifying picture of the three girls' lives emerged. It was a story of constant abuse, deprivation and poverty made all the more repugnant by the fact that the Golers lived only a few miles from well-to-do Valley towns where the children had contact with doctors, hospitals and teachers. The family was also well-known to social services, as many of them had been receiving welfare or disability payments. Somehow, through it all, nobody had noticed, or if they had they had paid no attention. It didn't take long before the names of other children, all cousins, began colouring the background. William had made regular and obscene use, not only of his daughters but also of his sisters' children, Pam, twelve, Sally, nearly nine and Annie, five. And Sandra and Donna told of watching William assault his nephews, nine-year-old Matt and Doug, fourteen.

Details were often vague and confusing, complicated by the tangle of relationships among the Clan. Lisa didn't understand many of the questions and she was so frightened and disoriented they dared not press her too much. Sandra babbled on about dates and places but she was difficult to pin down and seemed more interested in herself than what had happened to the others. But Donna's recall, despite the fear and anger making her nervous and edgy, was specific.

Just as he had when questioning Sandra, Upshall had a nagging feeling during the two days that there was more to the story than the children were telling him. But there was enough for the moment. Enough to arrest William Goler.

On January 23, 1984, Baxter Upshall and Ted Corkum left the New Minas police station for the Mountain. They wound their way up the Deep Hollow Road to the top of White Rock Mountain, then pulled into the yard of the Goler compound. They were a little tense, as any police officer is before an arrest, but they were no longer concerned about armed confrontation. They now knew that neither William nor any of the other adult Golers had been in serious trouble with the law before.

William Goler opened the battered door of the main house to Upshall's sharp rap and greeted the two men with a smile. To their surprise, he invited them inside as if they'd come on a social visit. They stepped directly up into the house; most of the front porch had rotted away long ago. Despite all his police training, experience and professional aloofness, Upshall was overwhelmed by the sheer number of people in the tiny dilapidated dwelling, at first glance eight or nine milling around, the confusion of shabby furniture, the mess and, underlying it all, the sewery smell of decay. "It was just terrible living conditions," says Upshall, his normally impassive face twitching. "They didn't have indoor plumbing that I can recall, certainly not modern indoor plumbing. Sanitation was bad. There was an old gentleman sitting in a chair—old Mr. Goler—and the flies were pitching on him, blue flies, all kinds of flies pitching on him." Despite working in a field where the underbelly of life is frequently exposed, Upshall felt an urgent desire to take a shower.

Rotten floorboards sagged beneath their boots as the two policemen told William Goler he was under arrest for having sexual intercourse with his three daughters and his nieces and nephews. As the charges were read, the police had some difficulty tearing their eyes away from the flies cantering about Charles Goler's face. William waited quietly for them to finish, then meekly left the house followed by Upshall and Corkum. He was so docile they didn't bother with handcuffs.

Fifteen minutes later, Upshall and Corkum were shepherding William into an interrogation room at the New Minas station. They explained the arrest again and asked if he understood. Once he had nodded, they read him his rights and William indicated he understood those also. Mountain people had a reputation for being simple and more than a little slow. Neither Upshall nor Corkum wanted to risk a mistake in police procedure getting this case thrown out of court—assuming it went that far.

The officers found William Goler strangely complacent, even smug, smiling from time to time when they tried to increase the pressure. It was as if he didn't believe they could touch him. When they confronted him with information corroborated by several children, he didn't budge an inch, adamantly denying ever having had sex with Donna, Lisa or any of their cousins. Whenever Sandra's name came up, he grimly pressed his lips together, refusing even to deny the charge or speak of her. It was as if she no longer existed. He claimed to be completely baffled by the children's stories. But he was quick to volunteer the information that his ex-wife Hazel entertained a lot and said he'd heard that her parties were wild affairs. The children visited her trailer from time to time and he was willing to bet that if anything funny had gone on that was where it had happened.

William's arrest created major, unexpected problems for the Goler Clan. As the most intelligent and articulate of his generation, he was the unquestioned leader and had been for many years. William was like a lion, head of the pride; his roar routed all pretenders. But the gene pool was so weak in the family that no young lion waited to take his place. Without their dominant male, the Goler Clan was paralysed.

It was a given to many in the Valley, including those in the medical and social services professions, that Mountain people were too backward to understand the law, government or any other kind of bureaucracy. But then few had ever met anyone like William Goler. Within hours of being arrested, William had contacted a lawyer from one of the top Valley law firms in Berwick, thirty miles to the west. Even though he had no money, he wasn't about to throw himself on the mercy of legal aid and risk being assigned any old lawyer. "I got the distinct impression that he was far from unintelligent," emphasizes psychiatrist Dr. Brian Garvey, then head of the Fundy Mental Health Clinic. "In fact I could tell he was playing the system like a violin. Most in the Valley thought these people just stayed on the Mountain. Not true, they were in and out of social services, doctors' offices and the hospitals more than anyone. They knew the system better than anyone. In some ways, they were the system—at least half of it."

What little organization existed in the Clan disintegrated in William's absence. The crisis hit them like a twister, churning the family inside out, creating divisions and leading them into long, ineffectual hours of argument about what to do. William's brothers, Cranswick and Henry, and his teen-age nephew, Billy, had difficulty keeping complex thoughts in their heads for even a short period. They needed to be forcefully briefed before they talked to the police, but there was no one to do it. Most of William's sisters were more intelligent than the brothers and a little more worldly, as they'd worked in the Valley in various menial jobs. But they were emotional and erratic; they needed to be kept in line. Charles Sr. just slumbered heavily in his chair, and Stella rushed around the house like a beheaded chicken, squawking piteously about her woes—the police, jail and her boy.

To complicate matters, William Goler made a grave error. He believed that the entire fuss was really all about him and Sandra. She'd been bucking his control for several years and tattling to the police was exactly the sort of thing she'd do. Hell, he thought to himself, she'd already done it once before, and the police hadn't believed her. As for Donna and Lisa, he was confident he ruled them completely. He believed that whatever they might have said under pressure, they would deny the minute they laid eyes on him. A single glare would snap their mouths shut so tightly they wouldn't speak for weeks. And if Sandra somehow summoned up the will to see the charges through, it would be her word against his. He didn't think anyone would believe a liar like his oldest daughter. But at the heart of William's miscalculation was where the battle line would be drawn. It would not be between him and Sandra but between him and his second child, three-foot-eleven-inch, forty-four-pound Donna—the only Goler bright enough and tough enough to challenge him.

In the days following William's arrest, Baxter Upshall quickly pulled in the rest of the Goler Clan for questioning. Initially, there appeared to be eight children involved. Based on the number of incidents Donna and Sandra had witnessed, he was sure some of the adults must know what William had been up to. There were simply too many people swarming over the Goler compound and too few places to hide for William's pleasures to go unnoticed. The police started with the immediate family and the list grew and became more complicated by the day.

Upshall used a simple interrogation technique, forcefully telling the adults he *knew* for a fact what William had been up to while implying that if they didn't tell him all *they* knew they could well end up being involved too. He was fishing but he netted a fine catch. "Their response was open to start with—'I know this or I heard this and so-and-so told me this'—which keeps the ball rolling. Finally we made the whole circuit amongst all the family. Their answers were trying to keep attention from focusing on themselves. They knew we knew something. It goes along with self-preservation. 'What can I do best to take the heat away from myself? I've got to make me look as good as I can.'"

In their rush to divert attention from themselves, the Goler adults spewed out a tangle of information about William. They had never done or seen anything themselves, they emphasized, but they had been told about certain things they were only too happy to share.

Stella Goler, William's forty-year-old sister, was the mother of three of the children William had been accused of assaulting—Doug, Pam and Sally. Her revelations were relatively harmless at first. She told the police that she'd seen twenty-year-old Charlie, her nephew, exposing himself to the children a few years back and once found William, wearing only underclothes, tucking five naked children, his own and hers, into bed. It was suspicious, Stella told them, and she made sure they knew she took the trouble to confront him. "That's an odd way to check them," she queried her brother.

The police interviewed Stella three separate times over two and a half days and each time she produced more information. "I have heard Willie [William] and others all talking about each of them screwing my Pam, and Willie as well saying that he was screwing Sandra," she confided. "Marge, my sister, if she was honest, can tell you the same thing." At the end of the third interview Stella left, cheerily promising to let them know anything else she discovered.

William Goler's arrest, coupled with the ensuing revelations about the other children, plunged the police and social workers into a brutal regime of fourteen-hour days as they drew up lists of people to interrogate and tried to figure out where they lived—no easy task since many had no phones, and if they were listed in the book their address was simply the name of the nearest community or a huge rural route.

Dale Germaine, assisted by other social services staff, ferried Sandra, Donna and Lisa back and forth from their temporary foster homes, talked to them, soothed them, accompanied them for the hours of questioning. There were more long hours of consultation with Upshall and Corkum about the best way to elicit information from the children. It was a delicate job. Sandra had become more sullen and less communicative. Once Lisa became a little more comfortable with them, she was surprisingly clear about events but because she was only seven they feared her testimony might not stand up in court. Upshall sensed, almost from the beginning, that Donna would be the key. She was still grudging with her disclosures but she usually knew dates and plenty of details. Best of all she was very difficult to shake once she'd stated something as a fact.

Still, the first week was tense with antagonism, especially from Donna. She had not seen her father or mother since she and Lisa had been taken from the school. She was angry at the way Upshall picked away at her life, scratching at layers of her memory, burrowing into her past like a determined tick. Her family was a powerful force in her life. Her only friends were family and the only thing she knew of people outside the Clan was that they looked down on her. Donna's sole experience with the outside world was school, which she loved with a passion but, like the rest of the family, she didn't mix with the other kids. She recognized how shabby and poor she was and she saw that the other children didn't want to sit next to her on the bus. It was just easier to keep to herself.

There were many torments in Donna Goler's life, not the least of which were her father's pleasures and tempers, but it was the life she knew—the only life she knew. Here in the Valley everything was different and the adjustment was hard. At the temporary foster home that she and Lisa shared, they could eat until they were full, and it wasn't all potatoes. She went to a restaurant for the first time in her life and was told to order anything she wanted. Until that day she'd never eaten a hamburger. She rode around in a clean car that had seats with no holes and didn't reek of cigarettes and squalid living. Her clothes were brand new, not other people's cast-offs or stale-smelling odds and ends scrounged out of the five-cent barrel at Frenchy's Used Clothes emporium.

Garbage was deposited in cans and then once a week hauled off in a truck. At home they just stuffed it into the attic until it was full or the stench became so foul the adults couldn't stand it any more. Then the children were ordered to clean it out. Though Donna had seen running water and a few times had baths or showers at the homes of Clan members with indoor plumbing, the availability of it was a treat. Flush toilets were a particular pleasure. On the Mountain the Goler outhouse was so rank, Donna sometimes felt like vomiting when she used it. And at night they urinated and defecated into a bucket and woe betide anyone who was clumsy when going about their business. Wanda Whiston dropped her used sanitary napkins into the same bucket and left it to the children to dispose of when they dumped the contents in the morning.

Part of Donna was awed and thrilled by the new life. Another part of her was waiting for the other shoe to drop—for the terrible vengeance her father had promised if they ever gave a hint about family business to outsiders. Whatever else William Goler was, Donna knew him to be a man of his word in such matters. She deeply feared her father, but beneath that corrosive ocean of emotion there was a tiny drop of love. William Goler was her father.

The roller-coaster of events and new experiences roared by Donna so rapidly she could hardly grasp what was happening. Throughout it all Baxter Upshall, the policeman, loomed like the great prow of Blomidon itself as it guarded Minas Basin. Everywhere she turned there he was, asking one last question, probing for one more detail. She hated him. But every now and then there was a flicker of something within her, a sensation of pleasure and pride. Donna, for the first time in her eleven years, was getting respect, not punishment, for her intelligence, positive reinforcement, not a smack across the face, for being smart. When she caught the look of appreciation in an adult's face, a little thrill burned inside her.

It was like throwing gasoline on a tiny flame. Upshall's questions were an irritant, an invasion, but they encouraged her to think, analyse and look at the strange new world around her. She told him more than she intended but she didn't tell him everything—she could not, even if she had wanted to.

Upshall came to rely on the slender little girl. In a universe of shifting stories, half-truths and outright lies, Donna was rock solid. Upshall had been uneasy about the case from the beginning. The strange disintegration of alliances within the Goler Clan when he interviewed them spelled one thing—complicity. Only the children, especially Donna, could clarify the fuzzy picture.

It started with one name, then another and another. At various times in their lives Donna and Sandra had seen virtually every member of their extended Clan having sex with their cousins. Upshall realized that no child within the Clan's grasp was safe. He had to get them out.

On January 30, they brought in Pam, the twelve-year-old daughter of William's sister Stella. Unlike Donna, Pam was an outgoing, social and gregarious girl eager to spin tale after tale about daily life in the Goler compound. "You couldn't shut her up with a two-by-four," Stella once said of her daughter. In a different world, the mercurial child might have become an actress. As it was, for the first time Pam had an audience hanging on her every word. She readily confirmed that Uncle William "screwed" her, then spilled out a dizzying list of over a dozen adults—family, friends and neighbours— who'd also "done" her in every possible way.

On February 1, Matt, Josephine Goler's son, was in his Grade 4 classroom when the principal came into the room. He asked the puzzled boy to step out into the hallway where his eyes widened at the sight of two uniformed policemen and a social worker waiting for him. "The police said, 'We have to take you into the police station for a little bit,'" he sighs, remembering back. "I figured it wasn't going to be that long. I didn't know what was going on. It happened so fast. I was afraid either I'd done something wrong or there'd been a death in the family and they had to tell me about it." Shortly after he arrived in New Minas, his frantic mother, Josephine, showed up demanding to see her son. He also spotted his two cousins, Jeff and Jennifer, Mary Goler's children.

Within eight days of William Goler's arrest, every child but one within the Clan had been apprehended and secreted away in foster homes and emergency shelters—ten in all, three boys and seven girls. It put a huge and sudden pressure on a small social services system accustomed to dealing with one or two children in a month, not ten in a single week.

Getting the confidence of the frightened, confused children was a difficult job, made all the harder since they came from the Mountain and had little experience with people from the Valley, let alone the larger world. All of them carried the distinct stamp of the Mountain in their voices, manners, hygiene and general knowledge.

Upshall wasn't entirely sure if they understood that they had been abused, let alone that it was wrong.

Two of the boys, Matt and Jeff, even when confronted with the other children's statements, adamantly denied that anyone had touched them. Upshall didn't know if their denial was out of shame, a need to protect the Clan or simply because that was how they had always lived. "Every other kid would go home from school and probably do what chores they had to do, have supper, watch TV, do their homework, go to bed, that type of thing. They went home and other things happened to them. But I don't know if they knew other kids existed a different way. That was a big barrier to overcome there."

Gradually, painstakingly, Upshall, along with Ted Corkum and Dale Germaine, convinced the children that what had happened to them on a daily basis was wrong and other kids didn't have to suffer through what was a routine part of their lives. "It took a lot of time talking to them, a lot of patience, befriending them," Upshall recalls. "The kids were somewhat intimidated by everything that was going on. The biggest thing was to take the guilt away from them. They were not the ones doing wrong."

A rhythm of questions developed: one child might shyly mention something witnessed and that fragment would be taken to the other children, who confirmed or embellished it. It was like building a card castle, every placement had to be gently and carefully made. Many of the children were fragile, especially the boys. The police had to be cautious about pushing them too far and asking them to put into words the terrible things that were normal occurrences. And all the children asked when they'd be going home.

What to tell the children about their future? It was a sensitive issue and still is today. "I did not tell them they would be going home. No! I did not," emphasizes Upshall, his voice rising. "I said, 'You can't go back home as long as Daddy's going to be doing this kind of thing. If Daddy or Uncle or Mommy or whoever the case had done things then they can't do it any more. We can't let you go back and have them do it. Now because they did wrong, they're going to have to go to jail. That's probably what's going to happen to them.' But at no point did I tell them that they would be going back home."

The fact, however, was that no one really knew for sure what would happen to the children. There were many long months ahead and the children were already being moved around within the system of emergency foster care, which wasn't set up for more than short stays. Adoption, foster care, institutions, return to their families—all of it was possible. So the children existed in a strange limbo, waking up each morning and wondering what was in store for them that day. And while no one knew for sure, most of those in the system suspected that the children would never be returned to their parents. But no one was willing to come out and say it, if for no other reason than that it was unlikely most of the children would have testified if the'd known they'd never be going home.

The children's revelations took their toll on the police officers. "Personally you felt very torn, very anguished for the children," admits Upshall thirteen years later, who confesses he became particularly attached to Donna. "You see, I had kids the same age and I would go home at night and look at my kids and think, 'How can anyone do this to children?' That aspect of it really tortured me and you sort of had to set that aspect aside and go on professionally. Go and do what you had to do. But I can still see this little face sometimes looking at me. She was just a little girl."

Early in the investigation Donna made a decision. She would trust Baxter Upshall. Since no one could tell her where home would be in the months to come, Donna took matters into her own hands. One day, after hours of questioning, she turned to Upshall, "Will you be my Daddy?" It's a request that still haunts him today.

At the peak of the investigation, the RCMP team led by Upshall was talking to more than seventy-five men, women and children over three generations, almost every one directly related by birth, marriage or common-law to the Golers. Though in many respects they were all simple people in a primitive setting, it added up to an extraordinarily complicated case. Family names were enough to drive the officers around the bend. Some of the children in the same family group still used the last name of their previous "father" while others used their current "father's" name though neither was their genetic father. In some families, the group of children were sired by two or three different men, none of whom was currently the "father." The women might, or might not, be using the names of the men they were currently with. Stella Goler, for instance, had been known by three different surnames and at the time of the investigation was living with a man, adding a fourth name to the list. To complicate matters, the same given names—Stella, Charles, William, Cranswick and Marjorie—appeared over and over within three generations.

As difficult as the family names were to follow, the relationships were even more twisted and complex. In one instance, a fifteen-year-old girl had a daughter who was raised with her mother as a sister. Both were sexually abused by her father, his brothers and his wife's brothers. Though only one of the Goler men, William, was actually married, his sisters had multiple partners, some of whom they married, some not. One sister, Marjorie, was married to Maynard P. while another was married to Maynard's father, Curtis, who was also the father of Hazel, William Goler's wife. And then there were two half-brothers, Billy, eighteen, and Charlie, twenty. Billy was Marjorie's son but Maynard was not his father. Similarly Charlie was Stella's son, though none of her three partners had fathered him, but it was well known in the family who the father of both boys was. "Nobody actually said it, but we all knew, we all believed my grandfather was the father of both of them," one of the Goler children admits today. "The boys knew too," Mary, Stella's sister, agrees, "but they didn't care."

As the interviews with the children and adults piled up, Upshall brought in an analyst from Halifax to keep track of the information and particularly the relationships. He spent weeks designing intricate charts and graphs trying to sort out the family connections while keeping track of charges, witnesses and victims. It became clear that everyone in the Goler Clan was involved, one way or another, as either a participant, victim, observer or simply someone who knew or suspected what was going on but would not, or could not, do anything about it.

Wives and girlfriends were passed back and forth, children—some as young as five years old—were prey. Gender didn't matter, the

Goler men were just as happy slaking their lust on boys as on girls. As for the act itself, anything went, but there clearly was a marked preference for anal sex among both men and women, and they liked to give and receive. Foursomes weren't unknown and Cranswick, William's younger brother, enjoyed including Cecil, his crippled older brother, by wheeling him in to watch him "doing" a child on the bed in the small room they shared. Cecil couldn't talk but his enthusiastic grunts and groans were approval enough for Cranswick. The children were handled roughly, heads forced into position, hair held and small bodies pinned by larger adult ones. Beatings were administered when they weren't enthusiastic. Occasionally a brother or cousin held a girl down for one of the adults. Afterwards they were told to say nothing or they'd "get a lickin'."

Two weeks after the second lot of children had been moved into emergency care, Baxter Upshall was ready. He selected and briefed five two-man arrest teams to bring in the dozen or so Goler adults who were charged, emphasizing that because the accused might not comprehend the charges they must be careful not to breach any technicality in bringing them in. Resistance wasn't expected but the sheer number of Goler men might lead to some trouble. On February 14, 1984, six cars sped to their various destinations.

Constables Sherman Dale Craig, a six-year veteran, and Al Botham, both from the New Minas detachment, were assigned to arrest Cranswick Goler, the biggest and potentially the most dangerous Clan member. Most of the children had told stories about his violence and viciousness. The policemen travelled in a marked car, in full uniform with side-arms holstered. It was a cold, overcast day made all the more oppressive by the bleakness of mid-winter on South Mountain. They drove into the rutted Goler yard just after noon to find confusion rather than menace. Other teams were already there, including Upshall, Corkum and another corporal, who was taking pictures of the houses and property.

Craig and Botham, who didn't know any of the Golers by sight, entered the main house through the open door and, amidst the squash of other officers, and Goler men and women, called out for Cranswick. A great bear of a man stepped forward sheepishly. He wore a heavy red plaid shirt with the sleeves cut off and a grimy T-shirt with a ragged baseball cap perched on his head. Cranswick Goler was twenty-nine years old; his clothes looked and smelled as if they were at least as old and had been worn continuously. Craig asked him to step outside, told him he was under arrest for sexual assault and read him his rights from a card.

Cranswick seemed puzzled by the reading of his rights, so they took him to their car and spent twenty minutes explaining and re-explaining both the arrest and his rights. It was a slow process because he was eager to discuss the charges and he kept asking irrelevant, disconnected questions. Finally they were satisfied he understood.

The two constables tried to keep Cran, as everyone called him, quiet during the fifteen-minute ride to the station. They wanted his statement to be as fresh and unrehearsed as possible with no suggestion that they'd planted ideas in his head with earlier conversation. In New Minas they ushered him into a stark nine-by-ten-foot interrogation room with a curtained window, a desk, three chairs and a government-issue, battleship-grey file cabinet. Then they left Cranswick to stew by himself for five minutes before returning to his happy greeting. The interview began with Cranswick on one side of the desk, Botham and Craig on the other.

The mood was amiable. "At the Goler residence, when we approached Cranswick we seemed to get along very well and set up what was like an immediate friendship. In fact, he made a comment in that regard," recalled Craig. "He was very co-operative. In fact, we had a real good relationship as we were dealing with each other and talking and he made a comment initially to Constable Botham and myself, he asked us how come we were such nice cops and different from all the other cops."

The minute they sat down, Cranswick, with no prompting, blurted out his story—it was partly a boastful tale of his conquests, which included every Clan child available, in every way conceivable, starting at age five, and partly a lament about how he'd been led astray by the children. It was a common theme in statements given to the police by the men of the Goler Clan. They were all incredibly forthcoming about their activities with the children, adding graphic details where none was sought and adding incident on top of incident to the astonishment of the police. According to their statements, the children were ready, willing and eager nymphomaniacal tempters and temptresses no matter their gender or age. "What can you do when they come on to you?" asked Rick Davison, Mary Goler's husband, helplessly, as if speaking for all of them. The Goler men attempted no other justification than that the children wanted it, wanted them.

Constable Botham recorded Cranswick's statement on a sheaf of lined foolscap but he had a job keeping up with him, not to mention keeping his breakfast down. Cranswick asked to see the notes from time to time, once correcting the misspelling of his name, then nodding approvingly as if Botham were a secretary taking dictation. Every now and then he'd stop and pore over what was written, as if he could read it. Like most of the Golers, Cranswick's education had ground to a halt long before he learned how to do much more than write his name. Finally, when he was eighteen years old in Grade 7, his teacher gratefully let him go.

Cranswick's most horrible revelations about the children were punctuated by a mean little giggle. Though they struggled with their own equanimity during the three-hour interview, the constables were dumbfounded by the good time Cranswick seemed to be having throughout, his playful joking around and the easy acknowledgment of his guilt. "I might as well be truthful," he shrugged when they began. "I might as well make it good. I know I'm going to get ten years out of it anyway." Craig responded neutrally, "I really don't know what you'll get, Mr. Goler. I couldn't say." The jokes came thick and fast with Cranswick. "If I knew you fellows were coming, I'd have baked myself a cake with a file in it," he said late in the interview.

Over the next week, twelve adult members of the Goler Clan were arrested, including eighteen-year-old Billy and twenty-year-old Charlie. Some were charged with as few as three offences, but William eventually faced thirty-three counts. And what caught the particular attention of the press, while titillating and shocking the public, was the arrest of one woman, Wanda Whiston, who was charged with eleven counts of sexual assault and gross indecency.

The charges represented an encyclopaedia of broken taboos. Fathers with daughters and nieces, brothers with sisters, uncles with nieces and nephews, and husbands, boyfriends and common-law spouses with whatever youngster they could lay their hands on. They were all criminal charges, more than one hundred at first, though nearly fifty more were added in the months to come. "Never forget that we could have charged them each time they did something. Then we would have been talking thousands of charges," Upshall observes dryly. If found guilty and sentenced to the maximum, the offenders faced close to one thousand years in prison.

Where and when it started is unknowable. Who took the first insidious step, three or seven generations ago—who first laid a hand on forbidden but inviting flesh? There were never-ending winter evenings spent in shabby houses with the wind whistling through the cracks, no money for diversions and entire families sleeping in a single room. There was the isolation of the Mountain and the certainty that no one in the Valley cared what went on "up there" as long as it didn't touch them. Perhaps it started when a wife fell ill or died during the birth of an eleventh child. Poisonous alcohol, loneliness, despair might have caused a man to turn to his sisters, daughters or sons for comfort, or to use them to express his anger at the world.

The Valley has always said the Mountain was born bad. Perhaps the sickness travelled to the land of the Acadians with the Planters two hundred years ago and all it needed was the right environment to let it blossom. However it started, it was all too easy to continue. With land too poor to farm, few jobs and insufficient education or motivation to leave, many of the Mountain families have only ever had one thing—each other.

Chapter Eight

A Bad Thing to Do
to a Little Girl

✦ WILLIAM GOLER SPENT THIRTY-THREE
days in jail, first in the basement "lock-up," Kings County's temporary holding cell in Kentville, and then in the provincial prison in
nearby Waterville. On February 21, 1984, the court granted him
bail of $500 and released him. Over the previous week, twelve other
Clan members, including Wanda Whiston, had been granted similar bail, which they cobbled together from meagre savings, ex-
girlfriends, boyfriends, husbands, wives and, in one case, a loan from
a legal-aid lawyer. They drove back to their Mountain homes or
shabby apartments on the fringes of the Valley.

All the children were gone. In the cluster of shacks that made up
the Goler homes on White Rock Mountain, the atmosphere was
strangely barren. Despite the filth and deprivation of the environment, it had always been enlivened by children, often more than a
dozen of them. No one could remember when there hadn't been children. Back in the fifties and sixties, when Stella and Charles's nine
babies were being born, the main house was stuffed with people and
smelled rankly of urine, feces and baby vomit. There was no money
for cribs and often five would sleep in a single bed. With no plumbing,

hauling water for baths, laundry and cleaning could take all day. Stella simply gave up and in the summer the toddlers went without diapers.

The Clan was smaller in those days, limited to immediate family, just Charles, Stella and the children, with rare visits from his brother Cranswick's family, who made the journey from West Brooklyn for special occasions. There were few houses within walking distance and the Golers had no car so going anywhere took hours. Charles would often walk down the long steep hill into the village of White Rock and wait until someone could give him a ride to where he wanted to go, usually into Wolfville for supplies, to one of the mills for a few days' work or to one of the Valley farms to pick apples during the harvest.

Stella rarely went anywhere. With her growing brood of children, she spent most of her adult life within sight of her small home. When the children were young, she wore a path to the creek fetching water for drinking, laundry and washing. In fine weather, she simply took the children to the creek, sat them down in the water and scrubbed them there. Later Charles dug a shallow well and made the job easier. They survived on game, fish, berries and whatever else they could scrounge from the fields and woods, augmented with basic supplies from town when there was money. Winters were the hardest. Often all eleven of the family would be marooned inside the half-finished house for weeks. Had it not been for the sheer number of bodies inside the inadequately heated structure, they likely would have frozen.

As the girls grew up, the first of them gave birth at twelve and the babies started coming again. There were at least eighteen grandchildren, four of whom, born to young girls, were terribly deformed, severely retarded or both. One died a few weeks after birth, another at five, still another lives in an institution and no one is quite sure what happened to the fourth. There was never a moment when the Goler homes weren't filled with children—until February 1984. The week the adults returned, Stella filled the clothesline with the few teddy bears and dolls the children owned as if to lure them back as well. For days they hung there, pegged to the sagging line by ears, hair and limbs.

———— ✦ ————

Once out of jail, William wasted no time circling the wagons. His incarceration had cost the Clan dearly. In the first days after his arrest everyone had drifted, unable to grasp what was happening and uncertain about what to do. Except for William, none had hired lawyers. No co-ordination of testimony had occurred, no strategy or tactics discussed. Each day, the Golers and extended Clan went about their business as if William were away for that day only and would soon return. Even after the adults were brought in for questioning and the children taken, they fretted and swore and railed at the authorities, but did nothing. It was only on Valentine's Day, when the other arrests began, that lawyers, ordered up by the court, appeared. But by then it was too late. Most of the adults, when confronted with the statements of the children and their adult kin, had either confessed, implicated each other, or both.

Ralph Curtis Kelly, for instance, admitted he "screwed" all the kids, male or female, whatever their age—"up their bums," "in their cunts," it didn't matter to him at all. "I've had sex with them all," he boasted. "I had screwed them all first in either 1980 or 1981, but then in 1982 I worked in Halifax and didn't screw them much then, but last summer I was off work and screwed them all a lot." Like Cranswick, he insisted the children wanted it, sometimes so badly they injured him in their eagerness to get it. Between bragging about his exploits, Ralph found time to implicate William, Cranswick, Henry and Billy while casting aspersions on the morals and chastity of the Goler women.

William called family meetings to find out what everyone knew and, most importantly, what had been said during questioning. This was a difficult task; the seeds of divisiveness had been well planted by the police. Scarcely a family member hadn't informed on the others and most of them had informed on William. He faced a virulent combination of guilt and fear, leavened by the habitual Goler hair-trigger tempers. As a result, Clan gatherings were acrimonious affairs punctuated by shouting and stormings in and out of Charles and Stella's house.

William berated his sister Stella for spilling her guts to the police. But Stella had her grandmother Ada's fury in her and she gave as good as she got, shrieking that the police had threatened her so that she'd had no choice. "What could a person do?" she shouted. After several tongue-lashings from William, Stella infuriated him even more by stubbornly clamming up, claiming that her lawyer advised her not to talk to him. The other sisters were also upset but William felt confident that they'd toe the line. Stella, his mother, fluttered around repeating over and over again, "They're gonna take my boys away . . . they're gonna take my boys away." "Shut up," he told her viciously as she moaned and wailed.

There wasn't much William could do with his brothers Cranswick and Henry, both of whom treated the whole business as a joke; neither could remember what he'd told the police except, of course, that he'd denied everything. Billy, William's eighteen-year-old nephew, moped around in a black mood proclaiming he was sick of it all and intended to go out and find a bit of fun. The other male relations were little more use with all their blustering threats and denials.

But William exerted his will. He convinced the Clan that every word they spoke was hurting them as much as him and he warned them that they had no hope of ever getting the children back if they kept it up. Within forty-eight hours of his release, all co-operation from the Goler Clan ceased. A few days earlier they had readily implicated one another. Now questions directed at both the accused and family members who had not been arrested were answered with denial or sullen silence. Even the lawyers had difficulty eliciting information and often had to remind their clients whose side they were on.

The family members all recanted their signed statements or confessions, claiming, in almost identical words, that the police had intimidated and confused them. Ralph Kelly said he'd been roughed up by the police. Similarly Cranswick accused them of intimidation. "Every time I tried to tell the truth they said I was lying." According to William's sister, Stella, "Baxter hit the desk with his fist and broke his watch in two pieces because he said I was lying to him. And I wasn't lying so they'd wanted to hear the damn lies so I told them some damn lies." She'd been browbeaten and threatened so she said she took the quickest route out. "Well, what are you going to do when you're under pressure? They wanted, they wanted to hear the truth, I tried to tell them the damn truth and they wouldn't believe me. They called me a liar, said I was lying to them. So what in the hell could you tell them?"

William briefed family members before subsequent interviews with police and debriefed them afterwards. He ordered the men to get their hair cut and clean their clothes and he was supported by the various lawyers. A bizarre wardrobe appeared over the next few weeks—paisley, plaid and polyester in a riot of colours—as Clan members strove to make themselves more presentable: shirts with long pointed collars, jackets and flared pants from two different suits married, dresses made from fabric popular over a decade earlier, wide belts in a thin-belt era.

Cecil was hauled out of his fetid bed and, for the first time that anyone could recall, was bathed, had his hair cut and his three-inch nails hacked off. His brothers were ordered to paint William's house, which they did in a cheery shade of sky blue, but they quickly tired of the unfamiliar work. Once the front of the house was finished they gave up, leaving one side half blue, the rest half bare boards or faded white from a spruce-up attempt many years ago. The effect was further spoiled by the fact that the boys cleaned their brushes on the unfinished wood interior walls. They also did some minor repairs, nailed wood over the most obvious gaps in the siding and attached trim around some of the windows.

One of the defence attorneys videotaped William's little house for the purpose of cross-examination. He hoped to demonstrate that given the door and window locations, the children could not possibly have seen what they claimed. But before he arrived to tape, William, hoping to mix up the children, rearranged the interior, added some items of furniture and removed others. He also tacked up cloth on the windows for curtains and separated the bedroom alcoves from the main living/dining area, with new cloth dividers. On the outside of the windows, he replaced the ripped, dirty plastic with something thicker as if to prove that nobody could possibly see into the interior from the outside.

The tactics boomeranged. Though some of the children were disoriented, so too were many of the adults who were not part of the immediate family and their lawyers. During testimony, several comic sequences were played out with no one quite sure which window, which door or which bed was being discussed. Finally the judge became so irritated with the chaos he refused to look at the tape any longer.

William was obsessed with finding the children. He was convinced that getting to just one of them would bring the rest into line. But they'd been hidden too well and he couldn't find a trace. Still, he was confident. In his heart William Goler didn't believe that any of the children could look him in the eye and still tell anyone anything about Clan business.

In early March, Rayburne McNeil, a second-year student in Acadia's Master of Divinity program and pastor of the Black River Baptist Church for the past three months, approached Billy Goler. Though he had been on the Mountain for only a few months, he'd already seen enough situations like the Golers' to feel the church wasn't doing all it could. He contacted Billy because, as the youngest charged, McNeil felt he might have particular need of advice and solace. Little did he know that the slender Billy, with strangely hooded eyes, lips pulled constantly into a knowing smirk and a "screw-you" tilt to his chin, was the wildest and least controllable, not to mention least convertible, member of the Clan.

Though the small, white, picturesque Baptist church in Black River was just a few miles from the Goler compound and the Golers called themselves Baptists, no one could remember a Goler ever attending. Nonetheless, Pastor McNeil bravely decided it was time for the church to reach out and take the initiative during this time of crisis. He was followed by another church member, David Long, a neighbour of the Golers, who began dropping over regularly to read the Bible to Cecil.

When William learned of McNeil's approach to Billy, he seized the opportunity, avidly taking up the pastor's suggestion of church and Bible study, even signing up for his own "discipleship program." The pastor was delighted with William's progress. "He has become open to the gospel message, has responded to it, I think genuinely. He has at times shared with me his testimony, his willingness, how God has changed him in various areas." Though William Goler never discussed the charges pending, let alone taking any responsibility for them or expressing even a shred of remorse, McNeil was convinced there had been specific improvements in his character. William had cut down on his cursing, he pointed out, was better able to control his temper and was "conforming more to society from my viewpoint. Like personal hygiene and things like that."

While William was undergoing his spiritual transformation, he got a stack of Bibles from the pastor and distributed them to the Clan. In the months and many court attendances to come the Golers made sure the books were plainly visible to the reporters and television cameras that eventually found their way to Kentville and into the brick Kings County court-house on the edge of the shopping district near the lazy-flowing Cornwallis River. William, in particular, always brandished his Bible and was quick to quote passages. Several charming photos and television news clips aired across the nation with the Clan members communing over their Bibles and discussing the words within, despite the fact that most of the men couldn't read. When one reporter told him that some believed the Bibles were a ruse to gain public sympathy, William, in a good imitation of a revivalist, declared, "The Bible is not a scam! God is not a scam!"

When William and the rest were charged, the Valley slowly began waking up to the evil festering in their midst. The local weekly, the *Advertiser*, more accustomed to covering weddings and community events than scandals, primly reported the basics, occasionally on the front page but usually several pages in: how many arrested, how many victims and the scant details of their bail or court appearances. In contrast, another sex story, but one involving the Valley and considerably less serious and far-reaching, merited full article status. It concerned a Kentville barber, Edward Brown, who had been fined $500 for exposing himself to a nine-year-old. When the residents discovered that the man was already on probation for a similar offence committed nearly three years earlier, they were horrified and disgusted that "the pervert" had been cutting their hair. "It's no

longer something that's just happening in California all the time,"
declared one of the forty marchers who picketed Brown's shop,
demanding "chemical castration" for the monster.

Meanwhile, no pickets showed up on the Mountain. There was
no public outcry or statement of concern about the children who'd
been raped, sodomized and brutalized in every conceivable way just
a few miles from the Valley. "Well, it *was* a terrible thing that happened to those kids," agreed one of the court officials, "but it wasn't
as if they were screwing other people's kids. They kept to themselves
and did their own." A lawyer for one of the accused offered another
opinion: "What you have to understand is that these weren't kids
like yours and mine. I'm not saying it wasn't bad, because it was, no
question. But you have to realize that these kids grew up expecting
that kind of abuse. Maybe they got used to it, I don't know. But it
wouldn't have had the same impact as grabbing a kid off the street
and doing those kinds of things. That was their life." Their words
reflected a common sentiment.

The arrests overloaded a legal-aid system accustomed to dealing
with one or two rape cases a year, at most. Thefts, bar fights, van-
dalism and wife beating were the bread and butter of legal aid. None
of the three full-time legal-aid lawyers had ever handled an incest
case before, let alone more than a dozen of them, with some of the
accused facing more than thirty charges.

Legal aid appealed to the Kings County defence bar for lawyers
willing to take one or more cases. A few days later, ten lawyers from
up and down the Valley met in the panelled library of Waterbury,
Newton and Johnson, a prominent Kentville law firm, to divvy up
the overflow. The terms were simple—$40 an hour up to a maxi-
mum of $500. There was no experience to draw on to determine how
close that would come to the real bill, but several lawyers expected
it would cover about half, not bad for a criminal case on a legal-aid
certificate, which never paid the whole bill anyway. Eventually,
William Goler's case alone rang up more than $4,000. In their hearts,
most of the lawyers believed the men were guilty, though perhaps
not responsible for their actions. And they felt the cases would be
fairly simple because most of their clients would simply plead guilty.

Two young lawyers, Eric Sturk and Curt Palmer, both natives of the Valley, agreed to take on three cases, including the toughest, William and Wanda. Sturk, short with a little of the street fighter about him, grew up on a farm near Berwick, a lovely village west of Kentville. In grubby jeans, a plaid shirt and with a touch of the farm in his voice, he could pass for a gas jockey—all useful camouflage for a bright young man practising law in the Valley. The tall, slender Palmer came from a well-to-do family and, though a friendly, open man, he could hold his own with any of his sharp-eyed, quick-tongued city brethren.

Sturk had already been approached by William, who telephoned him from the lock-up where he'd been held initially. William got Sturk's name from his sister Stella's current boyfriend, Gabriel Dodge, whom Sturk had once represented in a boundary dispute on the Mountain. "He just talked a little bit about the charges, very general," recalled Sturk. "Willie's original story to me was that if there was anything going on it might have been at wild parties that her [Sandra's] mother was having. And he told me that he had a lot of witnesses who could give him an alibi, which sounded very promising." Sturk adds ruefully, "His witnesses turned out to be two who were charged later on."

Palmer was assigned William's mate, Wanda Whiston, at the meeting. "I didn't see her as particularly sophisticated," recalls Palmer. "I thought she was a little more sophisticated than most of them but I saw her as withdrawn, a bit of a shy individual. Not particularly bright but not stupid. Average. She was as close to average as those people got. I think her intellect level was significantly higher than some of them."

Sturk, from a rural background, had known and met that backwoods class of people the Golers fell into—or so he thought. "I'd been up that road before and you see places, lots of places, where people live in basic poverty situations—part of it by choice. If you don't want to live off of welfare, you're better off to live out in the country where you can do a bit of hunting and you have some freedom and maybe you can choose your lifestyle." But nothing had prepared Sturk for this case. "It was my belief going through law school that you read about all these things in the criminal code like bestiality and sex with five-year-olds and all these kinds of things. But you didn't think that really happened, just that somebody sat down one day and wrote up all these things thinking there should be a law against that."

There were a lot of surprises in store for Sturk and Palmer, but the biggest was local reaction. "I like to think that we live in a pretty tolerant society, but this was the only case in my career, up to that point or since, that I've ever had people react violently when they found out that you were defending these people," says Palmer. Sturk adds, "I had people call me at home and say, 'Why are you doing this?'" Palmer wasn't prepared for the blanket condemnation, not only of the Golers, but of anyone willing to defend the Clan. "People would say to me, 'What, are you crazy? What kind of animal are you?' We got this attitude in the public very quickly that these people were guilty and you couldn't do anything bad enough to them and that if you were defending them, then you were a bad person too."

Sturk and Palmer quickly came to realize that the Goler cases fit neatly into the Valley's preconceptions about the Mountain. "One thing we are bad at in the Valley is we're very parochial in that people in Kentville sometimes look down their noses at people in Berwick and people in Berwick would look down at people in Aylesford and Waterville. Wolfville looks down on Kentville and everybody looks down on everybody on the Mountain," admits Sturk.

Sturk and Palmer recognized that Wanda's and William's cases were the bell-wethers for the rest. Their clients were probably the brightest of the group—a big disadvantage because the more intelligent, the more normal they appeared, the more difficult it would be to portray them as hapless victims themselves. The lawyers faced a dilemma in selecting which level of court would hear their cases, partly because no judges in the area had a track record in sentencing child sex abusers and partly because most in the legal system had already made up their minds about the guilt of the Golers.

Prior to the preliminary hearings, they heard an alarming report about one of the potential judges. A source at the court-house told them that the judge had called into the sheriff's office on another matter. As they were chatting, the Goler case popped into the conversation—not a surprise since nobody in the Valley, from lawyers to farmers, could stop talking about it. "I have to come down there tomorrow," the judge said to the sheriff, "and commit all these people for those despicable things they did to those children." At this point, the judge, who didn't try any of the cases in the end, hadn't heard a shred of evidence.

The man who would prosecute Sturk's and Palmer's clients was Jack Buntain. As Kings County's lone prosecutor, he handled virtually every aspect not only of William's and Wanda's cases, but all the accused except one—eventually sixteen of them facing nearly one hundred and fifty charges and requiring close to one hundred court appearances. It never occurred to Jack Buntain to call anyone in to help. Small, wiry and vigorous, Buntain moves like a man who believes he can catch up with tomorrow. There's no hint of the stereotypically relaxed small-town lawyer in his conversation or movements. Everything he does is done quickly, efficiently and with such certainty most wouldn't even consider questioning one of his decisions. Once the Goler cases crossed his desk, he attacked them like a terrier after a rat, determined to push them along and brook no hold-ups or interference along the way.

Since both their clients adamantly insisted they were innocent, Sturk and Palmer had two choices. After the preliminary inquiry before a provincial court judge to determine whether there was sufficient evidence for a trial, the case could be heard in either county or provincial supreme court by judge alone or judge and jury. Considering the reaction of the community, a jury trial was out of the question. They surveyed the available judges and settled on trial by judge alone—Donald Hall, a recent appointment to the county court bench. "He had done some prosecuting and he'd also done some defence work. We thought, hey, he's the guy to have a go at it, and he was duly appointed," says Palmer. "I think that turned out to be absolutely false.... It was like you were dealing with the Crown but also the judge too. What the Crown didn't fix up, the judge would do. If I have a choice, I avoid Judge Hall absolutely in sex-related crimes."

In preparation for the months of preliminary inquiries and trials, a small trailer was brought in and parked in the shade behind the court-house where the children could wait during the day, hidden from the curious until they were needed in court. They had a television to watch, books to read and a social worker to talk to, but it was hard to pass the hours. They couldn't leave because the court officials never knew when they might be needed. Some of the children, especially the younger ones, were in the trailer only a few times, but others, like Sandra, Donna, Pam and Doug, were there so often from April to October 1984 that the trailer became an unwelcome second home.

❖

On April 13, 1984, the day of her father's preliminary hearing, Sandra Goler walked from the trailer, across the parking lot and in the back door of the court-house. Led by a police officer and a social worker, she made her way up the back stairs and into the foyer outside the three small court rooms. An upbeat decorator had enlivened the roomy waiting area with great splashes of colour on the tiled walls as if to disguise the sombre business that went on behind the three doors.

The doors to court room number 2 swung open, and Sandra tentatively made her way to the witness box, carefully avoiding the eye of her father, who sat rigid and threatening as a cobra beside Eric Sturk at the front of the room. It was the same fourteen-year-old girl from White Rock Mountain who had lain beneath William as her sister Donna peeked in through the bedroom window. But she was different too. Clean now and wearing inexpensive but brand-new clothes, she had also shed her sullen, furtive look and seemed more at ease with herself. Throughout the trial, William tried to intimidate the children with his menacing facial expressions. Sandra solved the problem by never looking directly at him.

Sandra was sworn in, and Jack Buntain established her name, age and grade and asked her to identify her father. She quickly pointed at him, without really looking, then dropped her hand to her lap as if he might leap up and bite it.

Buntain: You had sexual intercourse with your father?

Sandra: Yes.

Buntain: And anal intercourse?

Sandra: Yes.

Buntain: Ah, did you engage in any other type of sexual contact with your father?

Sandra: Oral.

Buntain: All right, and how often did he do that?

Sandra: Oh, a couple of times.

Buntain: Just a couple of times?

Sandra: Yeah.

Buntain: Do you remember when the first time was?

Sandra: No.

Buntain: Now, to do this what would you have to do to your father to have oral sex with him? What would you do to him?

Sandra: Put his sperm in my mouth.

Buntain: And where would this take place—by sperm what do you mean? Is there another name for it?

Sandra: Dink.

Buntain: His dink. And what would you do to his dink when it was in your mouth?

Sandra: Suck it.

Buntain: Suck it. And did you do this willingly?

Sandra: No.

Buntain: All right, tell us how it came about that you did this. What would happen?

Sandra: Well, he'd take me in and he'd put it in my mouth and then he'd grab a-hold of my hair.

Buntain: Right and—

Sandra: So I couldn't get away.

Buntain: And would he say anything to you?

Sandra: He just said do it.

Buntain: And you'd suck it?

Sandra: Yeah.

Buntain: Until when?

Sandra: (No answer)

Buntain: What would happen, anything?

Sandra: Until stuff came out of it.

Buntain: All right and what would you do with that?

Sandra: Spit it out.

Buntain: Now did your father do anything to you that way?

Sandra: Yeah, he put his mouth on my vagina.

Buntain: Put his mouth on your vagina. And how often would he do that to you, Sandra?

Sandra: Only a few times.

Buntain: Only a few times. And when he put his mouth on your vagina, what would he do with his mouth?

Sandra: He'd just kiss my vagina.

Buntain: Did your father perform any other type of sexual act on you?

Sandra: Yeah.

Buntain: And what type?

Sandra: Anal and oral.

Buntain: Anal, and that's anal intercourse?

Sandra: No.

Buntain: What do you mean when you say anal, what would he do?

Sandra: He'd put his vagina, his sperm in my bum.

Buntain: In your bum. What did he put in your bum?

Sandra: (No answer)

Buntain: His what?

Sandra: Sperm.

Buntain: How would he put that in there?

Sandra: He just stuck it up.

Buntain: And how far in would he stick it?

Sandra: Just a little ways.

Buntain: Do you really mean his sperm? Is there another name for it that you can think of?

Sandra: (No answer)

Buntain: Now when he did this, could you feel anything?

Sandra: Yeah, it hurt.

Buntain:	And what did you feel in there?
Sandra:	His sperm.
Buntain:	And would you say anything to him when he did this to you?
Sandra:	Yeah, I'd tell him it hurt.
Buntain:	And what would he say?
Sandra:	He didn't care.
Buntain:	He didn't care. How do you know? What did he say?
Sandra:	Because he said, I don't care.
Buntain:	Sandra, can you tell me what all your father put in your bum?
Sandra:	Just his sperm and his finger.
Buntain:	His sperm and his—?
Sandra:	Finger.
Buntain:	Anything else? How could he get his sperm in there? With what?
Mr. Sturk:	I object, Your Honour.
The Court:	Oh, that question's all right.
	Mr. Buntain continues.
Buntain:	With what?
Sandra:	With spit. He just wet it and put it in.
Buntain:	What did he wet?
Sandra:	His sperm.
Buntain:	Sperm? And you don't know it by any other name?
Sandra:	His dink.
Buntain:	His dink? Okay. Thank you.

Sandra Goler's general testimony was given so matter-of-factly and with such assurance that Sturk saw little advantage in directly challenging the specific details of the alleged events. Instead he chose to try to create doubt about the dates, frequency and locations. In some cases, he had as many as half a dozen witnesses willing to testify that William wasn't even around when he supposedly assaulted his daughter. The fact that most of his witnesses were also facing charges was a problem, but if there were enough of them and they were good witnesses, then skilled questioning might overcome the disadvantage.

Sturk's biggest difficulty, one shared by all the lawyers defending the Golers, was producing alibis to match all the charges, some of which could have happened—according to the prosecution—any time, or several times, or hundreds of times over a five-year period. An alibi that might hold up for December 25, 1983, was suddenly worthless when the child testifying couldn't exactly recall whether it was 1983, 1982 or perhaps the summer, not winter. "I can remember going to court and making an application for particulars; the Crown already refused to give us anything more," Palmer points out in illustration. "The court said, 'These are children, they're young, their memories are expected to be bad, the Crown's given you all that you're going to get.' It was the pattern they were talking about. 'We're [the Crown] complaining about a couple of instances but if the truth were known, there were hundreds of these.' It went on from day to day. And it made it impossible to create an alibi. You threw that out the window."

It became a frustrating game of trying to pin tomato seeds with their thumbs. When Sturk asked Sandra if she remembered how many times her father had sex with her, she said no; later she said five or ten. She couldn't recall over how many years the abuse had taken place, then corrected herself and said it had started after her mother left. When pressed again about frequency, she revealed it had been ten or fifteen times a month. Constantly Sturk strove to attach dates and times to instances of abuse to give himself something to refute with a witness.

The defence of William Goler was made all the more difficult by Judge Hall, who adjusted the charges several times during the preliminary inquiries so that they conformed more closely to the prosecution's evidence. On one of the charges, he committed William to trial, even though the prosecution hadn't offered any evidence. Further, Sturk was brusquely dealt with when he asked for a delay because so few specifics were provided on the charges until the last moment that he wasn't able to mount an adequate defence.

Jack Buntain had problems of his own dealing with charges that seemed to change daily, children whose evidence was often precarious, and a concern that sympathy for the accused, because of their impoverished, deprived backgrounds, might encourage the court to be lenient in sentencing. Still, he at least had access to the children, had formed relationships with them and developed some skill in questioning them, something none of the defence lawyers had the opportunity to do since child witnesses were still a rarity. And, while the defence desperately wanted to pin down details, it was in Buntain's interest to leave things vague. All he had to do was prove, to the court's satisfaction, that the abuse had taken place.

Sandra's twelve-year-old cousin, Pam, Stella's daughter, was Buntain's next witness. The prosecutor quickly established her competence to testify and her knowledge of William Goler and his home.

Buntain: All right, and what did your uncle William do to you, Pam?

Pam: Put his penis in my arse.

Buntain: In your arse?

Pam: Yeah.

Buntain: And how often did he do this?

Pam: Every time I'd go up.

Buntain: Every time you'd go up. Now can you give me any idea how many times that would be?

Pam: No.

Buntain: And where would this happen?

Pam: Down his place.

Buntain: Down at his place. And anywhere else?

Pam: In the woodshed.

Buntain: In the woodshed. Whose woodshed?

Pam: His.

Buntain: Okay, do you remember when this started?

Pam: When I was eleven years old.

Buntain: Okay, when he did this to you, Pam, was there ever anybody else there?

Pam: Sandra.

Buntain: Sandra. I see. Did she see this happening? Do you know?

Pam: Yes.

Buntain: How many times did she see this happen?

Pam: All of them, all the times.

Buntain: Okay. And how would it happen? Would he ask you to do this or what?

Pam: Well, he would call Sandra in and Sandra would come out and tell me.

Buntain: Right, tell you what?

Pam: That he wanted me.

Buntain: And where did he want you?

Pam: In the bedroom.

Buntain: In the bedroom. Whose bedroom?

Pam: Sandra's.

Buntain: Okay. Anybody else's?

Pam: Just his own bedroom.

Buntain: His own. And when Sandra told you he wanted you, what would you do?

Pam: Well, he used to— Well, Sandra said that he had gum or candy for me and I went in and he had nothing at all.

Pam said the words with weary disappointment, as if the whole world were involved in a conspiracy to prevent her from getting her gum.

Buntain: All right. So when you went into the bedroom, what did he say to you, what did you do?

Pam: He, I started to come back out and he said, come on in for a minute.

Buntain: And did you go back?

Pam: Yes.

Buntain: All right. And what happened?

Pam: He took my pants down.
Buntain: Right. And did you try to stop him?
Pam: Yes.
Buntain: How did you try to stop him?
Pam: Well, I told him not to do it.
Buntain: All right—
Pam: 'Cause it was a bad thing to do to a little girl.

Sturk was left with few options. Undermining a child's story is tricky; press hard and he'd be seen as badgering the child, in this case one who'd already had more than her share of abuse. Even the most hardened, most unsympathetic judge would take a dim view of that. But if he didn't do his utmost to discredit the child, he wouldn't be fulfilling his responsibility to his client. To complicate matters, he never knew what to expect from a child on the stand—especially these children. One minute they were calmly reciting the most graphic sexual details, the next they were breaking down or freezing up over seemingly inconsequential matters like their place of birth or the clothing they wore on certain occasions. Questioning them was a little like driving in a demolition derby—he never knew when or where he was going to be blindsided.

Pam was that most dangerous of witnesses, a child rapidly becoming a woman. Her dark hair, now washed, was thick and glossy, framing an oval face and smooth, unblemished skin—surprising considering her wretched diet. Despite the awkwardness of her age, she moved with athletic fluidity, like someone comfortable with her body and proud of it. And her smile was a beacon, bright, wide and enveloping. Born into another world that smile would have taken her a long way. At times innocence radiated from her; other times, when you least expected it, the maturity of a woman with opinions of her own shone from her dark eyes. And like all the Goler women, there was anger lurking beneath the innocence. Sturk wasn't sure which Pam was going to answer his questions. He decided to go for the woman and try, as he had done with Sandra, to pin her down with dates and times. If he could shake even one of her assertions that an event took place on a specific date, he could call into question her devastating statement that William had sex with her every time she visited him.

Sturk: Now when was the last time you were at Uncle Willie's house?

Pam: Last Christmas.

Sturk: At Christmas time?

Pam: Yeah.

Sturk: Okay. Now, your uncle Willie's house, that's right beside your grandmother's house, isn't it?

Pam: Yes.

Sturk: And was it Christmas Day that you went there, was that the last time you went there?

Pam: Yes.

Sturk: Just on Christmas Day?

Pam: Yes.

Sturk: Did you go on New Year's Day?

Pam: Yes.

Finally, a point scored; every contradiction counted. Gingerly Sturk pressed on.

Sturk: Okay. So when you went there on Christmas Day did Uncle Willie do it to you that day, on Christmas Day?

Pam: Yes.

Sturk felt he was making progress. With lots of people in the house over Christmas, he felt sure his client could present an effective alibi, but first he needed to be sure Pam was going to stick to that date.

Sturk: And you are talking about the very last Christmas of last year, the one that we just had, that was just last Christmas? It wasn't a couple of Christmases

ago, it was just last Christmas that you're talking
about?

Pam: Thought you mean the other Christmas.

Pam had casually blown over the playing-card castle Sturk had
been so diligently constructing.

Sturk: Okay. There's a Christmas every year, isn't there?

Sturk allowed just the slightest hint of an edge to creep into his tone.

Pam: Yes.
Sturk: Okay. Last Christmas. The one in 1983. That's the
time you say that this happened. Is that right?
Pam: Yes.

Then Sturk noticed an odd interchange between Pam and the two
RCMP officers sitting watching.

Sturk: Okay. You're looking at Corporal Upshall, is he
nodding to you or...?
Pam: I'm looking at Ted [Constable Ted Corkum].
Sturk: You're looking at Ted. And is he nodding to you to
answer? How to answer?
Pam: No.
Sturk: You're looking at Ted. And is he nodding to you to
answer?
Pam: No.

Sturk admonished her sternly, feeling that this was one area he
could safely bully the witness without Judge Hall jumping all over
him.

Sturk: Now you just look at me, all right? Just you and me
and the judge and we'll—I'll ask the questions and
you look at the judge and tell your answers. Don't

look at Constable Corkum or the other constable,
okay. Now the last you stated at Christmas time
this happened, that's last Christmas. Is that correct?

Sturk sallied forth yet again, still trying desperately to elicit specific
details of the day that he could later refute or that Pam might con-
tradict on her own. He ran her through the minutiae of Christmas
Day—thirteen children, thirteen adults crammed into a few hundred
square feet for roast chicken dinner and presents with the children
playing red rover, go seek, red light–green light and mother may I.
On the face of it a normal, even mundane, Christmas.

Sturk: So you went in the house to see—no, don't look at
      Ted any more, look at me.

Pam: I'm not looking at him!

Sturk: You just look at me, okay? Now I'm the one that's
      asking you questions. And you asked Sandra and
      the other girls to come out and play?

Pam: Yes.

Sturk: And did they come out?

Pam: Well, Uncle Bub [William] called Sandra back in.

Sturk: Okay. He called Sandra back in and then what
      happened?

Pam: He told Sandra to come back, come outdoors and
      get me and I went back in and I said what'd you
      want and he said I want to screw you and I said I
      can't 'cause I gotta go outdoors and play. He said
      just take a minute.

Sturk: So then what happened? Were you in the house
      alone with Uncle Bub then?

Pam: Yes.

Sturk: Okay, so what did Uncle Bub do?

Pam: Screwed me.

Sturk: Is that all he did?

Pam: Kissed. Feeled me.

Sturk doggedly pursued Pam, trying to impeach her testimony by demonstrating that she really had no reliable memory of when these incidents happened. By dint of Herculean effort, he got her to agree that the incident with Uncle William had actually happened in the summer, not over Christmas, as she had earlier testified. But just as he closed in for the kill, he realized with a sinking heart that rather than discrediting Pam's recollection, all he'd accomplished through his painstaking questioning was to introduce an entirely new sexual assault into the record.

Two boys were on the witness list for the prosecution—Doug, Pam's fourteen-year-old brother, and Matt, William's nine-year-old nephew and the son of his sister Josephine. Both of them were tired. They had been waiting hours to testify, stuck in the small trailer parked behind the court-house. Worried about the alertness of his witnesses, Buntain appealed to Judge Hall for an adjournment to the next day.

Mr. Buntain: Your Honour, you're probably not going to be very happy with me at this point. During the break I asked the police officer to go to see the children. They are beat. One of them as a matter of fact has had to get up at five o'clock this morning in order to be here for ten o'clock and they've sat around for nigh on six hours and I understand that he's, well, nervous, that he's crying, that the others are tired. It's my view it's not fair to put them, to expect them to testify this late in the day.

The Court: Well, you'll have to try.

Mr. Buntain: Pardon me?

The Court: I think you'll have to try. See what you can do with them.

A drawn, sad boy entered the court room—Doug. From his red-rimmed puffy eyes it was obvious he'd been crying for hours. He was slight and shorter than normal, and his round face, highlighted by racoon circles under his eyes, made him appear younger than his fourteen years. Except for his sickly pallor and hunched, beaten demeanour, he could have been anyone's boy. Yet, along with the Goler girls and Pam, Doug was the most cruelly victimized of all the children. Again and again he was sought out and brutalized—sometimes by two or three of the men at once. Through some oversight, Doug wasn't taken into social services protection with the other children. When the accused Golers were released on bail, some of them re-offended with Doug.

He sat in the witness stand with his eyes fixed on his knees, looking as if he might vomit. He had trouble with basic details, he couldn't remember what province he lived in, let alone what county, and he spoke softly behind his hand as if he were trying to prevent his words from reaching the ears of his uncle William, sitting a few feet away, fixing him with his cobra stare. Doug didn't see his uncle's venomous stare because he didn't dare meet anyone's eyes that day.

Buntain: Now, at any time when you were at William Goler's house did he do anything to you?

Doug: Yes, he did.

Buntain: What did he do to you?

Doug: Well, he made me give him blow jobs—

Buntain: What do you mean by blow jobs?

Doug: Suck. And he screwed me.

Buntain: When you say screwed you, what do you mean by that, Doug?

Doug: Fucking me.

Buntain: And how would he do that?

Doug: Putting his cock up my bum.

Buntain: And do you remember the first time, when—how old were you the first time that happened?

Doug: Five or six.

Buntain: Would he ask you or would you just do it or what?

Doug: He asked me.

Buntain: He asked you. And how many times did you give him blow jobs?

Doug: Three or four times.

Buntain: Now, did he do anything to you, Doug?

Doug: Yeah, he screwed me up the bum. . . .

Buntain: And when he was screwing you up your bum as you call it, what happened?

Doug: He came his load.

Buntain: He came his load. What do you mean by that?

Doug: Sperm.

Buntain: Sperm. And what was he screwing you with?

Doug: His cock.

Buntain: His cock. And how far in would he put it?

Doug: About that much.

Buntain: You're using your fingers and it looks to me about four or five inches?

Doug: Um.

Buntain: All right. Would you feel anything?

Doug: Yeah.

Buntain: How did it feel?

Doug: It hurt.

Buntain: It hurt, did it? And would you say anything to him, Doug?

Doug: No.

Buntain: Did he say anything to you when he did this?

Doug: No.

Buntain: Now each time he screwed you up the bum, did he always put it in?

Doug: Yeah.

Buntain: Do you remember, Doug, if he used anything to help do that?

Doug: Yes, spit.

Buntain: Spit. And whose spit would he use?

Doug: His.

Buntain: His. And where would he, where would he put his spit?

Doug: In my bum.

Buntain: You told Mr. Sturk that you didn't want to tell anybody what this man had done to you because you were scared you might get in trouble.

Doug: That's right.
Buntain: Who were you afraid of, Doug?
Doug: Pretty near everybody.

Doug left the court room much faster than he had come in. His place was taken by his cousin, nine-year-old Matt. Tall for his age and thin, with long, piano-player fingers, he looked like a blond choirboy. Matt was eager to please. His anxiety to say and do the correct thing was palpable in his constant nervous smiles and slightly raised brows after each answer as if asking Buntain for approval. But fatigue had also settled into his face and Buntain moved him quickly to the point.

Buntain: Do you know William Dennis Goler?
Matt: Yes.
Buntain: And how's he related to you?
Matt: My mother was a Goler and she married a Paley and she had me and she turned back to Goler.
Buntain: So Mr. Goler here is your mother's what?
Matt: Brother.
Buntain: Do you remember when the first time was that something happened to you?
Matt: Summer.
Buntain: What summer?
Matt: Last summer.
Buntain: And what happened?
Matt: He, ah, played with my boat and put his boat up my bum.
Buntain: Now when you say boat, do you know it by another name?
Matt: No.
Buntain: What do you use it for?
Matt: Peeing.
Buntain: You said that he—and you mean Uncle Bub?
Matt: Yes.
Buntain: Played with your boat. How did he play with it?

Matt: He sucked my boat.

Buntain: He sucked your boat. Anything else?

Matt: No.

Buntain: Did you do anything to him, Matt?

Matt: No.

Buntain: Now, you said he put his boat up your bum?

Matt: Yes.

Buntain: Were you on something when he did that?

Matt: Ah, his bed.

Buntain: His bed. And how do you know he put his boat up your bum? How could you tell?

Matt: Because it hurt.

When Donna Goler, eleven, walked hesitantly into the court room, her father's head swivelled to watch her approach the witness stand. Waif-like and the size of a six-year-old, her arms were wrapped around a new Cabbage Patch doll as if she expected someone to snatch it from her at any instant. The testimony of her sister and cousins had been brutally plain, unvarnished by their inner feelings and usually delivered in flat tones. Donna was different. Her face mirrored her thoughts, the emotional war of her life and the nightmare of what she was about to do. Her answers were more prim, her descriptions less graphic, but there was an awareness about her beyond her years, as if she alone among the children had a glimmering of what the future would bring to the Goler Clan.

Buntain: Do you know William Dennis Goler?

Donna: Yes.

Buntain: And is he related to you?

Donna: Yes.

Donna stared straight ahead, breathing rapidly to contain the sobs rising in her throat.

Buntain: How is he related to you?

Donna: He's my father.

Buntain: Okay. Now did anything ever happen that shouldn't have happened between you and your father?

She brought the doll up to her face and wiped away the tears she couldn't hold back. Jack Buntain asked her again if something had happened and she gasped a faint yes.

Buntain: Now do you remember, Donna, the first time something happened?
Donna: When I was ten years, when I was ten years old.
Buntain: Okay, and what time of the year was it?
Donna: Summertime.
Buntain: Now the first time that something happened, Donna, where did it happen?
Donna: In Dad's bedroom.
Buntain: Right. And who was there with you?
Donna: No one.
Buntain: No one at all?
Donna: Just us.
Buntain: When you say us, who do you mean?
Donna: Me and Dad.

To this point, Donna had successfully avoided her father's penetrating eyes. Everyone, from the social workers to the police and the lawyer, had told her not to look at him, no matter what. But in the end, she couldn't help herself. She clutched her doll harder and her eyes flicked towards William Goler. "I'm gonna kill you," he mouthed. Her face drained white but she couldn't pull her eyes away. "I'm gonna kill you."

Buntain: And what happened?
Donna: I can't do this!
Buntain: Take your time. What happened?
Donna: I just know I'm not gonna be able to do this. I just can't. I still think a lot of Dad. I just can't do it!

Buntain: Do you remember the last time?

Donna: Yes.

Buntain: Before Christmas?

Donna: Yes.

Buntain: Can you tell me what happened that day?

Donna: I can't do it! I know he's guilty. Everyone else must know. We just going into this too much. I can't do it!

Donna's tears flowed hard and the sobs squeezed out of her with a stream of hiccups. Jack Buntain saw his case disappearing before his eyes. He simply couldn't afford to have Donna fall apart. Seven-year-old Lisa was so young and eight-year-old Sally unreliable, he couldn't depend on their testimony alone to convict. Sandra was steady but she could be withdrawn and fractious. Pam was, well . . . Pam, confused one minute, crystal clear the next. Doug would do what he could and the younger boys the same but their fear and anxiety always caused concern about their reliability on the stand. And in many instances, Donna was the only witness.

There was no question Donna was the key, either the victim or witness to nearly two-thirds of all the charges. Not only that but during questioning by the police and the prosecution, she had a clearer and more detailed recollection of events than any of the other children. Donna was that rare creature, a totally believable witness—she was perfect. And if she refused to testify, what would the impact be on the other children—Buntain didn't even want to think about it. He quickly asked for a recess, which this time Judge Hall granted.

The social workers, police and Buntain gathered around Donna in the anteroom but it was Baxter Upshall's quiet voice that caught her attention. He quietly asked her what was wrong. When she told him, between convulsive sobs, that her father was going to kill her, he reassured her. "No one's going to hurt you, I promise." Donna sobbed all the harder. "I can't do this, I just can't do this," she whimpered. Again Upshall's quiet voice responded. "It's up to you, Donna. But you have to decide."

Donna took a deep, shaking breath and by sheer force of will began to compose herself. What wasn't being said, had never been said, would never be said, but all the same was crystal clear, was that if she and the other children didn't testify they'd be sent back to the Mountain. Alone among the children, Donna had already decided that she never wanted to go back. She'd die up there, she knew it. Donna couldn't bear the thought of lying in one of those unmarked graves back on the Mountain.

> Buntain: When was the last time something happened?
> Donna: About a month before Christmas.
> Buntain: Of what year?
> Donna: 1983.
> Buntain: Now the first time that something happened, where did it happen?
> Donna: In Dad's room.
> Buntain: And what happened, Donna, that time?

Again Donna, unable to resist, looked over at her father. "I'm gonna kill you," he repeated silently, then he smiled. Donna felt bile rise in her throat but this time she didn't disintegrate. Drawing on an inner strength few adults and even fewer children possess, she continued.

> Donna: Do I have to look at him when I'm saying?
> Buntain: No, you look at me.

Donna inhaled deeply and held her breath for a moment.

> Donna: He kissed my front side and put his dink in my backside.
> Buntain: Okay. Now your front side, what part?
> Donna: Vagina.
> Buntain: Your vagina. Okay. Now who told you that word, where did you learn that word?
> Donna: My foster parents. I asked what the good names were.

Buntain: Right. Fast like, what's the bad name?

Donna: Do I have to say it?

Buntain: Yes, please, I just want to—

Donna: Bird.

Buntain: Your bird.

Donna: A bird.

Buntain: Okay. He kissed you there and he put his dink in your backside?

Donna: Yeah.

Buntain: And how did you know he did that?

Donna: I could feel it.

Buntain: How did it feel?

Donna: Do I have to answer that?

Buntain: Yes. How did it feel?

Donna: I don't know.

Buntain: How long did it go on?

Donna: Five minutes.

Buntain: Right. And were you on something?

Donna: Yeah.

Buntain: What were you on?

Donna: Bed.

Buntain: What about your clothes, where were they?

Donna: Down.

Buntain: And how did they get down?

Donna: Do I have to answer that?

Buntain: Yes.

Donna: I put them down.

Buntain: And what about your father's clothes?

Donna: He had his zipper down.

Buntain: His zipper down. Okay. Now did you do anything to him that time?

Donna: No.

Buntain: Okay. Did you tell anybody about that?

Donna: No.

Buntain: And did he say anything to you?

Donna: Not to tell anybody.

Buntain: Not to tell anybody. And did he say why not to tell
anybody, or something would happen?

Donna: No.

It was a baptism of fire for Donna, the first time she'd ever stood
up to her father and got away without receiving a beating or some
kind of sexual indignity. It felt good. When she finished testifying
she looked over at her father. William Goler still frightened her—
plenty—but her fear was just a little less intense. She tasted a new
emotion, hatred and loathing flowing in to replace the fear. It too
was good. For the first time Donna felt she might get out of this mess.

Donna didn't see him testify, but William Goler on the stand was
a far cry from the man who terrorized children and cowed the rest
of the Clan. Under Jack Buntain's questioning, he fidgeted and
fussed, nervously swinging back and forth on his chair like a
metronome, refusing to look directly at the prosecutor or the judge.
At one point he squirmed and twisted so much that he wrapped the
microphone cord so tightly around himself he could hardly move.

William denied everything, completely and utterly. He claimed
to "hardly ever see" Doug and said he didn't really know his other
nephew, Matt. As for Sandra, Pam and Donna, William denied that
he "at any time at any place sexually assaulted " a single one of them.
He said his family life was happy and his relationship with the children close. He couldn't for the life of him explain why they'd con-
spired to tell such awful lies.

Chapter Nine

Stella's Boys

✦ FROM THE END OF JANUARY, WHEN
she was taken under protection by Family and Children's Services,
to the end of June 1984, Donna Goler testified or was questioned as
many as seventy-five times, sometimes two or three times a day. As
the year progressed, her life became a stream of narrow facts defined
by sexual organs and other body parts. On the days Donna was sched-
uled to take the stand, a social worker delivered her and the other
children on the witness list to the trailer behind the Kentville court-
house. There they would meet Jack Buntain and Baxter Upshall, who
explained to the children whom they would testify against that day.
Then they'd go over the statements originally given to the police.

Sometimes there were tears when one of the children didn't want
to "tell" on an adult he or she especially liked or feared. Buntain and
Upshall took pains not to push the young witnesses, but the children felt the pressure of their expectations. Most of them sensed a
direct relationship between the food, toys, clothing and attention
they were getting and their performance on the stand. If they didn't
"tell," the treats might stop, they reasoned. There were also conflict-
ing emotions about their future. Some of the children were worried

that if they did badly in court they wouldn't be able to go home again. Others were afraid a poor performance meant they *would* be sent home. Depending on the child, either prospect was terrifying.

The worst part of her new life for Donna was missing school. In the first six months, she attended for only five days at the various places she and Lisa were lodged. The Goler children had never had any friends outside the family and for most of them school had always been a matter of surviving the teasing and taunting of the other students. But Donna, unlike her sisters and cousins, loved the regime of spelling and math—the letters and numbers she plucked out of her head and put where they belonged on paper. She loved the order, the structure. With letters and numbers she was in charge. Even with the disadvantages of her upbringing, Donna managed to maintain a C+ average and she dreamed of one day getting a magical A.

During February and March, Donna and Lisa lived in several different emergency foster homes before settling into one for three months in a small village forty-five minutes from Kentville. Donna saw Sandra, who was in a different home, only once or twice after they were apprehended and she didn't see her mother, Hazel, at all. It was a strange way for a little girl to live. Even so, Donna was beginning to believe she was important, needed. It was a good feeling; it gave her strength. She also had Lisa with her. The many people around her promised it would soon all be over and the two girls would be together in a nice home with clean sheets, their own beds, perhaps even their own rooms.

Donna's fear that her father would find her had lessened slightly. Though she still started at unexpected knocks on the door or when she caught sight of men who bore a passing resemblance to her father, the nightmares weren't so fierce or so frequent. But she didn't believe for one second, no matter what the police told her, that anything or anyone could keep him away forever. William Goler had indelibly imprinted upon her, with his fists, his feet and his reproductive organs, the fact that he was the strongest, most powerful man on the Mountain. Even though her uncles, Cran and Henry, hauled bigger sacks of potatoes and she'd once seen Henry, when drunk, beat her father into a bloody pulp, she knew in her heart that William Goler was invincible, that he would get her one day. But for now she felt safer than she ever had in her life.

Now that she was physically free of them, Donna found, to her surprise, that she had little compunction about testifying against the extended Goler Clan. For the first time, she admitted to herself how much she loathed most of them. She actually enjoyed the thought of getting back at them for what they had done to her and Lisa. She also recognized that some of her relatives were truly strange, even by Clan standards. Her cousin Billy, for instance, was cruel and crazy. Once an acceptable-looking, almost handsome boy, Billy at eighteen was rapidly coarsening into the prototypical Goler male. His eyes were hooding over, his lips thinning out into a permanent sneer and his jawline thickening. Billy always talked about "having a time" and where he was going to find one.

Billy cared for little except driving as fast as he could and doing disgusting things. One of his favourite tricks was to stand out by the mailbox on the side of the road, where he'd stick his hands in his pants, pull himself out and start jerking away, in full view of passing drivers. As he climaxed he'd bay like a dog serenading the moon. If a car came by at that moment, he'd fling the gooey handful at it, all the while standing with his pants open, his manhood hanging out and a wild grin plastered on his face. He loved that game.

The family called him Billy Goat because he was so randy—as randy as Donna's father William, but wild and uncontrollable on top of that. He'd been caught shoplifting in the Valley and he often stole money from his grandmother Stella and grandfather—or father—Charles. If they were foolish enough to object, he'd slap them around, stopping only when another family member inter-vened. When Billy availed himself of one of the children, he liked to hurt and terrify them. Pain was often part of his entertainment. Billy steered clear of Cran, Henry and William, but Donna didn't doubt that once he got a little more heft on him, they would have their hands full.

Cranswick was another family member Donna didn't mind expos-ing to the world. In fact, come to think of it, she'd be downright happy to put her twenty-nine-year-old uncle Cran behind bars. Of all the Goler men, he was easily the nastiest and most violent. If someone was "doing" or "punishing" one of the children, Cranswick seemed always to be there watching, giggling in the background, ready to join in. Cran giggled a lot; it was easy to make him laugh but there was usually a mean edge to it as if he loved to watch the children being humiliated and hurt. He treated his many nieces and nephews as playthings when he got the urge—which was often. Cran particularly liked to prey on the children who were more defence-less than the others, like Sally.

Sally, Donna's cousin and the daughter of Stella and Roy Hiltz, spent most weekends of her life at the Goler compound. She was a slow child, easily confused and intimidated. She could tell a coher-ent story away from the court, but as soon as she sat in the same room as her uncles she fell apart. The day Sally testified against Cranswick, she had trouble remembering her own name and said she didn't know what the Bible was, or what it meant to swear on it. Still, Judge Don Hall allowed Jack Buntain to proceed with his direct examination of her. He didn't get far. As he struggled to elicit whether she understood the difference between right and wrong, a truth and a lie, Sally's muttered responses became fainter and fainter. Finally, when she couldn't answer at all, Buntain gave up and excused her.

With Sally unable to speak for herself, Donna's testimony became critical. There was often more than one witness when a child was being abused, but this was one of several cases when only one per-son had seen what had happened and could take the stand—Donna. It was the summer of 1983. Donna had been washing dishes in the main house with some of her cousins. Her aunt had taken her grand-mother shopping and told Donna to fetch all the dirty dishes from the bedroom.

Buntain: Did anybody go upstairs with you?

Donna: No.

Buntain: All right. And Cran's bedroom, what's in that room?

Donna: A bed, all kinds of stuff. A stand, I guess.

Buntain: Is there a door into the bedroom?

Donna: Yeah.

Buntain: And this day what was the position of the door?

Donna: It was, well, halfway open.

Buntain: Why did you look in?

Donna: I was going in to get the dishes so I just went in or was going in.

Buntain: And where was Sally when you walked in?

Donna: On the bed.

Buntain: And where was your uncle Cran?

Donna: On top.

Buntain: Of who?

Donna: Of Sally.

Buntain: How long did you stand there?

Donna: Not very long really. I just went straight downstairs and I just said there wasn't any dishes.

Buntain: Now did you say anything to Sally or to Cran when you walked into the room?

Donna: No, well no, not really. I made a noise but I didn't say anything.

Buntain: All right. What kind of noise was it?

Donna: Well, the board on the floor, it was squeaky.

Buntain: Did Sally say anything to you?

Donna: Well, in a way, but she didn't tell me, came right out and tell me what happened. She just said, I was upstairs today, up in Cran's room, that's all.

Buntain: No, no. I mean when you walked into the room?

Donna: No, not then, no.

Buntain: Now when you walked into the room did Cran say anything to you?

Donna: I don't think he seen me....

Buntain: How could you tell from where you were that he was having sex with her?

Donna: Well, the only way I could tell, like what do you mean? I'm not sure what you mean.

Buntain: Well, you said you saw him having sex. What I'm

   trying to find out is how do you know that's what
   he was doing?

Donna: Okay, the bed, you could see the bed and he was on
   her and everything like that and you could just
   measure it up and he was bobbing up and down so
   he must have.

After Donna gave her testimony she left the stand, holding her
Cabbage Patch companion, Susie Lynn, hard against her body and
taking care not to look at her uncle. Throughout, Cranswick had
sat listening intently, as if he were watching a favourite television
show. Bearded, wearing a loud sports shirt and pink pants, he smiled
frequently, looking like an unkempt, colourful, amiable bear. To all
appearances, he was having an excellent time.

On the day Cranswick was initially questioned by the police, he
responded indignantly when they asked him if he had ever had sex
with Sally. "What do you think I am, sick?" Then he chuckled sheepishly, like a boy caught raiding the cookie jar. "Truthfully? Once or
twice. She was too small so I said to hell with her. I only tried her
a little over a year ago in summer. I always pick the warm times. Just
like the birds and the bees."

Cranswick freely, boastfully admitted to the police he'd "screwed"
everything that walked on two legs in the Goler compound—with
the possible exception of his brothers. When asked if he'd had sex
with Annie, the youngest at five years of age, Cranswick hesitated
for only a moment, then shrugged. "I might as well be a dirty old man,
down to the lowest. I've tried! She's smaller than Sally. I was at home
in Henry's bedroom. Henry was screwing Sandra in the other bed."
Cranswick might as well have been discussing a child's shoe size with
a store salesman, it was all so matter-of-fact. He listed all the different things he'd tried with Annie, despite the problem of her size,
detailing exactly how far he had managed to penetrate, vaginally and
anally, and how many times she'd performed oral sex on him.

By Cranswick's account, the children never "hollered," struggled
or cried and he never forced them. "I wouldn't hurt anybody," he
said piously. "I'm not that kind of guy." Instead the children were

"horny types" who "asked me to." And Cranswick was always happy to oblige.

Cranswick was largely indiscriminate in his use of the children, but his favourite was poor long-suffering Doug, his sister Stella's son. When Family and Children's Services removed the Goler children from their homes, they didn't make a clean sweep. For some reason, lost to memory, they didn't take Doug into protective custody. When the Clan was released on bail at the end of February, several of them returned to the Mountain and grabbed the first young body available—Doug. Both Cranswick and his brother Henry were eventually charged for re-offending with Doug. While Cranswick visibly enjoyed the testimony of the other children, he revelled in Doug, who sat in the witness stand pale and trembling, tears occasionally welling up and rolling down his cheeks.

Buntain: What happened, Doug?

Doug: He screwed me up my bum.

Buntain: How many times?

Doug: Twice.

Buntain: Now when you say he screwed you up your bum, what do you mean by that?

Doug: He fucked me up my bum. . . .

Buntain: Now how could you tell he was screwing you up the bum?

Doug: I was laying on the bed and he was on top of me.

Buntain: Could you feel anything?

Doug: Yes.

Buntain: What did you feel?

Doug: Him putting his cock up my bum. . . .

Buntain: Now did you do anything to him, Doug?

Doug: I give him a blow job.

Buntain: How many times?

Doug: Once or twice.

Buntain: Why did you do that?

Doug: I don't know.

Buntain: How did that start?

Doug: I don't know.
Buntain: Do you remember, Doug, the first time it happened?
Doug: When I was seven.
Buntain: When you were seven?
Doug: Yes.
Buntain: Where were you living then?
Doug: White Rock Mountain.
Buntain: And in whose house?
Doug: My grandmother's....
Buntain: How do you know you were only seven when it happened?
Doug: I had my seventh birthday.
Buntain: And where did it happen that time?
Doug: Up in his room, sometimes in Henry's room.
Buntain: How often would this happen?
Doug: Quite often.
Buntain: And would it always be this accused, this man?
Doug: Sometimes, and sometimes Billy and Henry....
Buntain: Did you ever tell anybody what this man was doing to you?
Doug: No.
Buntain: Why?...
Doug: He said I might go to jail.

The portrait of Cranswick Goler painted in newspaper articles and on the television was that of a harmless simpleton who, aside from trapping and hunting, wouldn't hurt a fly. His open, goofy manner, his habit of doffing his hat and bowing to the media, his relentless grin and his giggling all made him seem harmless. He told a CBC TV reporter he didn't understand what the charges meant or why the children were doing it. He said he just wanted to go home and live the same quiet life of "keeping to himself" that he'd always led. Sandra Goler had her own idea of just how harmless Cran Goler could be.

Buntain: Now did Mr. Goler ever do anything to you, Sandra?

Sandra: Yes.

Buntain: What did he do to you?

Sandra: He had sex with me and oral sex.

Buntain: How many times did he do this to you?

Sandra: Quite a few.

Buntain: Are you a married person?

Sandra: No.

Buntain: Do you remember, Sandra, the first time this happened?

Sandra: Yes. It was in the summer of '82.

Buntain: How do you remember that?

Sandra: Because he was the first person after my dad.

Buntain: And how did it come to happen, how did it start?

Sandra: He just told me that I was going to have sex with him.

Buntain: And what did you say?

Sandra: I said no and I said I didn't want to.

Buntain: And what did he say or do?

Sandra: He didn't care, he just made me do it.

Buntain: What did he do to you that made you do it?

Sandra: He just took a hold of my arms and sat me down on the bed.

Buntain: Did you say anything to Cran Goler when it was finished?

Sandra: I just said that I hated him.

Like most of the Goler men, Cranswick knew little of the world outside his family. His work experience was limited to occasional farm labour, mostly within the apple industry, and the odd stint at Long's Lumber Mill in White Rock. Except for one on-again off-again relationship with a woman from a different clan, he had no contact with women other than his sisters and nieces. He didn't need to. "When you make love to her, it's like making love to a girl-friend of your own," he said of his forced sex with his niece Sandra.

Cranswick Goler didn't plan his trysts with children. He took sex, as he did everything else in life, as it came. When it was available, he indulged; when not, he didn't bother. He didn't need to pursue the children since there were so many around the Goler compound and, according to Cranswick, they all wanted him—especially Sandra. "The first time I was at her father's place, back about two years ago. She wanted me to go down," he explained earnestly to a police officer. "She was half naked. It's hard to refuse something lying on the bed like that. She urged me to come on. She's a horny type."

The officer interjected, "Did you take all your clothes off?" Cranswick shook his head vigorously. "No! I don't take all my clothes off. Not even when I go to bed. Sometimes when I go to bed by myself, I take my pants and boots off." The officer tried again. "What clothes did you take off?" Cranswick replied patiently as if his interrogator was slightly slow. "I didn't take *any* off. Just pulled my zipper down. I got manners about myself."

Cranswick availed himself of Donna as well, but the young girl always made him uncomfortable. He could never completely cow her in the same way he could the others. There was always a spark of defiance about Donna that rubbed Cranswick the wrong way. "I don't like her anyway," Cranswick told police. Donna was the only one of the children he didn't "like" but that didn't stop Cranswick from making regular use of her. "I [screwed her] about three months ago. That was down in the basement, laying into a potato bin. No taters in it, though." When asked about the last time, Cranswick didn't have to stop and think. "Oh, I'd say a week or so before they took her. I didn't do very much that day. I wasn't feeling good. I just felt her up. I just tried and said to hell with her."

By June 1984, Donna, Sandra and Pam had become seasoned witnesses and even Doug, often hesitant and fearful, was improving. "They were growing on the job," ruefully observes Wanda Whiston's lawyer, Curt Palmer. But one child in particular was devastating the defence—Donna Goler. "She was killing us. Everywhere we turned she was killing us." On the other hand, fourteen-year-old Jeff never quite got the hang of revealing his innermost secrets. On the stand his face was pinched and white with distress and dread. He was old enough to be embarrassed and ashamed and he looked as if he'd like to crawl into a hole and die. There were certain things he would talk about, sometimes even offering up more information than was asked, but there were other dark experiences his young pride wouldn't allow him to reveal.

Buntain: ... When was the last time you were there [the Golers' house], do you remember?

Jeff: No. Before court and everything started.

Buntain: That was the last time you were in Cran's house. Now did something happen to you that day?

Jeff: Not that day.

Buntain: Not that day. Did something happen at any time between you and this man?

Jeff: About three years ago.

Buntain: What happened between you and Cran?

Jeff: Three years ago when we were living there and we used to have our own room and he used to have his room and when my mother went and got dinner and, er, breakfast and Cran went and pulled my pants down and then he pulled his and he put his penis in my rear end.

Buntain: Could you feel it in there?

Jeff: Yeah.

Buntain: You said, we had our room. Who shared your room with you?

Jeff: Just me, my mother and me and Jennifer.

Buntain: Jennifer. That's your sister?

Jeff: Yeah....

Buntain: Did he say anything to you, Jeff, when he came in your room that time?

Jeff: Well, he just did it, just told me not to tell nobody about it.

Buntain: Told you not to tell anybody about it and what did you say?

Jeff: Didn't say nothing....

Buntain: Now what happened on the second occasion, what did he do?

Jeff: He just done the same thing.

Buntain: Tell me again.

Jeff: He pulled my pants down, then he pulled his down and then he put his penis in my rear end.

Buntain: And could you feel it?

Jeff: Yes. . . .

Buntain: Other than putting his penis in your bum, did you do anything to Cran at any time?

Jeff: No! Positive!

Jeff suddenly spoke very loudly.

Buntain: Pardon?

Jeff: No, I'm positive!

There was a clear undertone of hysteria in Jeff's repeated assertion that he'd never done anything to his uncle Cranswick. Though apprehended along with the other children and placed in a foster home, Jeff steadfastly denied ever being abused. He, his sister Jennifer, Matt, his best friend, as well as Michael and the baby of the family, Annie, had been put together on a farm in temporary care. It was only after several weeks away from home that the events of his life began to press upon him.

Torn from their families, frightened and bewildered, the children did what they had always done, grouped together, backs to the world. No amount of warning from the police, Jack Buntain, social services or their foster parents could prevent them from talking and chewing over the upheaval in their lives. Eventually Jeff decided to tell his story too, but he would tell only one part—the least shameful part—to him. In a halting exchange he told his foster parents that he had something to say "about what was going on" and the police were called. Jeff joined the crowd of witnesses. But it was left to the other children to relate what it was that he refused to reveal.

On the stand Pam confirmed Jeff's testimony, then blurted out his secret.

Buntain: Pam, did you ever see Cran Goler do anything else to Jeff?

Pam: Then in Henry's bedroom Cran was giving Jeff a blow job.

Buntain: And where were you?

Pam: We were down, we go around the back of the house like so we can play. We were playing tag around the back of the house down by Willie's place and we could see right through Uncle Henry's window 'cause it's way open.

Buntain: How close to the window were you?

Pam: Really, really close.

Buntain: Now what's a blow job, Pam?

Pam: Putting the dink in, putting the dink in the mouth.

Buntain: So whose dink was in whose mouth?

Pam: Jeff's dink was in Cran's mouth.

Buntain: And what was Cran doing?

Pam: Sucking.

Buntain: Now other than on that occasion did you ever see Cran doing anything to Jeff, did you see him doing anything else to Jeff, at any time?

Pam: They were down in the woodshed, Willie's woodshed.

Buntain: And when is this other incident you're going to tell us about?

Pam: Last summer, yes. That was Jeff giving Cran a blow job.

The Goler boys were broken in at the same age as the girls, any-where from five to eight. As with the girls, Cranswick claimed they were all willing, even delighted, participants. "He took his own pants down," he said of Jeff during his original statement. "He didn't cry." After nearly three hours of interrogation, the police questions were as blunt and straightforward as Cranswick's answers had been from the beginning.

"Did you get him to go have a shit before you put your cock in his bum?" Constable Botham asked abruptly after Cranswick made a joke about going to jail. "I never asked him to but he did." Botham pressed a little more. "Why would he do that?" Cranswick shrugged. "I dunno."

"So he wouldn't shit on you?" Cranswick drew himself up—this was a manhood issue. "I'm not scared of a little bit of shit!" Later when asked if he put his fingers up one of the younger girls' bums, the man unafraid of a little excrement rose up in indignation. "No, I did not! I don't have gloves."

Similarly, while happy to make ready use of the boys, Cranswick's "manners" didn't allow for certain things. "Did you touch Jeff on the cock?" demanded one of the policemen. "No, I did not!" Cranswick replied indignantly. "I might go around screwing them but I don't feel them up, jerk them off." "Did you suck his cock?" "No, I did not! I don't go around sucking cocks!"

Like Jeff, Matt hated testifying. He often flinched slightly at the questions, as if the lawyers were firing darts at him and he hesitated with his answers, seeming to hope that the question and the questioner would just go away. Most of his responses were single words, but every now and then a torrent of detail erupted from him. They were little things, the colour of a blanket, a hook on a door, the sound or feel of something, an item of clothing, a favourite television show he'd been watching when called away—detail that tumbled from his lips like a protective shield as if the longer he spoke of such inconsequentialities the more chance he had of avoiding the painful facts.

Buntain: Now at any time when you were at Nannie's in White Rock and when Cran was there did anything happen between you and Cran?

Matt: Yes.

Buntain: What was your answer?

Matt: Yes.

Buntain: What happened, Matt?

Matt: Ah he, we were up at my room and there was a hook inside and he hooked it, there was a blanket,

he hooked the door and took my pants way down
and put his boat up my bum and sometimes sucked
my boat.

Buntain: Now when you say your boat, do you have another
name for your boat?

Matt: Ahem.

Buntain: What's another name for it?

Matt: I forget.

Buntain: What do you use your boat for?

Matt: Peeing....

Buntain: So you say Cran would put his boat in your what?

Matt: Bum.

Buntain: And how did it feel?

Matt: Terrible.

It all began to seem odd, words like cunt, cock, blow job and fuck
coming from the mouth of the tidily dressed, precise prosecutor Jack
Buntain. The defence lawyers, who didn't get as much practice with
the vocabulary, were all a little squeamish at first with repeating the
graphic words of the children, but they too soon became comfortable. Arse, dink, dick, pussy and bird came to sound almost commonplace as the weeks and months of testimony blended into a
litany of carnality. After a time the bits that stood out in sharp contrast were the small, mundane facts of the children's lives. In a world
where everything was twisted, the simple things seemed out of place.
They were also the things that sometimes hurt the most.

Once Jack Buntain asked Donna if she had a nickname. "Yes,"
she responded quietly. "Do I have to say it?" Buntain smiled, "Yes,
it's a nice nickname." "Oh please, Jack," she begged, embarrassment
flooding her face. "No, it's not!" "What is it?" he insisted. "Jack, it
is not nice, Jack! I don't like it." He wouldn't let her go. "Is it
Poochie?" Her shoulders sagged and she replied dully, "Yes."

Donna didn't realize that the other children sometimes referred
to her as Poochie in court and Buntain simply needed to establish
that they were talking about her. All she knew was that what little

privacy she had had been invaded when he spoke her name out for everyone to hear. Her family called her Poochie because she had trouble walking when she was young and scrabbled along the floor.

"Like a dog," her father would laugh derisively. "Like a fuckin' dog. Hey Pooch, c'mere Poochie!" Her mother told her she'd fallen down the stairs and broken her leg when she was little and that's why she crawled for so long. Donna hated the name, just as she hated the filthy dog Sheba her father kept chained up in the yard. She remembered three dogs, male and female, all given the same name. When William got angry at the children, he'd go out and get this Sheba, who surged and snarled and barked at the end of the chain like something gone mad. Whenever the children saw the dog, they fled but William would find them and corner them with the animal.

"Sic 'em," he'd yell at the dog, who slathered and drooled as he snapped hysterically at them. Donna was terrified her father would lose his grip on the chain. She was also terrified he would try to get the dog to mount her, as he once did with a naked Sandra while the men looked on hooting and howling with laughter.

Donna had come to terms with testifying against her father, her uncle Cran, her two older cousins, Wanda and the other men hanging around the Clan, but she faced a more difficult decision with her uncle Henry. Though Henry Goler was seven years older than Cranswick, the two brothers were like bookends, heavy lumbering brutes who were good with traps and had supernatural patience when fishing. Both said that fetching water from the well was their main job around the Goler compound. Henry's mind, however, worked even more slowly, more painfully than Cranswick's. In the words of one seasonal employer, his "intellectual capacity is somewhat limited." The court psychologist tested Henry's attention span, vocabulary and knowledge of common information and concluded he functioned "at a mentally retarded level," at best.

Henry, like all the Golers, could be fearsome if provoked and he had once been "thrown in the cooler" after a drinking spree and free-for-all. But unlike many of his brothers and other relatives, Henry had a thin vein of kindness in him. He dished out relatively few of the gratuitous smacks, kicks and beatings that usually accompanied the Goler Clan's conquests.

Though Henry's kindness was only relative to the cruelty of the other Golers, to Donna Henry was lovable. She adored hugging him and talking to him. He didn't have much in the way of a vocabulary and his conversation was so ponderous you didn't want to give him too many questions to answer, but Henry always had time to talk to her. And if he happened to be shambling by when her father was in one of his rages or Wanda was administering some "punishment," Henry would protect her. And every time Henry protected her, Donna loved him a little more.

But Henry had been bad too. Donna knew that, she'd seen it. Henry had admitted to the police that he'd "done" Sandra. "I put my finger in her bird. I tried to put my dink in her bird but I could only get it in there about an inch so I rubbed it on her bird and put my finger in her bird." Still, alone among the Goler men, Henry had never hurt her or had sex with her. Donna wondered about that. Sometimes she thought, or hoped, it must be because Henry was really her father—although that hadn't stopped anyone else.

Donna was in a quandary. She didn't want to testify against Henry but he had done things to Lisa that were impossible to forget. So, with a heavy heart, on May 10, 1984, at Henry's preliminary inquiry, Donna Goler, crying and unusually inarticulate, reluctantly admitted that she'd seen Henry put "his dink in Lisa's backside and in her mouth." But the little girl who'd been able to face down her father couldn't bear to see the sad, uncomprehending look on Henry's face. She refused to testify against him again.

Nor could Donna bring herself to tell on some of her older male cousins who had not been charged. They'd done the hateful things too, often egged on by her uncles, aunts or various other men who were always around, most of them either going out with her aunts, married to her aunts or formerly married to her aunts. When they hit their early teens, the boys' looks started to change and coarsen, as they metamorphosed from prey to predators, from boys into Goler men. This process was often kicked off by the boys "helping out" one of the older men.

Buntain: Who is Kenny?

Sandra: My cousin. Cran came down and Kenny held my arms up so that Cran could have sex with me.

Buntain: How old would Kenny be, have been then?

Sandra: Thirteen.

Buntain: How old were you then?

Sandra: Thirteen....

Buntain: And you say Cran came down, did he say something when he arrived there?

Sandra: He was just standing there talking to Kenny and then they were joking around and they were whispering and then Cran said he was going to have sex with me and they pushed me on the sofa.

Buntain: What were you doing at this point that your arms had to be held?

Sandra: I was trying to push him off.

Buntain: Did you succeed?

Sandra: No.

Buntain: And when they had you down on the sofa and Kenny was holding your hands what was Cran doing?

Sandra: Having sex with me.

Buntain: And again you mean?

Sandra: Putting his penis in my vagina.

Buntain: And how long did that go on for?

Sandra: Not very long because they flicked the lights at our place and we knew that somebody wanted... they wanted somebody, so Cran went.

Buntain: This time, just to make sure that I'm clear, this time when Kenny was there holding your arms, whose house were you in?

Sandra: Mine.

Buntain: Now what do you mean they flicked the lights out, Sandra, what do you mean?

Sandra: Well, the people at my grandmother's house just pulled the plug out.

Buntain: Why would they do that? Does that mean something to you?

Sandra: Yeah, that somebody was wanted up to my grandmother's house.

Buntain: I see. So when the lights started to flick, what happened?

Sandra: Cran went out. He said, "I'm wanted," so he ran up.

Buntain: And did he come back?

Sandra: Yeah.

Buntain: And what happened when he came back, Sandra?

Sandra: Then he held my arms while Kenny had sex with me.

Buntain: When he pushed you down on the sofa, did he say anything to you? Would there be any discussion between the two of you?

Sandra: No. He just called me a lot of names. He said I was going to do what he wanted to do.

Billy had once been prey himself, and now he was one of the worst offenders. An eager, even fanatical, participant right from the beginning, Billy didn't need to serve time as a helper. One day when Sandra and her cousin Pam were upstairs in the main house tidying up for their grandmother, Stella, Cran motioned his nephew Billy, then sixteen, to follow him and they went up after the girls. They each grabbed one, pulled them roughly into Cran's bedroom and ordered the protesting girls to take down their pants.

Ten minutes later when the men were finished, they released the children and sent them on their way. As Sandra and Pam bolted from the room, a rare idea popped into Cran's head. He and Billy took off after the girls, snaring them before they were halfway down the stairs. "We ain't finished yet," he commanded. Laughing they dragged the girls back to the bedroom, switched partners and went back at it.

For a time the Goler boys were on the cusp, simultaneously abused and abusers. Kenny was a case in point, and even Doug was going through the Goler changes. By rights they should be stopped. But too many times Donna had seen her cousins bent over, pants around their ankles, protesting at the invasion, while one of the adults plunged away at them. She would not tell on them.

Chapter Ten

And the Rest

✦ DONNA GOLER ADDED IT UP. IT was early June 1984, and after a few more days of testimony she would be officially rich. Like all witnesses the children were paid two dollars a day. She calculated it wouldn't be long before she hit the magic one hundred mark. One hundred dollars, more money than she'd ever imagined, let alone seen. And there would be more as she'd been told the preliminary inquiries and trials would likely spill over into the fall and possibly winter. She still found it hard to believe that she would be given this money although Jack Buntain, the prosecutor, and Baxter Upshall, the policeman, assured her that would be the case. Needing confirmation, Donna asked her foster mother, who told her that there would indeed be a cheque and that she would put the money in the bank for her where it would be safe.

Not a chance, no way, never, Donna thought. No one was going to get their hands on a penny. It was hers. She would keep it, hide it, take care of it all by herself. And when the time was right, she would take some of it and buy another Cabbage Patch doll, maybe even two, perhaps twins, to keep her first one, Susie Lynn, queen of the patch, company. One hundred dollars added up to a brand-new family.

Donna had split her life into two distinct parts. In one compartment lived the little girl who sat in the big chair and told of the life she and her sisters and cousins had led for as long as she could remember. In another was a little girl who ate regular meals, wore clothes that didn't stink and washed every day. No one had hit her in nearly five months, no one had yanked her pants off or stuck their fingers or their members into her private parts.

One of Donna's few good memories of her life on the Mountain was the mysterious benefactor who dropped off boxes in front of her house in the middle of the night. Inside were good second-hand clothes, shoes and occasionally toys. The first time it happened one of her aunts grabbed the box and claimed it, dispensing all the clothes to her own children. From then on, Donna kept her eyes peeled for the treasure, and hopefully a glimpse of the person who dropped it off. She was always the first to look out the window in the morning and if there was anything there, she'd be out the door and back again so quickly no one even realized she'd gone.

Donna wondered if it was the same angel who had paid for school lunches for herself and Lisa. Neither William nor Wanda bothered to send them on the bus with anything to eat, but one day the lunches began. She was afraid to eat anything the first day just in case she'd be accused of stealing. But the teacher told her not to worry, that the lunch was all paid for. Donna often fantasized about her mysterious benefactor, conjuring up a Prince Charming who'd one day swoop down, gather her in his arms and take her away.

✦

Along with Donna's father, older cousins and uncles, the court also mowed through the extended Clan—the legion of men who tramped in and out of the children's lives. These husbands, ex-husbands, common-law husbands and husbands-to-be of her aunts used the children with much the same sense of ownership as did her father and uncles. When they congregated, it amused William to demonstrate his power over the children with games like the mailbox race.

It usually happened when the men had crammed into William's tiny house. There would be lots of laughing, shouting and arguing and often angry proclamations of some indignity committed by a Valley person or a government official "for no reason t'all." If there were plenty of children about, William might suggest a little diversion, a race. The children would be corralled and ordered to run from the house to the mailbox and back. Even when they have no hope of winning, the simple joy of a contest thrills most children. But the mailbox race brought no happiness or anticipation to the Goler children's eyes. William's rules were simple—the first child back to the house was given a free pass from the sexual attentions of the Clan for that day.

Donna may have been very slow to start walking when she was younger but that mailbox drew her like a powerful magnet. She ran not only for herself but for Lisa too. Lisa couldn't run, she was slow and fell down again and again. In a singular moment of pity, her father allowed Donna to race for both of them. She seldom lost.

The men loved this entertainment, and they'd joke about it for hours afterwards.

One of the many men hanging around the Goler compound was Roy Hiltz, a strange, wizened little creature with dreadful teeth, small, close-set eyes and pockmarked skin. Hiltz looked rather like a poorly groomed rodent wearing thick spectacles. No one could remember exactly when he came into the picture but once joined to the Clan, he never left. First he married Mary, William's sister, and fathered two children, a boy and a girl. After a tempestuous and violent five years he left, eventually getting together with Mary's sister Stella, then living in Blue Mountain. She already had three children by the late Cecil Kelly who'd been killed in a car accident. With Roy she had one more child, Sally. Hiltz was a short, almost fragile-looking man, but he had a temper that ranked with any of the Golers'.

When Roy Hiltz moved in with Stella Goler, he used her two sons Kenny and Doug as his personal whipping boys. "He left some wicked marks on those kids," confirms Stella. Hiltz beat Kenny so many times that the boy ran away constantly and then, when he was twelve, for good. He moved in with his uncle, Lawrence Kelly, another member of the Goler Clan who was later charged with the rest of them. Doug, two years younger, wasn't so lucky. Hiltz preyed on him, tortured him, sometimes sending him into convulsions with the severity of his beatings. "Roy beat hell out of him," Stella says matter-of-factly. "He'd go right wild like."

Doug too kept running away and either the police or social services kept returning him like a stray dog. Once Doug was so badly beaten that a male social worker felt compelled to tell Roy "to keep his damn hands off him." Recognizing the hollowness of the threat, Hiltz ignored him.

But the "wicked marks" didn't just appear on the boys' flesh. Since he rarely worked, Roy Hiltz had a lot of time on his hands that he used to control even the simplest activities of his family. "I hardly ever let the children out in winter, because my husband wouldn't let me," Stella explained. "He said they'd only lug snow in so I just made up my mind to keep them in most of the time. Just the minute my children wanted to go outdoors, he'd beat the hell out of them and make them stay in the house and everything else and what was I going to do?"

Perhaps because he seemed so small and harmless to outsiders, Roy Hiltz, fifty-four years old at the time of the charges, was treated relatively leniently by the criminal justice system. He was never called to account for the years of beatings he inflicted on the children and faced only three sex charges: one count each of buggery, sexual assault and gross indecency against only one victim, Donna's younger sister Lisa.

Hiltz had been arrested on February 16, two days after most of the Clan had been brought in. At the station, Constable Botham asked how often he had put his "cock in Lisa's mouth" when she was five years old. Hiltz corrected him. "*She* put my cock in her mouth," though he couldn't exactly remember where it had happened. "Must have been making my water and she came out and grabbed it and started sucking." At first Hiltz denied having anal sex with Lisa. "*She* may have thought I did. She was brushing her bum up against my cock." Botham asked, "Why would a little girl brush against your cock?" Hiltz shook his head in puzzlement. "I don't know. Don't know why they do it."

On the stand Lisa could barely speak. After Jack Buntain got past her name, most of his questions elicited only inaudible whispers. Though Lisa had known Roy Hiltz all her life and could point him out with a trembling finger as he sat in the court room, clad in a bright striped shirt, she claimed to have known him only for several weeks. When Buntain asked Lisa exactly what Hiltz had done to her, she broke down into terrified sobs. Buntain tried to console her, reminding her that she was safe in the court room and asking who was frightening her. With what seemed to be her last reserves, the seven-year-old again pointed directly at Roy Hiltz.

Hiltz helped himself to Lisa several times in William Goler's house. Once Donna used the ladder to look in through the window. Another time she crept into the house to peek through the hole in the curtain draped over the doorway to the bedroom. Sometimes she just listened, waiting for Lisa's agony to be over so she could comfort her. Donna despaired over her inability to protect Lisa but she'd often seen what Hiltz had done to Doug—she didn't dare intervene. There was nothing she could do about it—until now.

Donna calmly testified that she'd repeatedly seen Roy Hiltz "having sex with Lisa. Putting his cock in Lisa's mouth and in her backside." Darrell Carmichael, Hiltz's lawyer, tried to discredit Donna by implying that with the number of men hanging around the Goler compound, there was no way she could be sure that it was Roy Hiltz she'd seen.

Carmichael: Now Donna, did you ever see any other men having sex with Lisa?

Donna: Yes.

Carmichael: Who would they have been?

Donna: Ah, Billy— Do I have to mention all of them?

Carmichael: Well, how many would there have been?

Donna: Two or three. Billy and Cran and some other people. Two or three.

Carmichael quickly moved on as it was clear Donna would have no difficulty distinguishing between her hulking uncle Cran and the diminutive Hiltz.

Carmichael: And the first time you were at the police station, had they asked you about this sort of thing?

Donna: Yeah, but I didn't say anything about it.... I said it didn't happen, but I lied.

Carmichael: So why did you tell the truth the second day when you hadn't the first day?

Donna: Because, well, I was going over it in my mind and I thought, well, since I moved I should tell the truth instead of keeping it on my mind. It wouldn't be really fair to my sister and everything, for her helping me out.

Carmichael: And what sister was that?

Donna: Sandra Goler.

Carmichael: Sandra Goler. And how did you think it would be helping her out to tell this?

Donna: Well, I thought it would help me first.

Carmichael: How would it help you?

Donna: I'd get it off my chest. It'd be all over with.

It was Donna's first admission that she owed a debt of gratitude to Sandra for what she had once called "ratting" on her family. In the past Sandra's attempts to get away had only resulted in punishment for Donna and Lisa, and Donna had hated her for it. Now, months after they had been taken off the Mountain, Donna was beginning to realize that, perhaps for the first time in her life, her sister had done her a favour.

Donna had told her best friend and cousin Pam about what she had seen between Lisa and Roy Hiltz, but she knew better than any of the children just how ridiculous telling the other adults would be, particularly her father and Wanda.

Carmichael: Did you think they would not believe you either?

Donna: Well, if they did they'd just say something to Roy and that'd be it 'cause they did probably the same to Lisa. They did the same to me.

Carmichael: This is your father who did it?

Donna: Yes.

Carmichael: And your mother as well?

Donna: Wanda. In a way, yes, not the same way but in a way.

Carmichael: She was sort of your stepmother, was she?

Donna: You wouldn't call her that. Just call her the maid.

Carmichael then tried to discredit Donna's motivations for testifying. Some of the lawyers had begun to suspect that the children's co-operation was being purchased with the multitude of treats showered on them—the accused were sure of it. "They bribed them kids, by taking them to Zellers," laments Mary Goler. "They bought 'em stuff, bribed 'em good like. Who wouldn't say what they wanted them to say? They're just kids, like any other."

Even if it wasn't a deliberate attempt to buy their testimony, the lawyers felt the children might say anything, just to keep the unaccustomed bounty coming. Carmichael asked Donna if she had been promised anything if she took the stand. Donna's simple and definitive no forced him into a different line. He hoped to make the case that Donna's testimony was her way of improving her situation. He was partially successful but the poignancy of her answers brought into sharp focus how little these children had, and how meagre were their hopes.

Carmichael: You're in a foster home at the present time?

Donna: At the present time, yes.

Carmichael: And do you know where you're going to go from there?

Donna: Not exactly.

Carmichael: Do you think you might stay there?

Donna: In a way I want to move to a different place where there's somebody my age and I guess my sister.

Carmichael: And do you think how you testify here today might have a bearing on whether you'll go where you want to go?

Donna: I don't know for sure but I hope I did pretty good.

During his trial, Roy Hiltz became something of a media star. He spoke an odd, almost incomprehensible form of English, slurring his words as if he were holding something in his mouth. Though an absolutely awful-looking man, Hiltz's cheery demeanour and obvious helplessness charmed the media, who, because of a court-ordered publication ban during the preliminaries and trials, had no access to testimony about him. Jan Van Horne, a wire service photographer, recalls him as being "sweet," "childlike" and so eager to please she had difficulty believing he could harm anyone. Like the Golers, Hiltz was never seen without his Bible.

When a television reporter asked Hiltz if he knew what incest meant he replied quizzically, "Insects?" The reporter repeated the correct pronunciation, incest. Hiltz again screwed his face up and struggled hard. "No, no. Can't say's I do. Nope." It was a routine he was happy to repeat time and again. Hiltz claimed he didn't understand any of what was happening and several times appeared ready to cry. In all he presented the image of a very backward man who had been plucked from all he knew for no reason that he could comprehend. He was a pathetic, sad and vulnerable figure—at least to those covering the case.

Another individual operating on the fringes of the Goler Clan was forty-one-year-old Rick Davison, who married Mary Goler in 1980. Compared with Roy Hiltz, her first husband, Rick was a saint. Mary described Rick as "a good provider" who gave her "the happiest and most settled time" of her life. She fondly recalled family camping trips, fishing trips and visits to a nearby park, all orchestrated by Rick. What she failed to remember or said she had no knowledge of was her husband forcing her son Jeff into oral and anal sex. Rick was also charged with similar offences against Matt, Mary's nephew.

Earl Johnstone, twenty-three when he was arrested, followed his cousin Rick into the Goler Clan. Not long after Rick had moved in with Mary Goler and her two children Jeff and Jennifer, Earl took up with Josephine, who was living in Blue Mountain near her sister Stella. Like most of the other men who slipped into the Clan's circle, the Johnstone clan had been linked to the Golers for several generations. One of Rick's sisters was married to one of William's cousins and on Stella's side (William's mother), the name was connected to the generation that produced her mother Ada, "who walks the road."

Like the rest of the Clan, Earl went along with the arresting officers peacefully. At the police station, he happily drank several cups of tea and willingly answered questions during a three-hour interrogation by constables Ted Corkum and Mark Boileau. And like the rest he implicated the others willy-nilly. "He was quite talkative, very co-operative," recalled Constable Corkum. "He indicated different persons that he had seen, had witnessed doing different things to different children and different acts that he himself had been involved with."

Earl was right at home with the Golers' squalor and deprivation; he had grown up in a similar situation. As a boy, living in a one-room shack with his mother and alcoholic father, there was little he could do to get away when his father used his fists on him or ordered him to drop his pants and give his old man some pleasure. He found little relief at school where he was teased and shunned by his Valley classmates and virtually ignored by his teachers, who more or less left him in Grade 2 until his size and age forced them to suddenly promote him to an auxiliary class at Horton District High School, skipping seven grades in the process. After a torturous year there Earl gave up. No one worked too hard at convincing him to stay.

It was remarkable that he lasted so long in school since he'd been on his own from the age of ten when his mother walked out on him, his two sisters and his permanently sodden father. That was 1970 and social services stepped in to assist his mother but left the three children to drift from one relative to another, often spending only a night or two on a blanket on the floor before moving on. But somehow Earl Johnstone got to school nearly every day. Apple picking and potato digging kept him alive throughout his teen years. He'd go on a tear now and then, but he ran up against the law only once after he slashed the tires of someone who crossed him. He was just out of his teens when he walked into the bosom of the Goler Clan. It was as close to family as he had ever experienced.

Earl freely admitted to the police that he felt Pam's crotch once in the living room of the main Goler house in White Rock. "She was hinting around for it like a she-cat," he maintained, denying politely but vehemently that he'd had any sexual relations with her. Strangely enough, he admitted that he regularly "blew" and "jerked" eight-year-old Matt, the son of Josephine. "What do you mean by 'blew him and jerked him'?" demanded Corkum. "Blow job is when I put his penis in my mouth and jerked means, penis in my hand and jerking it," Earl obediently replied.

Earl also disclosed that Josephine, Matt's mother, had caught him in the act more than once. But Josephine stood by her boyfriend Earl because "he's not that type of man." She indignantly denied that anyone could get their hands on her child, "because I don't leave my son alone with anybody, and I'm always checking on my son even if he is outdoors playing alone. I'm very stric' and I watch over him very closely, 'cause he's the only son I've got. I think too much of him to let him out of my sight too much, so even if he is outdoors alone then I still check him."

By the time Earl Johnstone met Pam, Stella Goler's daughter, the girl was already well used to the rites and rituals of the Goler Clan. She had come to assume that every man would use her as her uncles and cousins did and she discovered that with some men who weren't blood relations, there were occasional benefits like candy or a few dollars tossed her way. Fighting or protesting only got her "smucked" across the face or grimy fingers embedded in her throat.

Like Josephine, Pam's mother Stella angrily dismissed charges that Earl had "screwed" her daughter, claiming that she had only known Earl Johnstone for a short time and that he'd only been in her home once to help his cousin Rick drywall the kitchen. Earl had never, according to Stella, been into any other room of their three-room shack. Moreover, the house was always so full of people he couldn't have done anything without being observed.

> Buntain: Okay, and how many times did you see him in your house? Do you remember?
>
> Pam: No.

Buntain: Do you remember what he was doing there, why he was there?

Pam: Came out to visit us.

Buntain: All right, and was he doing anything else while he was there?

Pam: He screwed me twice.

Buntain: He screwed you twice. Now when you say he screwed you, what do you mean by that?

Pam: Put his dink in my cunt.

Buntain: How did you know he did that?

Pam: I could feel it.

Buntain: All right, and where did this happen, Pam?

Pam: In Mum's room.

Buntain: Both times?

Pam: Both times.

Buntain: All right, and what did it happen on?

Pam: The bed.

Buntain: The bed. How did you come to go into the bedroom? Somebody say something or what happened?

Pam: See, I go in there to listen to the record player.

Buntain: Yes? And is that what you were doing both of these occasions?

Pam: Both times.

Buntain: And how did Mr. Johnstone come to be in there?

Pam: He likes to listen to the record player.

Buntain: Okay. And whose idea is it to screw?

Pam: His.

Buntain: All right, did you agree to this?

Pam: Yes.

Buntain: Did you want to do this?

Pam: Yes.

Buntain: All right. Was there anybody else in the bedroom with the two of you on these two occasions?

Pam: No, but Mum caught us, Mum and Sally caught us.

Buntain: Both times?

Pam: Yes.

Buntain: Okay. What happened when Mum and Sally caught you?

Pam: She was very mad.

Buntain: Who was?

Pam: Mum.

Buntain: All right, and when you were on the bed the first time what happened to your clothes?

Pam: Just pulled down.

Buntain: What clothes were pulled down?

Pam: My pants and panties.

Buntain: And who pulled those down?

Pam: I did.

Buntain: You did. What about Mr. Johnstone's clothes, what happened to those—do you remember?

Pam: No.

Buntain: All right. Were any of them taken off, do you remember, or down?

Pam: Don't know.

Buntain: All right, how did he get his dink out?

Pam: His zipper.

Buntain: Okay, now when your mum caught you did you hear her say anything to Mr. Johnstone?

Pam: No.

Buntain: All right, now, Mum and Sally caught you, you say. Do you remember, Pam, if on any of those occasions there was anybody else in the house?

Pam: Josie [Josephine], Matt, Dad, Doug, Kenny.

Buntain: And where were they when you and Mr. Johnstone were doing this?

Pam: Some of them was outdoors.

Buntain: And where were the others?

Pam: Josie and Mum was making cookies.

Though Stella was "very mad" when she twice caught Pam having sex, it wasn't Earl Johnstone who was the recipient of her ire. "I got a licking after," Pam recalled sadly. To Johnstone Stella said nothing.

Lawrence Kelly, fifty-one, so meek and used-up looking that he seemed like a man of seventy or eighty, was one of the few who voiced the slightest concern for the welfare of the children. "I didn't come in her," he earnestly told the police about one of the girls. "I pulled it out and came on the floor. I had to let it go somewhere. I couldn't leave it in her. I was afraid I'd knock her up. She's only young, too young."

When the police officer asked why he'd had sex with such a young girl, Lawrence Kelly responded quickly. "Because I was horny and she wanted me to. You would too if you never had it for seven years." He also claimed that he did ask her if she was willing and to prove the point he added, "All you had to do was take it out and shake it at her and she got right sexy. She would make faces and smack her lips and things like that."

Eugene Brown, thirty-six, was another man from the Mountain who slithered into the Goler Clan. The Browns settled in the Greenfield area of South Mountain at least one hundred and fifty years ago. Today, one mailbox after another in Greenfield carries the Brown name. Eugene didn't quite measure up to Goler standards. "He wasn't a pro," recalls Donna. "He came into the family and he wanted to be like the rest of them. But he was too nice. I think he felt he had to pay for it with money or candy or cigarettes. He didn't just come in, grab you, slap you around or smuck you and do it. He'd try to talk you up a bit first."

Unlike most of the Goler Clan, Eugene Brown had been steadily employed for eleven years even though he was illiterate and the court psychologist described him as "functionally retarded." Brown tried out several of the children and when arrested was charged with assaulting seven of them. But he settled on Pam as his favourite, "screwing" her fourteen or fifteen times. She was also readily accessible since Brown was "seeing" her aunt Marjorie and the girl was happy to take money, usually ten dollars, in exchange for submitting to him.

Gabriel Dodge was also a regular and, like the rest, found his entree into the Clan through the sisters. His roots on the Mountain date back to the late eighteenth century when a British sailor took up a land grant in the new world. Dodge's branch of the family ended up trying to farm the rock and acid soil of Blue Mountain, which today is a dejected little strip of shabby homes interspersed with the odd neatly kept bungalow. The forlorn air pervading the place reeks of abandoned hopes.

Gabriel's mother, twenty-three years younger than her husband, bore seven children, four of whom lived to adulthood. The family survived by raising a few cattle and chickens supplemented by income from cutting trees. On the Mountain names like Mary, Edith, Esther, Fred and John were common, but the Dodges gave their children unusual names like Karl, Ivan, Phyllis and Gabriel. Two of their children, Perry and Theresa, died in their first four months and tragedy visited the family again in 1970 when Gabriel was eleven. He woke up in the morning to find his brother Ivan hanging from a rope tied to a beam in the bedroom the two boys shared.

Even for a "kid from the Mountain," twenty-five-year-old Gabriel Dodge was slow, though considered to be one of the most amiable fellows around. He was teased and tormented about being dumb all the way through school and he eventually dropped out at the age of sixteen because "they suggested I stop." By then all he'd learned was to write his name. Gabriel was always a mild boy, anxious to please but quick to blame everyone else if something went wrong, which it frequently did as his life lurched from one crisis to another.

At twenty-one he raped a girl who lived next door. As he was with almost everything else in life, Gabriel was puzzled by the charge, claiming that the neighbours made the accusation because they were "jealous" of the Dodge family, which had recently acquired a "new" second-hand truck. The judge took pity on him for his child-like manner, giving him a suspended sentence with two years of probation. Shortly afterwards, the mother of the raped girl moved into the Dodge farmhouse. Not long after that Stella and Roy Hiltz moved to Blue Mountain and Gabriel met up with the Goler Clan.

Gabriel was charged with sexually assaulting a single child, Pam, Stella's daughter. The court psychologist asked him if he understood what was happening to him. "A sex charge," a puzzled Gabriel replied, "and I can't figure it out." He told the psychologist that he felt sorry for Pam because "she ain't all there." When asked to explain he continued, "Because of the way she goes on and is low on the mental side because her stepfather beat her." During questioning by police, he told them he had sex with her because she asked if she "could have a piece" and "came on" to him.

Stella Goler, who was freed of her husband Roy Hiltz shortly after they moved to Blue Mountain in October 1983, furiously dismissed the charges, loudly insisting that Gabriel was only an occasional visitor to the house and never alone with Pam. And, in any case, Pam told nothing but "a pack of lies" and wasn't to be believed on any count. Stella neglected to mention that she and Gabriel had been living together almost from the moment she moved to Blue Mountain.

All the Goler men portrayed the children, even the five-year-olds, as determined tempters and temptresses, but thirty-eight-year-old Ralph Kelly, who started "screwing" the children four years earlier, took the portrayal to the extreme. Ralph boasted to the police that he'd "had sex with them all" and they all wanted him so badly, they often hurt him in their eagerness to seduce him.

Pam, when she was nine, "started playing with my rod and got it hard. She wanted me to put my rod in her and I took my zipper down. She put my rod in her mouth and got it hard, then I put it in her cunt and screwed her. She pulled her pants and panties down and we screwed standing up against the wall." The next time "all she had on was a T-shirt. She laid there and spread her legs wide open. She played with my cock. I took it out of my zipper and put it in her cunt and screwed her. I had put my cock up her ass the time we screwed [before] as well. She didn't suck my cock the second time."

Ralph started with Sandra when she was nine or ten. "She followed me over to the well to see what I was doing—some damn reason. She started rubbing my cock. I took my zipper down and she rubbed it until it got hard. She took her bottom off and she never had no panties on. She laid on a blanket or coat and I got on top and put my cock in her cunt and screwed her. I screwed her one other time near the well. The next time she had slacks on and a light blouse you could see through. You could see her tits, no bra on."

It didn't matter how young, the Goler girls were able to have their way with Ralph—dozens of times. In addition to numerous encounters by the well, in the woodshed and the various bedrooms in the Goler houses, the girls enticed him to "screw standing up in the water... up above our bellybutton," in a "hammock," on an "arm-chair," in a "tent" and when "I was watchin' 'All My Children' on the TV. She got my cock out and got it hard, she left her dress on but fired her panties on the floor. She straddled me, put my cock up her ass and rode me back and forth."

The boys weren't immune to Ralph's charms either. The first time with Jeff, then ten, was the summer of 1983 in White Rock. "I was piling wood when he came down and slapped me across the ass with a piece of wood. I told him it hurt and to stop. I shook him and he grabbed me between the legs, it brought tears to my eyes. Then he started rubbing my cock and got it hard, then he asked me to put it in his bum." Doug, when he was nine, "asked me in his bedroom and told me to lay down. When I did he started playing with my cock. He put my cock in his mouth and got it hard, then he shoved my cock up his bum. He told me that he liked it. That it felt good."

✦

Of the sixteen originally charged, seven were born Goler and the remaining eight—one had all charges dropped—were Clan regulars, most of them attached by marriage or a common-law relationship to the Goler women.

Chapter Eleven

The Women

✦ WANDA WHISTON WAS TWENTY years old in January 1979 when she embarked upon her odyssey of self-discovery with William Goler. Over the next five years, she evolved into the rarest of criminals, the female sexual predator. Born as Wanda Joyce Schofield in 1958, she could trace her family back to the seventeenth-century Scovills, if she cared to. The Scovills were Planters who moved to the Mountain within a few years of arriving in the Valley from Connecticut. They settled in Black River, not far from White Rock. The clan multiplied rapidly, making their name one of the most common on South Mountain within three generations. At least a dozen Schofields intermarried with descendants of Rolen Rogers and several became connected with the Golers when they established themselves on South Mountain.

Wanda came from an average-sized Mountain family with six children—an older sister and brother and three younger brothers. Slight and dark-haired, she appeared, to outsiders, to be shy and self-effacing. But there was a wildness and a hunger at her core. Wanda's mother called her "headstrong" and, though Wanda denied it, the police suspected she'd been abused as a child. At sixteen she was arrested for shoplifting and placed on probation. She failed Grade 9 that year, then transferred into a vocational secretarial program at Horton District High School. Although her IQ scores put her in the bottom 10 percent of all people her age, Wanda seemed much brighter than the numbers indicated. At least one teacher thought that "with application" she might become a good secretary. But typing didn't suit her any better than academics so she tried graphic communications, which brought her to the end of Grade 11 when she quit.

Wanda left home at the age of eighteen to wait on tables in the Valley. At nineteen she married a man who, according to Wanda, loved the bottle more than her. The marriage lasted a bare eight months and left her with the Whiston last name. Afterwards she worked at a series of odd jobs including baby-sitting, housekeeping and a three-week stint as a dishwasher at the legendary White Spot where Valley people had been coming for fish and chips, burgers, pie and milkshakes since 1946. She met William Goler through her father who, like some of the Goler men, did seasonal work at Long's Lumber Mill in White Rock.

In January 1979, Wanda moved into William's house to clean for him and care for the children while his wife, Hazel, by then a well-worn twenty-six, was in hospital having her tubal ligation. The girls can't remember Wanda ever cooking a meal or lifting a cleaning rag but they do recall her immediately slipping into William's bed. Of course, there wasn't anywhere else to sleep, except the floor or the bed shared by Donna, Sandra and Lisa. Wanda later insisted she intended to leave when Hazel came back, only staying on "because Mrs. Goler wasn't well." Hazel declares heatedly that she was perfectly well and more than a little surprised to find the younger woman replacing her. "That bitch," she growls. "That bitch turned him aginst me. I'd like to take a stick to her if I could."

When Hazel returned, William Goler's house, filled with fury and tension at the best of times, became a minefield. The children tiptoed around carefully, never knowing what might detonate one or all of the three adults. Hazel lashed out, picking fights with Wanda, muttering obscenities at her under her breath and often provoking William into one of his rages. At times the three of them were all screaming and swinging at each other as the children cowered in corners or under beds.

At night William, Wanda and Hazel crammed into the same small bed, snarling and snapping at each other like penned dogs. Sometimes Donna woke up to the sound of her father "goin' at" Wanda while Hazel clung angrily to the edge of the bed, each squeak of the springs underlying her rejection.

After a few weeks of trench warfare, Hazel left without a word. The days went by and the children wondered when she would return. In many ways it was better with her gone—the fighting declined. On the other hand, they had to put up with Wanda. Half child, half woman, her mannerisms would be adult one minute and eerily immature the next. Her conversation was an odd blend of truculent teenager and the gutter with a disconcerting bit of shy, nice girl thrown in occasionally for confusion. She carried around a small doll and talked to it constantly, asking its opinion, discussing things with it, sometimes taunting or teasing the children using the doll as an intermediary. It was spooky and Donna stayed out of her way as best she could.

When Hazel came back to White Rock after staying for a while with her mother, the fights broke out again, and once more the children were caught in a no man's land between the warring adults. And so the winter of 1979 dragged on. Hazel left and returned several more times, often carrying away with her the imprint of William's fist on her face and body as she walked or hitch-hiked down Deep Hollow Road towards the Valley. Once a police officer picked her up. Thinking she was drunk, he offered to take her back home. Hazel blazed at him, spewing a jumble of incoherent words, ranting about Wanda and William and vowing to kill him if he dared take her back up the Mountain.

Finally Hazel demanded that William choose between her and Wanda. He laughed in her face and said Wanda wasn't going anywhere. Hazel could either join in, shut up or leave.

Just before Easter the weather warmed, teasing with spring before winter's tail end snatched the promise away. Donna and her sisters were playing outside when Hazel told them she was going away again.

That in itself wasn't surprising. Their mother had come and gone many times in Donna's lifetime. The first time she simply handed three-month-old Lisa to Donna and walked out the door. "I thought she was going into the yard or something," Donna recalls. "I stood there with Lisa in my arms waiting for her to come back. She never said a word." Hazel was gone for months that time, returning with no explanation. What was surprising about this latest departure was the fact that her mother was actually saying goodbye. "I can't take you with me this time," she said, though as far as they knew she had never tried before. "I hope I'll see you again, okay? Goodbye now. Bye girls." With that Hazel Goler left for the last time.

Donna knew better than to question her father about Hazel. It was obvious she was leaving because of Wanda. She directed a virulent beam of hate at both Wanda and her mother. Hazel, her mother's first name, had always been part of Donna's name and her cousins often called her Hazel instead of Donna. The day her mother left, Donna exorcised the name, turning on anyone who dared use it when addressing her.

Hazel had virtually no education but like the rest of the Clan she had more than a passing familiarity with the social services system. She now realized she would never dislodge Wanda but she did go to legal aid, enlisted a lawyer and tried to get custody of her children. Her efforts were doomed from the start. "Hazel was, well, she was what you might call mental," a social services worker said years later. "We all knew her and she never had a chance to get those kids, not from day one."

Sandra wanted to live with Hazel but William forbade it, though he did allow her to visit from time to time. The day of the custody hearing in 1982 Sandra, as the oldest, went into Kentville to testify in Family Court. Donna and Lisa were sent to stay with Wanda's cousin. It was one of the happiest days of Donna's life. The cousin had a clean house, running water and an indoor toilet. There were lots of children to play with and, best of all, no mailbox game. She didn't really understand why Sandra had to go into town with William and Wanda but she hoped none of them would ever come back so she and Lisa could stay with Wanda's cousin.

The Family Court judge granted custody of Donna, Sandra and Lisa to William Goler. No one can quite remember or understand why, and no one wants to examine the ruling too closely, in light of ensuing events.

Hazel tells a rambling story of being told to get a larger apartment, which she claims she did, only to lose custody anyway. If anyone visited the William Goler home to evaluate living conditions no one within Family and Children's Services is willing to admit it now. In an ironic twist, the judge who made the decision to leave Sandra, Donna and Lisa with William and Wanda was Don Hall. Two years later, as County Court judge, he would hear what William had been doing to the children he had left in William's tender care.

Wanda Whiston bewitched and entranced William Goler. Suddenly the Clan leader had a consort. Hazel had never been able to raise herself from the bottom of the Goler pecking order; Wanda started at the top. "My mother hated sex," explains Donna. "Wanda would do it anytime with anyone. All my father had to do was point to the bedroom and she'd be in there with her pants down." Wanda did what she pleased when she pleased around the Goler compound, with William backing her to the hilt. She swore like a sailor, worked on the cars alongside the men in greasy coveralls and then turned into a girl again, whispering to her doll. On the rare occasions when the children dared disobey or provoke her, Wanda simply announced she was going home, then hit the road. When that happened, William's wrath shook the walls of the little shack. Donna took special care to avoid her father. If she got in his way, he liked to stomp on her thin legs.

Wanda took to the Goler way with gleeful and indiscriminate abandon. To a deviant, the Clan offered a cornucopia of sexual delights. The first time Wanda reached for Sandra Goler was just after Hazel left for the last time. Sandra, then ten, her sisters and cousins were playing in the single room that served as kitchen, dining room and living room when Wanda grabbed Sandra and marched her into the bedroom.

"You're coming in here with me!" Wanda announced. "They seen her push me down on the bed. I told her to stop it," Sandra testified.

"They [the other children] said stop and they were crying. I tried to push her away and told her to stop it but at ten you can't do anything. She had her stomach against my leg. She was leaning on the floor—like the bed's only low. She just put her mouth on my vagina, sucked it. She made me do the same thing to her, she had ahold of my hair."

There was no hiding it, even if Wanda cared to. In fact, she made a point of displaying her conquests of Sandra in full view of the other children, as if instinctively understanding the power of modelling in shaping their behaviour. Sandra was the oldest girl and by repeatedly abusing her in front of the younger, impressionable children Wanda ensured they would be more malleable when their turn came.

The last time Wanda "used" Sandra before her February 1984 arrest "was basically like the first time, like all the rest of the times. She forced me to do oral sex on her and then she did it on me." Sandra no longer struggled but then Wanda, who was strong despite her diminutive size, left her no options. "The doors were locked and she would have caught me and I had a hard time getting the latch open when I wanted to go to school, getting the hook up so [she] would have caught me before I got out." When Wanda finished with Sandra, she sent her away with a dismissive flick of her wrist. Sandra stood up, pulled her clothes on and walked out of the house to wait morosely for the school bus.

Shortly after she initiated Sandra, Wanda reached for Pam, Sandra's cousin, "fingering" her and kissing "my cunt—she made me kiss hers." Wanda liked an audience. Cranswick often sat in.

Wanda worked her way through the Goler girls like a thresher through a field of ripe grain. She introduced Donna to her hungers shortly after she turned ten. But Donna's fierce loathing of Wanda made it necessary for the older woman to apply a strong lever to force Donna to do her bidding. Eventually Wanda used a mix of humiliation and fear, with an underlying threat, to bring her into line. If Donna displeased Wanda, say, by waking her up in the morning, she ordered the girl into the bedroom for "punishment." When such punishments were announced, the rest of the children disappeared, lest they be included.

Wanda told Donna to go inside, strip down and wait on her knees. After a suitable pause to allow her to ponder her sins, Wanda appeared, doffed her clothes and began roughly probing and poking at the little girl, her fingers invading her "backside and frontside," all the while telling her she was only getting what she deserved. Donna quietly whimpered but, like Sandra, she had long ago given up active resistance. Earlier attempts to fight had only resulted in thrashings—Wanda preferred to use a length of bicycle tire. And if she persisted, Wanda simply told her Lisa would get Donna's "punishment" instead. That was a thought Donna couldn't bear.

Donna never for a moment considered complaining to her father. "Then Dad would come in and I would have got in more trouble," she told the court. "I was afraid I was going to get in trouble again, and the same thing was going to happen." Those on the periphery of the Goler case seemed perplexed by the children's inability to get help; the underlying inference seemed to be that they didn't really try very hard. "Do you think we children gave up our bodies willingly?" Donna asks angrily today. "People believed that, they still believe it because of who we were. I fought, we all fought. It was wrong and I knew it was wrong."

But who was a Goler child like Donna to tell? Her father and Wanda? Her uncles, who were also assaulting her? The various hangers-on who similarly preyed on the children? Her aunts, who had mastered the art of looking the other way? The authorities who were paid to protect them and were also looking the other way—or worse? Donna and the rest of the children knew that Sandra had run away from home twice and was brought back, first by a policeman and then by a social worker. Both times she told them what her father was doing to her; they returned her anyway, to terrible beatings. Donna also told a teacher who in turn informed William that his daughter was saying terrible things about him. It didn't take Donna, or the other children, long to get the message that there wasn't anyone who would help. It was a body- and soul-destroying predicament for a little girl.

One day in the summer of 1983, Sandra, Donna and Lisa were picking blueberries in a field near their house when they heard

Wanda bellowing for Lisa, who immediately left her bowl of berries and went to the house. Concerned, her sisters followed. Not daring to go inside and see what was going on, they quietly propped the old wooden ladder against the house. Taking turns peering in, they saw the little girl on her back across the bed with a naked Wanda on her knees holding Lisa's legs apart. Her top and socks were still on, her shorts and panties hanging from one ankle. Wanda grabbed Lisa's head and rammed it against her crotch but Lisa put up a furious struggle. Not even Wanda's clouts and threats could stop her terrified wailing and squirming. Wanda finally gave up, pinned her down and performed oral sex on Lisa, who lay there sobbing.

The last two girls to be "done" by Wanda were Donna's cousins, Sally, eight, and Annie, five. She bribed the pliable and slow-thinking Sally to get what she wanted. But she designed other motivations for the much younger Annie. "I'm going to tell my mommy," Annie promised the first time Wanda touched her. "If you do I'm gonna spank you," threatened Wanda, adding for good measure, "I'm gonna take you down the old house and leave you there." Annie was terrified of the windowless shell where Stella and Charles had lived in the forties and fifties. Though they had given the house to Henry, it was too ruined even for Golers to inhabit. Rats had taken up residence long ago and at night bats swooped silently in and out through the gaping boards. One of the children told Annie that Cecil "went cripple" because he slept there overnight, emerging twisted, bent and unable to speak. She never struggled against Wanda again.

Wanda didn't limit herself to the girls. "I was visiting Nannie and Papa and went down to see Sandra and Pooch and Lisa," Matt, who was seven at the time, testified. He played with the girls in the main room until Wanda summoned him into the bedroom and cornered him. "She played with my boat and she tried to stick her fingers up my bum." Then Wanda "put my boat in her bum."

Donna scooted over to the shower curtain and peered in through the hole to see Wanda pawing a protesting Matt. "She was putting her finger in his backside and later on, about a minute later, she has his dink in her mouth." Lisa came over for a look. Donna grabbed her hand and dragged her sister away, telling her not to say anything about what she'd seen. "You don't want to get smucked, do you?" she asked sternly. Lisa shook her head. "Okay, so don't say nothin'. Just leave it be." Donna knew if Lisa inadvertently let slip that she'd watched the assault on Matt, Wanda would be quick to react. It had nothing to do with secrecy or privacy. Wanda didn't care about that, but she liked to be in control of who watched and when.

After Matt, Wanda tried out his eight-year-old cousin Michael, Marjorie's son. As she did with Donna, Wanda announced she was going to punish the boy because he'd been bad. The first time it happened Annie (Michael's sister), Lisa, Donna and Michael were all playing in the main room when Wanda issued her declaration. She barked out an order to Donna to keep Annie and Lisa out of her way. Donna sneaked over to the plastic curtain and peeked around it. There she saw Michael lying on his stomach while Wanda worked him over with her fingers. She commanded him to roll over. "I only looked for a minute and then Wanda had his dink in her mouth, and that's called a blow job," Donna solemnly testified.

Wanda first took Jeff when he was eleven. Tall and gangly, Jeff was an obliging child who, when excited, talked faster and faster until his words spilled over each other in an indecipherable torrent. His branch of the Goler Clan was living with the grandparents, Stella and Charles, that summer. One day the boy made the mistake of entering one of Wanda's favourite lairs—the woodshed. She asked Jeff to help her carry some logs up to the house, and being an obedient boy he quickly obliged. With his arms full, he tripped over a piece of wood and Wanda pounced. She quickly latched the door and leapt on the surprised boy with the ferocity of a jaguar. "She pulled her pants down and she had pulled mine and started going back and forth and everything."

Wanda clamped onto Jeff's penis with an intensity that brooked no opposition. "She puts all the pressure on you too," complained Jeff on the witness stand, talking as fast as an auctioneer. "She puts all her pressure on it, so I can't move." He did his best to avoid Wanda and "all the pressure she puts on it" but he was no match for the woman, who waylaid him at her whim.

One Christmas, most of the Goler Clan was congregated in Stella and Charles's house when Wanda sidled over to Jeff, covertly slipped a hand under his sweater and began massaging his chest and tweaking his nipples. After a time, Wanda suggested a trip "down cellar." "Well, she just wanted me to help her carry some wood up, I thought she really meant this," Jeff recalled ruefully. "I just went down, went down to get an armload."

Again Jeff tripped. Wanda "started doing dirty stuff.... She put her fingers up my rear end." Once again, she used an agonizing grip on Jeff's penis to maintain control. "I tried to push her away," he lamented, "but she kept on putting more and more pressure on it, on me to go close to her.... I was crying, had a lot of pain in it, quite a lot of pain." Wanda liked the pain, particularly Jeff's reaction to it; her sessions with him lasted as long as an hour.

Doug fell to Wanda just like all the rest, but unlike the rest Wanda enjoyed teasing and tempting him, offering him cigarettes for a "fuck." A stern taskmaster, she directed him to "kiss her and feel her breasts" and when she was ready, commanded him to "screw her both ways, fuck her front and back." After Doug did his duty, he'd meekly ask for his reward, only to have Wanda laugh harshly at him and say, "I ain't gonna to give you any."

Doug had lived a life of constant dislocation. When he wasn't in the hospital for treatment of severe epilepsy, he spent his time bouncing from one member of the Clan to another. Like his older brother Kenny, he had an independent streak, running away numerous times after being beaten to a pulp by Roy Hiltz. But unlike Kenny he always came back, either on his own or with the help of the police or social services until he finally moved in with his uncle Lawrence Kelly. Doug's docility made it seem he didn't care what was done to him, was even willing, but humiliation settled inside him like a tumour.

Doug's school tests showed him to be so slow few children his age would score below him. But his intelligence never had fertile ground in which to develop. What the tests didn't show either was Doug's thoughtfulness, the spark of caring left inside him that hadn't been entirely extinguished, and his eagerness to please. During the trial and all the months he and the other children were ferried back and forth from their foster homes to the police station and court-house, he rarely broke out of his silent shell. But one day, when one of the foster parents delivered Donna and Lisa to the court, he grabbed her by the sleeve. "Are you taking Donna?" he asked shyly. He spoke so softly that the woman was forced to ask him to repeat what he'd said. "I hope you're taking Donna," he said. "She should have a nice home."

William's role in Wanda's adventures was a curious one. At all times, he was the enforcer backing up her wishes, but when she wanted privacy he ushered the kids up to "Gram's." Sometimes he observed covertly. Other times, with her knowledge, he stood and watched the action. But he was ambivalent about her relationship with Doug. One day he'd watch and say nothing and the next he'd beat up Doug after Wanda had been sated.

Within weeks of the Goler Clan's arrest, people up and down the Valley were claiming they'd always known such things went on among "those hillbillies" on the Mountain. Still, they were scandalized to learn that one of the offenders was a woman. Curiously, nothing was said of the other women in the family. Most assumed they, like many women in abusive relationships, were too downtrodden or terrified to do anything about it. But Baxter Upshall believed right from the beginning that some of the mothers and aunts of the children were more than passive bystanders and that the pattern of incest went back at least two generations.

The men gave him the first specific clues. "She told me she had screwed her brother before," Lawrence Kelly told the police about one of William's sisters. "I told her she was sick for screwing her own relations. She said it didn't make any difference and that she wasn't sick."

Lawrence's brother Ralph was also forthcoming about the relationships between the Goler men and another sister. "She told me about her brothers screwing her. She also said about her father, the old man, screwing her sister." When the police asked if the women knew what was happening to their children, Ralph replied, "They either saw it or were told but they knew."

Cranswick was happy to give his own eyewitness account. "Have you ever screwed your sister?" the interrogating officer queried. "Yes," Cranswick replied matter-of-factly. "I only screwed her three times. It was in my bedroom about six or eight years ago. She wanted to do it and I agreed on it." When the police pressed him about his mother or his other sisters, Cranswick became uneasy and denied he'd ever touched them. "'Cause it's about as crazy as you can get," he explained. "What would you do if you found out who told us these things?" the officer asked. "What's the law about killing sisters? You'd better lock me up right now, then," Cranswick growled. Later he said that he'd been kidding. "I wouldn't hurt anybody. I'm not the murdering or hurting type."

One child told the police she'd been held down by her mother the first time she'd been raped by her father but later retracted her story. All of the others also said they'd told their mothers or aunts. Most of the children described incidents in which the sisters had seen or heard what was happening to them. Ten-year-old Jennifer was visiting White Rock with her mother, Mary Goler, when Eugene Brown, then Stella Goler's boyfriend, dragged her into a bedroom and forced her to fondle him while he rammed his fingers into her. As they left that evening in their car, Jennifer confessed to her mother what had happened.

"Why are you talking that way!" her mother blazed. "He wouldn't do no such thing. You just shut up about it." Jennifer sadly concluded years later that her mother's refusal to accept her story was simply because her sister was going out with Eugene and "she didn't want no trouble stirred up in the family."

Sandra Goler went to her mother, Hazel, and revealed that William was "using me as a wife." When Stella caught Earl Johnstone, her sister Josephine's boyfriend, having sex with her daughter Pam, it was Pam who got the "licking." Despite what the children said to the women, they all claimed they knew nothing and had never seen anything happen to their children. On the stand Stella, alternately unco-operative and defiantly angry, denied that Pam, Doug or Sally had said anything to her about being molested by anyone. And she couldn't remember the fact that Pam turned over some of the money paid to her by the men.

Buntain: Why would she make that up?

Stella: Why in the hell didn't she tell *me*?

Buntain: Can you give us any reason as to why she would come here and swear under oath and make that up?

Stella: How would I know because she never told me the truth since the day she was born.

Buntain: Right. Did she know what the truth was—did you teach her to tell the truth and what—

Stella: How could you teach a child that did not listen or did not care? You cannot teach a kid that won't listen.

Buntain: So are you telling us she didn't know, doesn't know the difference between the truth and a lie?

Stella: I have my damn doubts.

Buntain: And Doug came here under oath and told us this man did the same thing to him.

Stella: He's never told me anything about it either.

Buntain: Would he have any reason to lie?

Stella: My children always did lie to me.

Buntain: Would he have any reason to lie under oath, in that chair that you're sitting in this morning?

Stella: He probably would lie.

Buntain: Why?

Stella: How would I know? They got the answers to that, not me.

The only Goler woman who took any action at all was Josephine. When Matt revealed that his uncle Cranswick was "being bad" by "poking" him in his "bum with his boat," Josephine moved out of Stella and Charles's house, "because they were dirty."

Baxter Upshall had no doubt that the women were aware of what was going on and he suspected some of them had been involved, but initially he had nothing to charge them with. Early in the winter of 1984–85 the police got their first break against one of the women, Josephine. Even though barely eight months had passed since the first arrests were made and despite the fact that no charges had been laid against his mother Josephine, Family and Children's Services had already put Matt up for adoption. Like the legal system, the child welfare system was working at record speed to erase the Mountain problem. "I guess I was lucky," he said later. "Some of the other kids went from place to place. I just had the one foster home and then my parents adopted me."

Robert Whyte and his wife were kindly people. Born-again Christians with warm hearts, they took to Matt very quickly. His wife could not have a child and they wanted to adopt. Matt, though older than they preferred, seemed to need them. His big eyes and almost comically big ears gave him the look of a friendly rabbit. It was his adoptive mother Matt first confessed to, about not only his mother but his aunt Mary. Nearly a year had passed since he'd last seen his home or family. Both women had already begun to seem like people in a dream to him. When his new parents suggested the boy talk to the police, Matt reluctantly agreed. It was the right thing, the Christian thing, to do, they emphasized.

Matt hesitantly explained how his mother would suck his "boat" and "put her finger up my bum." She warned him not to tell anyone, a caution the boy took seriously because "I was afraid of somebody hurting me." Matt also testified that his aunt Mary "would suck my boat" while her children were upstairs playing records at Josephine's place. When he complained to his mother about Mary's nautical adventures, she stopped him from watching his favourite show—"The Duke boys" ["The Dukes of Hazzard"]—for a month.

There were two apartments in the rickety house on the edge of the Valley where Matt lived with his mother. The lower floor was occupied by his best friend Jeff; Jeff's sister Jennifer; their mother, Mary Goler; and her husband, Rick Davison. It was a cosy arrangement with much to-ing and fro-ing among the families. That is the way they had always existed, with a constant flow of Clan visitors and children staying over with cousins, aunts, uncles and grandparents. Most weekends they went back to the Mountain and during the summer camped in the Goler compound in a small trailer they set up there.

Mary liked to pin her own son Jeff on the bed with her 230-pound bulk, forcing him to kiss and touch "her boobies and stuff." Then "she wetted her vagina and wetted my rear end and started going back and forth" with her fingers. When Jeff was five or six, his mother put his penis "in her mouth and then she would try and put it against her vagina." At first Mary was unable to achieve pene- tration because "I was too small." Later, as Jeff got older, that proved to be no problem.

In case Jeff should ever be tempted to say anything about his home life, his mother would lock him in a small closet for an hour or two "just so I would remember not to tell nobody." Other times his mother gave him presents to ensure his silence. Jeff, like all the children, had no one to confide in, no one to turn to. Even if he hadn't been physically frightened of his stepfather, Rick, the "good provider" was also buggering him and forcing him into oral sex. And Rick paid the same attention to Matt, who was also being used by Rick's cousin, Earl Johnstone.

Until Sandra's revelations, no one cared much what was hap- pening to the Goler children. No doctors, teachers, police officers or social workers investigated their lives. They were Mountain. As their ancestors had been condemned and abandoned by the Valley and the church when they moved onto the Mountain more than two hundred years before, so were these children left to live in a sit- uation everybody believed could not be changed.

Chapter Twelve

The Other Side
of the Clan

✦ DURING THE FIRST MONTHS OF 1984 the main topic of conversation from one end of the Valley to the other was the Golers and their dark secrets. Rubbernecking on South Mountain became a Valley pastime. Hoping to spot a Goler, or some "hatchet-face," the curious drove up Deep Hollow Road, slowing at each shack, pointing, laughing—and sometimes more. Rocks were thrown, garbage strewn and shotgun blasts shook some of the shabbier dwellings. Even a few of the better-kept homes with nice cars in the yard and neat lawns ended up with giant penises spray-painted on their windows. The owners of one house on White Rock Mountain woke in the morning to find "Cunt Mountain" spelled out in rocks on their front lawn. Mountain gawking also spread to other communities.

Murrille Schofield of Gaspereau was, in the words of one Wolfville resident, "either a character, a crackpot or a seer, you never knew with him." Wonderfully literate with a fine, dry sense of humour, Schofield penned many witty letters to the local newspapers. After one particularly bad weekend when "sightseers" dumped garbage near his property, he fired off a complaint to the *Advertiser*. "The mess consisted of parts of an aluminum door, car parts, a rubber tire, plastic junk, bottles, cans and, according to that colorful and artic-ulate mountain man of the last century, Nate Atwell, 'pots, kettles and chains and every uvver damn fing.'" Things got so bad on the Mountain that one White Rock resident put up a sign, We Are Not Golers! But still the interlopers came.

The Goler cloud enveloped that entire section of the Mountain. Chris Long, owner of Long's Lumber Mill in White Rock, still flares at the mention of the Golers and their trial. "It got pretty unpleas-ant for us living and working up here," he snarls. "People had this attitude about White Rock and it was like everyone was part of it, part of what they did. People seemed to think we should all have known. Well, I knew several of the Golers and I never had a single hint of anything going on." The worst part of the notoriety, accord-ing to Long, was how it further entrenched the gulf between Valley and Mountain. A cartoon appeared in the newspaper showing a newlywed couple from the Valley driving past Deep Hollow Road leading up to White Rock Mountain. "Do you love me enough to live up there?" the groom asked the bride. At a PTA meeting in Hantsport the father of two boys and a girl joked, "Martha's been gone visiting her folks for two weeks. I wished I was a Goler tonight."

White Rock residents were reluctant to admit they lived there because people assumed anyone living within five miles of the Golers must have plenty of salacious details to add to the meagre informa-tion coming from the court room. "I got right sick of people asking me," says Becky Barkhouse, who lived on White Rock Mountain near the Golers. "Everyone figured you could tell them stories about what was going on. And if you didn't tell them nothing then they figured you were just like them. They branded you, just like that."

The court-imposed publication ban ensured that none of the tes-timony leaked out, forcing the public to rely on their imaginations. Every conceivable sin and degradation was attributed to the Golers. It was as if two hundred years of South Mountain badness, the folk-tales of inbreeding, deformed babies, dreadful diseases, mental retar-dation, immorality and every other vice imaginable, could all be blamed on White Rock and the Goler Clan.

But what the good folks of the Valley didn't know, what had never come out, was the existence of another branch of the Clan, living a bare twelve miles away in West Brooklyn at the eastern end of the Mountain. Charles Goler, William Goler's father, was born in 1905 in West Brooklyn, one of the many small settlements sprinkled over South Mountain. His father, Henry Goler, was a descendant of Munday Goler, the freed slave who came to Nova Scotia after the War of 1812. Munday spelled his last name with an "e" but several generations later the Golars of West Brooklyn changed it to an "a."

Charles Goler had a younger brother named Cranswick, born in 1915. Their mother's name was Mary Walsh, a sister of Ada "who walks the road." But within the family it is believed that the two boys were sired by different men. Which one was the true Goler, the son of Henry, and which one was not? The children and grandchildren of both men suspect that Charles was the illegitimate one, but who fathered him is a matter of debate. There are, however, some clues. The murky oral history of the Goler Clan says Charles's father went by the last name of Pickles. And in the archives of Acadia University in Wolfville there is a pencilled notation on a 1950 South Mountain population survey adding Pickles, in brackets, beside Charles's name.

Pickles is not a Mountain or Valley name. The Golars of West Brooklyn were Methodists, unusual in an area dominated by Baptists. Cranswick, for example, is a classic Methodist name. The nineteenth-century Methodists were tireless missionaries who gloried in the challenge of marching into Baptist, Catholic or Jesuit strongholds and converting as many souls as they could. In the Valley, conversion was a tough job as the Baptists, by the 1870s, were well-entrenched with churches and parishes. The Methodists were not daunted but they did make more converts on the Mountain, which had no churches and enjoyed only occasional visits from itinerant ministers. Most of the Methodist missionaries, called "aliens" by one Baptist minister, stayed only a year or two.

There were no hotels on the Mountain, then or now, and no Methodist church, so ministers habitually overnighted with their flock—a situation that caused much tut-tutting among their religious competitors. After all, the Methodists were known to have a lax moral code since they not only encouraged blacks to become part of white congregations but allowed mixed-race marriages. There was a joke repeated in Baptist circles, prior to the First World War, whenever a baby was born to an unmarried girl whose family were not Baptists. "Has the look of a Methodist, don't you think?"

Between 1898 and 1907, three such missionaries, all Pickles and likely related, preached throughout the Valley and Mountain communities. At least one of them was in the vicinity of West Brooklyn in 1904 when Charles was conceived.

The strongest evidence that Charles was not a Goler by blood is the fact that Cranswick, though younger, inherited the family's hundred-acre farm on West Brooklyn Mountain when his father, Henry, died. Shortly thereafter, Charles moved to White Rock Mountain, began spelling his last name with an "e" instead of an "a," married his first cousin Stella Walsh and started producing the children who would become infamous as the Goler Clan. "It'd be funny, wouldn't it?" muses Lucy Golar, who married one of Cranswick's sons. "All them people thinks everything bad on the Mountain is the Golers' fault. But here it is, maybe they're not Golers at all. If William and the rest of them were Pickles, then our name wouldn't be black as mud, the Goler name would have some pride to it. That'd be something. Things'd be different, that's for sure."

Cranswick Golar remained on the farm in West Brooklyn, scratching a living tending cattle and growing crops. In 1936, he married sixteen-year-old Ruth May Atwell, whose Mountain roots went back to the time of Rolen Rogers and Hannah Jeffers. The Atwells and the Rogers had married back and forth for generations. Ruth May had many hard-of-hearing and deaf cousins, aunts, uncles and siblings. In 1957, a geneticist studying the phenomenon concluded that the Atwells were among the original carriers of the gene that had spread deafness over the Mountain. Ruth May and Cranswick had six children and the same geneticist's field notes suggest Cranswick fathered another child with one of his daughters. The oldest child, Eric, drowned at the age of eighteen. One daughter, Hazel, had a baby when she was thirteen. Hazel stayed at home and her child, Alberta, was raised as her sister. Even today Alberta frequently refers to her mother as her sister. Another daughter, Heather, had a deaf child named Wendy, also born out of wedlock. Ruth May and Cranswick had three more children—Dennis, the second oldest boy, Norma, the oldest girl and finally the youngest, Fred, born in 1957.

Cranswick Golar died of cancer in 1966 at the age of fifty-one. Ruth May, five years his junior, continued living on the farm and worked seasonally in canning factories and apple orchards, relying on social assistance to put food on the table the rest of the year. Though Ruth May had never gone to school, she recalled often reading the Bible to her children and raising them to know the difference between "right and wrong." She was an incredibly tough, self-sufficient woman with an intense suspicion of outsiders and any institution or organization, be it a school or a government office. She refused to see a doctor or go to a hospital throughout her life, no matter how dire the circumstances. In her fifties, Ruth May fell and broke her back but brushed aside her children's attempts to get medical attention for her. "Get away from me! I'll heal it myself," she told them firmly. "I know more than any damn doctor."

Though the food in the Golar household was basic, there was always enough. Everyone worked the farm and clothing was continually recycled. They had no indoor plumbing until the 1970s, but the family takes pains to point out "at least we kept ourselves clean, not like the others," referring to their White Rock cousins. Still, there are many similarities between the two branches. They disliked outsiders, had few friends outside the family and shared a predilection for anger and violence. Alberta recalls her grandmother Ruth May, who raised her, flying into rages and beating her with a pitchfork. She also fled from cuffs and blows dealt out by her uncles. And two of Cranswick Golar's children admit that there have been incestuous relationships within the family.

But there is one sharp difference between the two sides of the Clan. What distinguishes them from each other is a sense of striving, of ambition, that somehow took root on the Cranswick Golar side. It is a determination, among some of the children, to escape the destiny laid out for so many of the Mountain-born.

By all accounts, Cranswick Golar was a prodigious worker. His half-brother Charles, though diligent on occasion, never worked more than seasonally and seldom at all after he turned forty. Cranswick served with the Canadian Army, but the closest Charles ever got to active service were scuffles on the Mountain after a night of knocking back bootleg hooch. Norma, Cranswick's oldest daughter, married and moved to Florida. The Mountain-born and -bred might drift into the Valley, another county or even Halifax, but leaving the province, let alone the country, was almost unheard of. Dennis, Cranswick's oldest surviving boy, graduated from Grade 12 and went on to get his stationary engineer's ticket. The qualification, combined with Dennis's steadiness on the job, has ensured him full-time employment his entire adult life. But among all of Cranswick and Ruth May's children, it was Frederick Gordon Golar who stood out the most.

Fred was a lonely young boy, acutely conscious of how poorly he lived, compared with most of the children he went to school with. His threadbare, dated clothing, badly cut hair, old shoes and twangy speech marked him indelibly as Mountain. Fred was so embarrassed by his family and living conditions that he never brought any friends home. He recalled little affection during his formative years, "he was never really loved, hugged or kissed," but he well remembered being "fondled" by an older sister and having a sexual relationship with a female first cousin. Sex, according to Fred, was always spoken of freely in the home and "no taboos" were placed on it. He later told a psychiatrist that there had been "incestuous relationships" within his immediate family.

Fred finished Grade 12 and left home at eighteen; initially it seemed as if he would lead an unsettled life of constant change. For a couple of years he kicked around working at a variety of jobs like apple picking, and he too had a stint at the White Spot restaurant in New Minas. The turning point came in 1977 when, at the age of twenty, he landed a job with Minas Basin Pulp and Power, in part because his older brother worked for a sister company. Like Dennis, Fred proved to be a good worker who took direction well and was amicable with his fellow employees. His supervisor was convinced the young man would go far, and he did. In 1982, Fred became an inspector for the provincial Department of Labour and Manpower. He began working towards his first-class standardized certificate of stationary engineering and talked about taking over from the provincial chief inspector when he retired.

At this point nothing about Fred Golar seemed to match his background. He skied, did a bit of modelling in Halifax and acted in a Kentville community theatre group. Fred also looked after himself, eating well and swimming several times a week to maintain the lean, muscular body he'd been blessed with. He and his brother, Dennis, looked very much alike, square jawed, even-featured men with intelligent eyes and warm, ready smiles displaying straight white teeth. Family photos look odd when Fred and Dennis are in the picture. Their handsome faces stand out in stark contrast to their rougher, coarser relatives, whose eyes are often magnified by thick glasses and whose skin shows the ravages of poor nutrition.

Though Fred's school years were friendless, once he left home girlfriends and sexual relationships came easily. Young women found him attractive but he was never satisfied with any of them for long, breaking off most of his relationships after a short time. One girlfriend lasted two and a half years but he ended that relationship in 1983. Afterwards he became depressed about the difference between him and his peers. While others were settling down and starting families, Fred couldn't make himself care about anyone that deeply. He said he contemplated suicide and was despondent enough to begin seeing a psychiatrist to help him through his depression. But it was a rare glitch in a life moving ever onward and upward. As Fred climbed up the ladder, he saw less and less of his family, who felt he was taking on "airs" and "getting beyond himself" with his fancy new clothes and Valley ways.

On May 20, 1984, Fred, then living in Hantsport in the Valley, paid a fateful visit to the Mountain.

It was a beautiful late spring day, perfect weather to get his car washed, Fred thought. He dropped by his sister Heather's house, also in Hantsport, and asked his fourteen-year-old deaf niece, Wendy, if she'd like to come with him to the car wash in Falmouth. Though she was deaf and had little intelligible speech, the family had developed their own method of communicating with a combination of gestures, lip reading and a crude form of sign language. Wendy was delighted to accompany her twenty-six-year-old uncle on an outing, but as fate would have it there was a long line-up when they arrived at the car wash. They decided instead to go and visit with her grandmother, Ruth May, and the rest of the family in West Brooklyn on the Mountain.

"On the way, we started fooling around with each other and feeling each other," Fred recalled. "It just went too far this time." According to him, Wendy opened her pants in the car and eagerly dove into his. "I had on sweat pants and they were open. She had a hold of my penis. Jacking or jerking it off. She was doing this part on her own. I didn't have to tell her." En route to West Brooklyn, Fred drove by a small brook and pulled over. "We went to the brook to clean up," he told the police. "Wendy emits a strong odour. That's what got us there."

Fred helped her wash up, then she willingly followed him to some nearby bushes. "We took our pants down. I took mine down. There was no resistance. I didn't want to come inside her so I didn't put it in all the way. I didn't want to hurt her." When they were finished, Fred said he helped his niece wash off some mud that clung to her pants and the two of them, laughing happily, walked back to the car. It was, Fred assured the police, an enjoyable interlude with his young niece. "That's why it was such a shock to me that she went and told," he said sadly. "She had a real smile on her face when I gave her flowers. She held on to them," he emphasized.

Fred drove his niece to West Brooklyn and her grandmother's house. Wendy asked Ruth May if she could go and see her aunt Hazel, who lived nearby. She needed to tell someone what had happened but it didn't occur to her to talk to her mother, who was more like a sister to her. With a combination of slurred, deaf speech, gestures and tears Wendy got the message across. Hazel was furious at her brother. Relations among the Golar siblings were often strained at the best of times. Fred's brother and sisters felt he thought himself too good for them, and now, thought his sister angrily, he turns around and does this. She picked up the phone and dialled the RCMP.

It was nearly 10:00 P.M. by the time the police picked up Fred Golar. He was stunned and stared unbelievingly as they read him his rights. In the police station, he babbled and stammered that he had just got carried away and that "this time" they had gone too far.

"God, I feel terrible!" he moaned. "I guess I'm like all the other Golers. No! I take it back, I won't ever be like them. I really care about people. I'm just so sorry for all of this."

By the time Fred Golar's case went to preliminary inquiry in September 1984, Darrell Carmichael, who had earlier defended Roy Hiltz, had become an assistant to Jack Buntain in the prosecutor's office. Buntain had ramrodded all the other cases through but, because this one didn't bear any relationship to the White Rock Golers, he handed it over to Carmichael. Fred Golar assured Carmichael that he wasn't related to "those Golers." Carmichael wasn't really sure, but on the surface there was little to connect him to the Clan. "I was struck by how different Fred Golar looked and acted," he recalls. "He seemed very middle-class, almost suave."

Carmichael faced a challenge with his primary witness, the victim Wendy. Though she was deaf, she had a small amount of residual hearing, sufficient to give her some lip-reading skills. When the speaker talked clearly and slowly, she could comprehend simple sentences, particularly if she remembered her hearing aids. That day she forgot one of them. Questioning a child in court can be tricky at the best of times; add in Wendy's deafness and the complication of an interpreter who had difficulty fully understanding her signing, and you had a bit of a three-ring circus. At several points during the testimony, judge, prosecutor, interpreter, defence lawyer and Wendy herself were all attempting to clarify a given point. A particular quagmire developed over her complex family tree.

Wendy had no trouble stating her name, age and where she lived. And when asked to identify Fred Golar, she quickly pointed to the young man sitting quietly in a well-cut grey jacket. It was when Carmichael asked her if they were related that the trouble began. "My mother is his sister, no, my sister, I have one sister and he [Fred] is…" After several more efforts trying to untangle the relationships, Wendy looked helplessly over at the interpreter. "Could you please say it for me?" she signed. After about twenty minutes of effort from all concerned, the court established that Fred Golar was, in fact, Wendy's uncle. But the judge was never able to pin down just who was Wendy's mother, who was her grandmother and whose house she was living in at the time of the incident. But Wendy was crystal clear on one point: events hadn't unfolded as Fred Golar claimed.

Carmichael: What happened in the car from the time you left Falmouth?

Wendy: Fred put his hand down on me.

Carmichael: On what part of your body?

Wendy: Not on the upper part, down below.

Carmichael: And what part of the lower part of your body did he put his hand on?

Wendy: Right there.

She pointed at her crotch. Carmichael directed the interpreter to ask if Wendy knew a word for that part of her body. The girl shrugged.

Carmichael: Do you know a name for it?

Wendy looked at the interpreter, who signed the question again. "The name for down there? Do you know the name?" Wendy frowned nervously and nodded. The interpreter encouraged her. Wendy raised her hand and slowly fingerspelled the word, "P-U-S-S-Y."

Carmichael: Did you leave his hand there?

Wendy: I didn't understand what you said.

Carmichael: When Fred put his hand on your pussy?

Wendy: He wanted to do it more.

Carmichael: Okay. And did you do anything with his hand?

Wendy: Fred put his hand, pulled my hand, on his pecker, Fred pulled my hand over to his pecker.

Carmichael asked her if she knew another word for pecker. Wendy squirmed uncomfortably and began to spell with her fingers again. "C-O-C-K."

Carmichael: And at the time that he put your hand there did he—
Wendy: He held my hand on there.
Carmichael: Did you try to pull your hand away?
Wendy: Before, when Fred put his hand on me I pushed it away. After Falmouth, I tried to push it away.
Carmichael: And did you say anything to Fred when you pushed his hand away?
Wendy: I said no, no. . . .
Carmichael: Were his pants up?
Wendy: The zipper was down and his pecker was up. The pants were up but open with his pecker up through.
Carmichael: Now what happened after the car stopped?
Wendy: And Fred took me by the hand, pulled me down and pulled my pants down.
Carmichael: And where did this take place? . . .
Wendy: There were some trees with land and that's where he pushed me down. I covered my face. Fred pushed me down and had sex.
Carmichael: Now did you say anything when Fred pushed you down?
Wendy: No. It hurts. Sex hurts.
Carmichael: Ah, what do you mean by, he had sex with you? What did he do?
Wendy: Fred took off my pants, pushed me down on the grass, on my back. Fred took his pants down and had sex with me, took his pants off.
Carmichael: And what does it mean to have, that he had sex with you, what did he do?

The interpreter responded, "Sex, the sign that she is using is showing the finger going into a hole, that is the sign they use."

Carmichael:	Okay. Ah, what part of your body was hurt, you said that you were hurt.
Wendy:	The sex hurt. It hurt inside....
Carmichael:	Was there any bleeding as a result of him hurting you?
Wendy:	Yes.
Carmichael:	And what part of your body was the blood coming from?
Wendy:	It was on my pants after I pulled them up.
Carmichael:	But what part of your body did the blood come from?
Wendy:	Blood from my pussy.
Carmichael:	How did you feel about what Fred was doing to you that day?
Wendy:	Hurt.
Carmichael:	Why did you let Fred do that to you?...
Wendy:	Because Fred pushed me down and had sex, I just covered my face.

The psychiatrist who had previously treated Fred Golar prepared a report for the court. "In my opinion, Mr. Golar finds it extremely difficult to commit himself to anything permanent in his life, whether that is a career or a marriage, or whatever. He seems to need constant change, and his orientation in such things seems to be largely selfish." The psychiatrist noted that Fred claimed not to enjoy his life but doubted whether he suffered from "sexual deviations."

Throughout the trial, Fred had steadfastly maintained he was not related to the White Rock Golers. Both his mother, Ruth May, and his brother, Dennis, confirmed that to the court. His mother said Fred was a "good boy." She vehemently denied that anything like this had ever happened in the family before because she had brought up her children properly and watched over them carefully. Ruth May didn't know that her son had already admitted that there had been "incestuous relationships in the family."

Ruth May and Dennis also neglected to mention that Dennis's brother-in-law was Rick Davison, the husband of Mary Goler and one of the Clan members who had been arrested for sexual abuse of the Goler children.

The effect, on both sides of the Clan, of sex charges against so many family members was like acid thrown indiscriminately over them—lightly scarring some, destroying others. Less acid landed on the West Brooklyn branch of the family—but it's there all the same, twisting and buckling their lives. Even though they protected themselves as best they could by successfully denying a kinship with the White Rock Golers, the similarity of their name was sufficient to suck them down into the pit that swallowed up so many lives in 1984. The newspapers did not report Fred Golar's arrest, let alone uncover any connection to the White Rock Clan, but whispers, jeers and innuendo followed his brother, sisters, in-laws and other relatives for the next thirteen years.

"I don't know how they find out, but they always do," laments one of Cranswick Golar's granddaughters, who has never used the Golar last name and has no obvious connection to the family. "And I get treated like a piece of human garbage. Men feel like they can grab me and paw me, molest—do whatever they like whenever they like. And the women are even worse—what they say to me. And I had nothing to do with this thing."

To those innocents on the periphery, it is a prison sentence without end.

PART THREE

Chapter Thirteen

Conviction

✦ INCEST, THE ANCIENT TABOO, HAS
survived countless millennia. It has always been the most private of
crimes and one of the best hidden. Cloaked in shame, incest victims have carried their dark secret deep within their souls. The Goler
trials shone a brief though not typical light on an old story.

In the end they were all convicted, though on only a fraction of
the more than 150 charges originally laid. The brooms wielded by
the police, social services and the courts swept the offenders and victims off the Mountain in record time. Less than a year after William
Goler's arrest, preliminary inquiries, trials and sentencing were complete for all but two of the fifteen accused. There were appeals in
most cases, sometimes by the Crown and often by the defence, which
dragged things out for a few more months, but by the middle of 1985
most of the offenders were behind bars and the Valley and the Mountain had been purged.

WILLIAM GOLER

The Clan leader originally faced thirty-three separate charges—
enough, if convicted, to jail him for several lifetimes. He denied to

the end that he had done anything wrong and repeatedly claimed his problems were somehow related to wild parties his ex-wife Hazel had while the children stayed overnight with her. He had no explanation for his many nieces and nephews also testifying against him except to imply they had been led astray by his own children, the police and social services. In one memorable CBC television interview, he accused the Valley people of similar crimes. "As far as I'm concerned, people in town or anywhere else have done as bad if not worse." This was as close as William Goler came to acknowledging what he'd done to the Clan children. Increasingly articulate as his preliminary inquiries and trial wore on, William became adept at casting himself as the victim of a hypocritical system obsessed with persecuting people from the Mountain.

Fittingly, the Clan leader's own case proved to be the bellwether. After the preliminary inquiries, William was committed to stand trial on August 1, 1984, and face six charges, with twenty-seven more pending. Believing it would be impossible to assemble a sympathetic jury, Eric Sturk, his lawyer, advised him to elect trial by judge alone. Twelve witnesses were called by the defence and prosecution. Though he mounted a spirited defence, Sturk made little headway in discrediting the children's credibility or recall. "Where the evidence of the children varies in material particulars from that of the defence witness, I have accepted the evidence of the children," Judge Hall concluded.

Dr. Denton, the court-appointed psychologist, had determined the children were, at best, well below normal intelligence and many of them "retarded," but Judge Don Hall strongly disagreed. "Certainly, I would consider them to be of average or above-average intelligence among witnesses I see appearing from time to time in proceedings of this nature or criminal proceedings in general." Hall had some reservations about the accuracy of Pam's and Doug's memories but he was convinced that both children were doing their best to be honest. He also concluded that Sandra Goler was believable. But in Donna Goler, he found a witness who was as credible and solid as the granite of South Mountain. "I formed the opinion that Hazel Donna Goler was an exceptionally bright child, very aware of what was going on in this proceeding and intellectually mature for her years."

Judge Hall wasn't nearly as impressed with the defence witnesses, most of whom were also charged with similar offences. He did allow that some had tried to give their evidence in a "fair and proper manner," but he believed that others "were not being completely honest and frank." The defence, in closing arguments, contended that William's dreadful poverty, isolation and long-established family traditions should be taken into account. Rehabilitation and "cultural re-orientation" were called for, not punishment, they argued. Judge Hall was having none of it. "Deterrence," he maintained, was the only way to protect the community. On August 3, 1984, Judge Hall found William Goler guilty of all six charges. He sentenced him to seven years in prison, which he would serve in a federal institution, in this case the Kingston Penitentiary.

At his sentencing the other twenty-seven charges were still outstanding, but once William Goler was convicted on the initial six counts, the legal system curiously lost all enthusiasm for pursuing the remainder. Some were dropped for "lack of evidence" while the rest were stayed, although the bulk of the charges involved the same combination of witnesses whose testimony had convicted William Goler on the first six counts. With two exceptions, Cranswick Goler and Rick Davison, the same inexplicable pattern was played out again and again with the Goler Clan. After the initial convictions, the prosecution of further charges wasn't pursued—no matter how solid the evidence. It was as if the Crown tacitly felt the Golers had been punished enough and, in any case, didn't know any better. "After all, it's just a way of life among that clan," Jack Buntain, the prosecutor, explained to the *Toronto Star*, "and it's been so for generations."

William's appeal was denied and by January 1985 he was behind bars in the Kingston Penitentiary, the first time he had ever left Nova Scotia and one of the few times he'd ever left the county. Because sexual crimes against children are treated far more harshly in jail than outside, prison officials were deeply worried about the reception William would get from his fellow prisoners. Other Golers had already been harassed at local lock-ups and provincial jails. One beating sent William's nephew Billy into hospital and forced officials to charge the man involved. "To be honest, we weren't sure what would happen," recalls one guard. "No one's going to admit this but we were a little worried about the reaction of prison workers as well as prisoners. They hate this stuff. You can murder your mother and have a good time here. Screw your kid and you're toast." William was placed in protective custody and carefully watched.

Throughout his time at Kingston, William Goler distinguished himself by not distinguishing himself. The terror of the Goler children was so quiet, biddable and inoffensive that guards and prisoners alike left him alone. "I am sure that if he was sentenced to stand for seven years by the prison garage with his hands in his pockets and not move a muscle that is exactly what he would have done!" exclaims one guard assigned to Goler's unit for most of his stay. "He defined the words model prisoner." Another guard laughs when he recalls William's first meal. "I'll never forget what he said: 'The food's great!' That broke us up. I know guys who have worked here for thirty years and they can't remember anyone ever saying that."

In March 1986, another prisoner sent a letter to Claire Culhane, founder of the Prisoners' Rights Group in Vancouver, on William's behalf.

> I'm a fellow inmate on the same range as William and he has told me all his problems, I have written letters to the Minister of Justice and to the Solicitor General for him and all to no avail, as they don't seem to give a damn about his situation.... since he has been here he has been Adamant that he is innocent and the children has lied....
>
> Needless to say at his trial it was more of a Kangaroo court and as to his part in it, from what I'm told, he says his Lawyer the Crown the Judge just ignored him and did the trial as if he was not even present. He had no concept as to what they were saying or doing to him.
>
> He was more like a child in the room as he understood nothing they were telling him. Also I might add that William is a SLOW LEARNER and it takes some time a lot of explaining to

him so he will understand the meaning of what your telling him. He is not retarded just slow.

William suggested that a system be set up that allowed a couple, like him and Wanda, who had also been convicted, to serve their time together. "Sounds great," seconded his friend, "as I too have a wife over there [Kingston Prison for Women] and if there had been such a prison she and I would still be together, but she become a lesbian and now I have lost her to them."

William asked how to get additional visits with Wanda when she was released. (The regulations permitted one supervised family visit every three months and one "open" visit monthly, which would enable them to see each other without a barrier between them.) William also accused the penitentiary officials of "tormenting" Wanda with "head games" by telling her that when she was released she would never be able to live with William again. Culhane's intervention sped up the processing of William and Wanda's request, though Willie Gibbs of the Correctional Service of Canada dismissed the "head games" accusation as "unfounded."

Culhane also went to bat for William against CBC's "Fifth Estate," which aired a documentary on the trials in 1986. She castigated the program for not including the information that a thirty-seven-signature petition, initiated by David Long, a neighbour and member of the Black River church, declared that the residents of the Mountain would welcome William back and were eagerly "looking forward to your homecoming. Our Church is badly in need of you." Strangely, the petition named not only William Goler, but also his three sons, though no one on the Mountain was aware he had any, despite his often repeated desire for a male child.

In 1987, when the health of Charles Goler, patriarch of the Clan, worsened, William once again turned to Claire Culhane for help. "I am some worried about my family who are sick," he wrote with the help of a different prisoner. "And I may never see them alive again unless I can get someone who can help me.... My dad is dying with cancer and he is 81 years old, and a short time ago he had his leg taken off up above the knee. And the news I got a few days ago is that he won't last much longer. My mom is going in the hospital in a few days. Her heart is bad and she is about to have a nervous breakdown. No matter how many disappointments I get I try to go on. But things are adding up and I can't take it much longer."

Charles Goler died in 1987 while his sons were still in jail. William served his entire seven years steadfastly refusing to acknowledge guilt or express remorse. When he returned to the Mountain, he and Wanda Whiston lived for a time in the infamous blue house, which had stood unoccupied for years. But eventually, when it grew too decrepit, they joined his mother, Stella, and his brother Cranswick in a new house built by a government program designed to clear out some of the worst Mountain habitations. His parents' house was torn down while William was in prison, as was the original homestead—the abandoned, rat-infested heap that had scared the children during most of their early lives. The new house was built while William was in jail on the condition that the blue house be torn down also, an order Stella ignored.

"That's justice, don't you think?" says Donna in disgust. "We get raped and they get a nice house with heat and a toilet." In late winter 1997, someone towed away William's shack to be used as a garden shed.

The Goler compound is quiet these days. No longer do waves of relatives and friends constantly flow in and out. But if you stand and look at the clearing, its emptiness stares back like the eyeless sockets of a skull. A sterile fury emanates from the compound, making you want to move on quickly.

William's trial and rapid conviction badly rattled the rest of the Clan. Their various lawyers had counted on leniency because of their clients' deprived circumstances, low intelligence, lack of education and professed confusion about the charges. Additionally, they were hopeful that the children's difficulty in pinning down dates and times might make it hard for the judge, or the jury if there were one, to convict them on specific counts. But after Judge Hall brushed aside those arguments and sentenced the Clan leader to seven years, there was a flurry of changes in pleadings. "The system was gonna screw us, no matter what we done," explained Rick Davison. "I figured I'd be better off saying I done it but I never done nothing."

Eight of the Clan changed their pleas to guilty while four—Crans-wick Goler, Earl Johnstone, Rick Davison and Roy Hiltz—believing they could beat the charges, elected to go to trial. Fred Golar from the other branch of the Clan pled guilty from the start and two of the women, Mary and Josephine, were yet to be charged. Regardless of the plea, none of them, except Fred Golar, expressed any remorse. "How could we say we were sorry," erupts Rick, "when we didn't do nothing wrong!"

The legal system pushed along the trials with astonishing speed. Less than a year after they were arrested, fourteen of the accused, including Fred Golar, had been sentenced. In contrast, two other cases involving sex with children in the province, one in Halifax and one on the south shore, lasted almost two years each though there was only one victim in one case, two in another and a single individual charged in both. "It seemed like when we got to the rest of the trials and preliminary inquiries [after William], everybody wanted it over and done with," recalls Donna.

"They'd be telling you you'd be testifying about something and then suddenly it was dropped. After the preliminaries they weren't as careful, they didn't want to draw it out. They were in a hurry. Jack would say, 'Let's get it done.'"

Though Donna's testimony was specific and detailed, many of the charges against the Clan with herself as victim were dropped. "They kept telling us they were trying to move things along, get it done, so's we could have a life again. I can understand that in one way but most of us ended up with shitty lives anyway. They were in a real hurry to put all of them in jail but they weren't in such a hurry to make sure we were looked after properly. I never wanted anything for free but they were spending a lot of money putting them away; I think they could have spent some to make sure the kids that needed help got help. They just got rid of us. I could have survived a little longer to get them convicted on all those charges. If they'd asked me I would have said stick it to them as hard as you can. We deserved that much."

Though they're careful not to say so, the police were far from happy to see so many charges, which represented hundreds of hours

of investigation, abandoned willy-nilly. This was particularly annoy-
ing because the 150 original charges had represented only the tip
of the iceberg. "I could have laid a lot more," Baxter Upshall, the
lead investigator, confirms with an edge to his voice. "The charges
that were laid were one charge for an act. If they committed buggery on the children three times, they were charged only once. If
they committed oral sex on the child twenty times, they were only
charged once. If it was an actual sexual act with the child, they were
only charged once, regardless of how many times it happened. I felt
that the child should have the right to at least one charge laid for
everything that happened to them. The children had been very
traumatized."

BILLY GOLER

Billy pled guilty to five of sixteen charges facing him on September 28, 1984. Alternately defiant and sulky throughout the proceedings, the nineteen-year-old showed not a flicker of contrition.
He received four and a half years for sexual assault, buggery and
incest. In April 1985, he successfully appealed his sentence and it
was reduced to three years. While in jail, Billy reverted to the role
of victim he'd shed just a few years earlier in the Goler Clan as he
became the target of repeated assaults.

When Billy returned to the Mountain in 1988, the Clan compound was eerily silent with most of the adults still in prison and all
of the children gone. For long stretches, there were only him and
his grandmother Stella, who spent most of her time moaning about
the loss of her "boys" and cursing her grandchildren for "what they
done." Billy had grown up with perpetual activity. In the absence of
his playmates, his quest for "a time" became ever more difficult and
desperate. Shortly after he was released, Billy Goler, then twenty-
three, died in a car crash.

CHARLIE GOLER

Facing thirteen charges, Charlie, twenty-one, eventually pled guilty
to three counts of sexual intercourse with girls under fourteen and
one count of buggery with a young girl. The judge considered Charlie's

youth and the fact that he had told the court he'd been abused himself as a young boy by Clan members. He noted that such abuse was
"commonplace" in the Goler Clan and that "victims grew up to be
offenders." He was sentenced to six months on each charge of unlaw-
ful intercourse and five for buggery for a total of twenty-three months
plus three years of probation after that. Charlie appealed his sentence to the Supreme Court of Nova Scotia in June 1985 but was
denied. He served his time in the Kings County Correctional Centre not far from White Rock.

Charlie Goler now lives quietly in the Valley. But the sight of him
still sends chills through the hearts of his victims. One of them was
in a local shopping mall when she whipped around babbling hysterically and begged her friend to hide her. "I'd come across Charlie," she explains in a low whispery voice. "Until I laid eyes on him,
I'd sort of hoped they was all dead, though I knew they weren't. I
didn't want to see him again. Charlie done terrible stuff to me."

✦

On January 4, 1985, Judge Don Hall passed judgment on a whole-
sale lot of ten Clan members: Wanda Whiston, Earl Johnstone,
Lawrence Kelly, Henry Goler, Ralph Kelly, Cranswick Goler, Rick
Davison, Eugene Brown, Gabriel Dodge and Roy Hiltz. To save time,
and his wind, the judge made general comments covering all ten
before sentencing each specifically.

As Hall declared that the Clan's "despicable" conduct had caused
harm to the victims "from which they will never recover," any lingering hope that the offenders' deprived circumstances would
encourage Hall to be lenient was dashed. "I am satisfied beyond a
shadow of a doubt that the offending parties knew that what they
were doing was morally wrong and legally wrong and that they were
doing harm to the children in violating and using them for their las-
civious purposes as they did," he stated firmly. Hall did, however,
acknowledge that he believed the ten accused "did not look upon
their abhorrent and criminal behaviour with the abhorrence and
revulsion that the mainstream of society does." He said he had
reduced the sentences of those who pled guilty and therefore saved

the children from the "discomfort and apparent agony" of testifying again at trial after they had taken the stand in the preliminary inquiries.

WANDA WHISTON

Wanda was charged with twelve counts, eventually pleading guilty to two of gross indecency and six of sexual assault. She received six months on each count, for a total of four years. Wanda served her time, much of it in protective custody, at P4W, the Kingston federal prison for women. There she was known as a quiet, co-operative prisoner who caused no trouble. Prison officials recall her as being shy but possessing a pleasant sense of humour and the ability to avoid either joining or aggravating the various gangs operating within the prison.

Like her mate, William Goler, Wanda stoutly denies to this day that anything happened between her and the children, even though she pled guilty to the charges. She is still living with William at the Goler compound. They have had no children together.

CRANSWICK GOLER

Originally charged with twenty-seven offences, Cranswick Goler eventually faced only seven counts. He pled not guilty and elected to be tried by judge alone. Don Hall convicted him on buggery and gross indecency against Doug, whom he used "like a chattel for the most degrading purpose." Cranswick was sentenced to fifteen months for buggery and six months for gross indecency.

A year later he received a further three and a half years: six months each for three counts of buggery and one year each for two counts of sex with a female under fourteen. This time the Crown appealed. Calling Cranswick's merciless use of the children "repugnant" and "done with the full knowledge they were wrong" the appeal court bumped his second sentence to five and a half years, giving him even more time than his brother William, the Clan leader.

Along with William, Cranswick was the most brutal and vicious member of the Clan. He joked, boasted and giggled his way through his arrest, his statement to the police, his preliminary inquiries and his trial. He remained convinced throughout the proceedings that the children were no more capable of hurting him than the rabbits he so adroitly snared. That they could and did has created a core of bitterness in his simple and once carefree life. Cranswick had a heart attack in 1997. After recovering in the Kentville hospital, he returned to the tiny house in White Rock that he shares with William, Wanda and his mother.

HENRY GOLER

Originally facing eleven charges, Henry pled guilty to three: two of sexual intercourse with a female under the age of fourteen and one of buggery. The rest were stayed. Though Judge Hall noted that Henry's plea saved the children from further testimony, he could not "see any substantial difference between this man and most of the others." Henry received two years for each count of sexual intercourse and one year for buggery, for a total of five years. He successfully appealed his sentence, which was reduced to three years.

Today Henry lives alone in a run-down area on the outskirts of the Valley. "He don't do much of anything that I can figure," one of his sisters says. "But then Henry were always a little touched up here. Know what I mean? Not much he can do, I s'pose."

EARL JOHNSTONE

Judge Hall handed Earl Johnstone a guilty verdict with the rest, convicting him of one count of sexual intercourse with a female minor and one count each of sexual assault and gross indecency committed against Matt. Hall gave him a three-year sentence to be served in a federal institution. Johnstone appealed on October 4, 1985. Three judges of the Supreme Court of Nova Scotia examined the evidence and overturned two of his three convictions. The judges concluded that the case involving Pam was "unreasonable and cannot be supported on the evidence," and they criticized Judge Hall for suggesting, in court, that the burden was on Earl Johnstone to refute the charges rather than on the Crown to prove them. "In doing so he misdirected himself on a question of law. The unsatisfactory nature of the evidence does not warrant a new trial." It was a scathing denunciation of a fellow lodge member—the judicial equivalent of a two-by-four across the brow of Don Hall.

To add insult to injury, the appeal court pointed out that Judge Hall had decided the two offences Earl Johnstone was convicted of committing against Matt were actually a single offence that had occurred on one occasion. But, having made that decision, Judge Hall failed to make the correct legal adjustments to the charges. It was a basic error, one that a first-year law student should have spotted. "In view of that finding the convictions on both counts cannot stand," ruled the appeal judges. "There was a single act which, with deference, could only sustain one conviction." They did allow the conviction for gross indecency to stand. Several of the defence lawyers who had been frustrated by the constant changes in charges, sometimes facilitated by the judge to fit the available testimony, received some small comfort from the decision.

After serving his time in a provincial jail, Earl Johnstone returned to the Mountain to live with his mother. He was a young man when he went to jail and now, in his late thirties, he finds the fall-out from the case still sticks to him like napalm. Though his name is not normally associated with the Golers, people always manage to find out. The parents of a recent girlfriend refused to let her have anything more to do with him after they discovered who he was.

RICK DAVISON

Forty-one-year-old Rick Davison initially faced charges of buggery and gross indecency against Sandra Goler. He pled not guilty to both and elected trial by jury. Although Judge Hall had convicted Rick's cousin Earl on the evidence of Pam alone, he found her testimony as an eyewitness inconsistent in Rick's case. He also had doubts about Sandra Goler's reliability. Once again it was left to Donna Goler to nail down the details that would send Rick Davison to jail. "I rely on her evidence completely," intoned Hall, "and accept her version of events that she claims to have observed through the window of her aunt's bedroom as being completely accurate. I reject the evidence of the accused and his protestations of innocence."

On January 4, 1985, Judge Hall sentenced Rick to one year for buggery and six months for gross indecency. He appealed and lost.

Then, in February 1985, six months after Jeff and Matt belatedly came forward, Rick was charged with three more counts: one each of sexual assault and gross indecency against his stepson Jeff and one of gross indecency against Matt. He was found guilty of all three counts and sentenced to a further eighteen months. In March 1986 the Supreme Court dismissed Rick Davison's appeal on the second set of charges.

"If anyone's a victim, it's me," laments Rick. "I am not that kind of guy. If I did those things, I would have the guts to say so. I would feel bad if I had done it, and the only good thing is I know I didn't do it."

Bad luck has dogged Rick Davison since he got out of jail more than a decade ago. He was always known on the Mountain as a good, reliable worker who never shirked even the most menial of chores. The Levy family, who own a lumber mill just outside Gaspereau, were happy to have him back and for a while it looked as if he would quickly shed the stigma of the case. He continued to live with his wife, Mary Goler, and their lives began to knit together, though the scars of the trials and the loss of Mary's children to foster homes remain raw and a constant topic of conversation to this day. Then in 1990 a car accident left him badly injured. Though he has recovered from the accident, Rick still doesn't walk well, his vision, poor since childhood, has worsened and he relies on Mary to shepherd him through life. He is a short, slight man with a gentle-looking, myopic face. You have to pay close attention to him when he talks as his words slip and slur through the gap of his missing front teeth.

Rick Davison's particular sorrow is the loss of the five children he says he voluntarily gave up for adoption when his first wife died in a car accident. "People say I had to give 'em up," he says, his voice quavering and his eyes watering. "Ain't true. I didn't. I coulda kept them but I hadda do what was best. I couldn't look after them. That was all, see? I sat 'em down and 'splained it all. It were best, I told them." Rick's face collapses in agony as he tells his story. When he recovers, he adds that he was in contact with some of his children until "someone told 'em I was a sex criminal. Now they don't want nothin' to do with me." Court documents indicate that his wife died two years after Family and Children's Services took the children away from them.

LAWRENCE KELLY

Lawrence Kelly was charged with having sexual intercourse with a child under the age of fourteen, his niece Pam. Like most of the Goler Clan, Lawrence Kelly confessed to the police but later recanted, claiming he'd been bullied and threatened. But when pressed on the stand during questioning by Jack Buntain, Kelly admitted everything in his statement was true, except "the sex part." Further, Kelly acknowledged there had been times when he was alone with Pam, contradicting his own alibi, Roy Hiltz, who had sworn up and down there was "no possibility" Lawrence Kelly could have had intercourse with Pam because the two men were in the kitchen together talking at all times on the day in question. "As to the evidence of Mr. Hiltz, that is in conflict with the statement made by the accused, I can only conclude that his memory must have failed him on certain parts of his evidence." It was as close as Judge Hall ever came to suggesting that any of the defence witnesses were lying.

Hall sentenced Lawrence Kelly to two years less a day. Kelly appealed. On September 12, 1985, the appeal court reaffirmed the conviction but dropped his sentence from two years to one, in part because "no force was used by him and . . . the girl co-operated in the act and has suffered no ill effects mentally or otherwise." Curious reasoning, considering that it was well-known, even in 1985, that the ill effects of sexual abuse could take years to surface. In any event, neither Pam nor any of the children were assessed to determine the "ill effects" they might have suffered. Today Lawrence Kelly, sixty-five, is stricken with Alzheimer's and lives in a long-term care facility.

ROY HILTZ

Roy Hiltz, then fifty-five, was charged with buggery, sexual assault and gross indecency against his niece, seven-year-old Lisa Goler, who was so frightened of her uncle she couldn't testify against him. Again Donna Goler provided the key testimony. In the end Hiltz pled guilty to a single charge of buggery and was sentenced to one year.

In 1993, Roy Hiltz was pardoned by the National Parole Board and his record wiped clean. The Criminal Records Act requires complete erasure of any indication that the individual was convicted and demands other jurisdictions, both provincial and federal, comply with the "spirit of the legislation." The man who, his former wife testified, repeatedly beat and brutalized his stepchildren, can now work in a day-care centre with no one being the wiser. Emboldened by Hiltz's pardon, several members of the Clan are contemplating applying themselves.

RALPH KELLY

Initially, Ralph Kelly, the man who described to police in vivid detail how he'd "screwed them all a lot," faced eleven charges. During his various court appearances, there was considerable difficulty pinning down his exact relationship to the Goler Clan. He was variously described as being a close family friend, a family member or a "one-time stepfather of one of the victims." In fact, he was one of Stella Goler's boyfriends, being "married" to her sometime during the 1970s. Ralph pled guilty to three counts: two of sexual intercourse with a female under fourteen years and one of buggery. The remainder of the charges were stayed. Don Hall handed Kelly two years for each sexual intercourse charge and one year for buggery.

Kelly appealed to the Supreme Court of Nova Scotia, which reduced his sentence from five to three years on June 5, 1985. The appeal judges placed considerable emphasis on the fact that Ralph was "dependable and a hard worker" and his "low cultural background" played a role "in the commission of these offences." The appeal court concluded that the "total sentence unduly emphasizes the element of deterrence and does not give sufficient consideration to rehabilitation and the background of this particular offender."

Rehabilitation was, however, a long way from the judicial mind during the Goler trials. With two exceptions none of the accused were recommended for any counselling or rehabilitation program.

EUGENE BROWN

Eugene Brown pled guilty to four charges: two of sexual assault and two of having sex with a female under the age of fourteen. Donna described Eugene as "not really a pro." His desire to be friends with his victims did set him apart. In fact, compared with the rest of the Clan, he was something of a saint. In one of the sexual assaults he "merely felt the private parts and the breast of the child through her clothing" and in the other he "tried to put his hands inside the child's panties and felt her breasts." Eugene also paid his underage victim, Pam, for his fourteen or fifteen encounters with her and often gave candy to the other children after having sex with them. Nonetheless, Judge Hall sentenced Brown to two years for each of the two charges of sex with a female under the age of fourteen and three months each for the sexual assaults, which he characterized as "of a relatively minor nature."

Eugene Brown, aged forty-one, died of cancer in 1989 shortly after he was released.

GABRIEL DODGE

Hulking twenty-five-year-old Gabriel Dodge was one of the most popular men on the Mountain. Everyone liked his sweet disposition and his harmless demeanour—except his victims. Nor was Judge Don Hall immune to Gabriel's childlike charms. Eric Sturk, Dodge's defence lawyer, convinced Hall that, though Gabriel did commit sexual assault, it should not be punished with severity because his victim, Pam Kelly, was willing, even though she was only twelve at the time. Most of the accused were evaluated by the court-appointed psychologist as having a "low mental age" or being "border-line retarded," but in the case of Gabriel, unlike the rest of the Goler Clan, the judge considered it a mitigating factor.

"The accused, according to the information that has been presented, suffers from a learning disability, his education consisting of grade seven in an adjusted class and according to the report of Doctor Denton he is functioning at the mental age of 12 to 14 years. As Doctor Denton says, he had the mental age of or similar to the accuser." Though Pam's deportment, knowledge and emotion on the stand clearly indicated she wasn't functioning at her chronological age either, Hall did not consider the fact that Gabriel Dodge had been assaulting a child who was likely closer to ten mentally, not twelve.

"There is no violence involved," Hall noted. "It also seems rather bizarre that the victim was the party with the greater sexual experience"—Pam's sexual experience being repeated forced intercourse and buggery at the hands of the Clan.

Despite Gabriel's having a previous conviction for an indecent assault on a woman, and showing absolutely no contrition for his previous and current acts, Hall sentenced him to a year in jail and, following his release, probation for another year. After his release, Gabriel moved back to the Mountain. Few associate him with the Goler trials but if they do, doubt that he ever actually did anything wrong. He lives with William's sister Stella, and their household now functions as the focus for the truncated Goler Clan, as Stella and Charles's house once did. People and cars come and go constantly and there are usually children about as several of the victims who have returned to the Mountain have children of their own.

FREDERICK GOLAR

There isn't a trace of the Mountain about Fred Golar. With his neutral accent, educated conversation and smooth manner, he is the antithesis of the Goler Clan. Though William is his cousin, he successfully denied any kinship to the White Rock Golers as did his brother, Dennis, and his mother. The police didn't make the connection either and though Darrell Carmichael, the prosecutor, suspected there must be some kind of relationship, he never established it in court. As a result, Judge Hall dealt with the twenty-seven-year-old rather differently from the rest of the Clan.

"It is significant," he said in sentencing, "that the complainant did not cry out or do much to inform the accused that she was not consenting to the sexual act. I was satisfied, however, that she did not consent and that the accused was reckless and uncaring as to whether she was consenting or not." Hall took into account Fred's "lustful exuberance" and the fact that Wendy "continued to be friendly with the accused after the act was completed."

Hall was disturbed by Fred's relationship to Wendy, their age difference and her vulnerability because of her deafness. But, despite
Wendy's testimony about her emotional turmoil and the blood and
pain caused by her uncle's penetration of her, Hall was confident that
"the complainant did not suffer any permanent trauma of a physical or emotional nature." This conclusion was in sharp contrast to
his earlier sentencing decisions when he said the children of the
White Rock Clan had been irreparably damaged.

Hall was impressed by Fred's blameless criminal and employment
record and by the way he had so ably managed to overcome childhood poverty. "I am deeply of the conviction that if I am to err in
this case it should be on the side of leniency," he stated. "In my view
the element of deterrence can be served by imposing a relatively short
term of incarceration. The rehabilitative aspect of the sentence can
be obtained, in my view, if the accused is able to remain in his present employment and the imposition of appropriate terms in a probation order. I will seek insofar as I possibly can, to avoid making it
necessary for him to lose his present employment. It seems to me that
if he were to lose his present employment because of his action on
this occasion it will certainly destroy his career and may well destroy
him." A number of the men on the periphery of the Goler Clan,
notably Eugene Brown, had been continuously employed for years,
but that didn't stop the judge from giving them stiff sentences.

Judge Hall sentenced Fred Golar to serve ninety days of impris-
onment on weekends, starting at 7:30 P.M. on Friday and ending Sunday at 6:00 P.M. He also gave him two years of probation, which
included his jail term, and ordered him to continue psychiatric counselling and treatment. The Crown successfully appealed and Fred
Golar's sentence was increased to six months of straight time.

As he was then, Fred Golar is still the most successful member of
either side of the Clan. When he left prison, he resumed his work
and soon moved out of the province to continue in a similar field.
Today he has children of his own and is well respected by his employers. His Nova Scotia family has almost no contact with him as he
has worked hard to create a new life for himself as far away from the
Mountain as possible.

JOSEPHINE GOLER

On May 14, 1985, a jury found Josephine Goler, thirty-three, guilty of sexual assault and gross indecency against her son Matt, when he was between the ages of six and nine years old. She was sentenced to twelve months. On March 20, 1986, her appeal of both conviction and sentence was dismissed.

Today Josephine lives on the slopes of the Mountain and remains in close contact with the Clan. She has a boyfriend, a job in the Valley and her son back. Matt visits her regularly in his efforts to re-establish his family.

MARY GOLER

Mary Goler, then thirty-six, elected to be tried by judge and jury. On June 26, 1985, she was found guilty of committing common assault and gross indecency against her son Jeff and gross indecency against her nephew Matt. She was sentenced to twelve months in a provincial correctional centre. Ten months later the appeal court upheld the two gross indecency convictions but overturned the conviction for common assault.

Mary, like Josephine, has a job in the Valley, where she now lives. The apartment she shares with her husband, Rick, looks nothing like the compound on the Mountain where she grew up and spent a great deal of her adult life. It's tidy, though jammed with knick-knacks. The furniture is inexpensive but well cared for and clean. There is little in their lives to connect them with where they came from, though they still make frequent trips to the Mountain. Today Mary is literally half the size she was during the trial and doubts whether any of the children who have not returned to the Mountain would even recognize her.

Until 1997, Mary thought her life was slowly but surely being returned to her. Rick was recovering from his terrible accident and she was seeing her daughter Jennifer on a regular basis and her son Jeff occasionally. Then the shadow of the trials cast itself over her again when a social worker phoned and informed her she wasn't to see or baby-sit her daughter's child without supervision or without undergoing rehabilitative therapy. "I wouldn't take him up there," she protests plaintively, referring to the Mountain. "I got more sense'n that. I jus' keep him near me and look after him good like. Rick too. We oughta get those charges overturned. We could, you know! Anyone can see we done nothing wrong. They was all aginst us. It was all over before it began."

Fourteen years after it was over, the Annapolis Valley still tingles faintly with the aftermath of the Goler Clan trials. Those who lived through them, whether they were actively involved, fascinated observers or revolted bystanders, recall it as an endless period of shame for one of the most beautiful places on earth. "We got to be known as the incest capital of the world," muses Wendy Elliott, a long-time columnist with the *Advertiser*. "I don't think it did much for the tourist trade," she adds wryly.

Looking back, people in the Valley remember dozens of articles, documentaries, radio reports and regular television bulletins: a media frenzy sensationalizing the grimmest aspects of the cases. Most who were around at the time would agree that they were virtually assaulted by the media. But the Valley is a place where one reporter asking a single unwanted question is regarded as if he or she were a herd of persistent, insensitive gnats feeding rapaciously on the under-belly of life, twisting facts and distorting events.

In truth there was astonishingly little coverage locally, nationally or internationally. Aside from a twenty-minute CBC "Fifth Estate" documentary, one extended local television report and several short summations, details and opinions surrounding the cases were scanty. Though there was a single national wire service feature story and one national magazine story and a few paragraphs in an American tabloid, the "hillbilly sex ring" cases were largely buried in back pages and brief wire service reports for the duration—especially in Nova Scotia.

Chapter Fourteen

In the Shadow of
South Mountain

LISA

✦ DONNA GOLER WAS WRONG. ONCE
the machinery of the law and social services had the children in their
grasp, there was no chance she and her favourite sister would ever
live together permanently. Finding foster or adoptive homes for a
single Goler child was hard enough, let alone placing siblings
together. At first there was a series of what Donna calls "one-night
stands," she and Lisa sleeping in a different bed virtually every night.
They even stayed a few nights at social workers' homes when there
wasn't enough time to drive them to their temporary shelter after a
particularly long day spent with police and lawyers and in court.
Then the two girls were moved to a short-term foster home at the
east end of the Valley for three months, after which Donna moved
in alone with the sister of that foster mother. The social worker and
the new foster mother both told her that Lisa would be joining her
soon, and the girls looked forward to being settled in their new life
together.

One day late in the summer of 1984 Donna was getting ready for
one of her treasured visits with Lisa when her foster mother abruptly

told her the day had been cancelled. Lisa was gone. Just like that—gone. No warning. No chance to say goodbye. Just gone.

The foster mother explained that a nice couple in Halifax was adopting Lisa. She would have a lovely home with another child to play with and lots of clothes and toys—they even had a piano. Donna was stunned. Everything seemed to drain out of her in a few seconds, leaving her so weak she thought she was going to be sick. Today she feels that she was systematically lied to by the social workers, that they never had any intention of leaving the two sisters together, or at least knew it would be impossible, despite their, and the police's, many promises to the contrary. Her suspicions centre on the fact that her new foster parents didn't immediately bring Lisa into the house along with her. After all, they were a well-off professional couple who had fostered or adopted twelve children over the years.

The couple from Halifax were a doctor and her husband, an officer with the armed forces. Shortly after they adopted Lisa, the man was transferred to a new posting in Ottawa. Not only did Lisa have a new home and family but a new province—a lot to take in for a child who'd left the Mountain only a few times in her life.

Lisa's adoptive parents had no real idea of what the little girl had been through and the world she grew up in was so foreign to them Lisa might as well have come from outer space. They didn't realize that their new child, while not mentally handicapped, was certainly "slow" and at times difficult to control, the result of either genetics or environment or both—no one would ever know. With all the expectations and ambitions of a middle-class upbringing, they assumed that good food, a happy home and the stimulation of educated people would draw Lisa out of her shell. But no amount of window dressing could alter what had been done to Lisa. Her new parents thought her slowness was simply reticence and they could not begin to identify, let alone fix or erase, the turmoil inside her as a result of her brutal impoverished early childhood. She needed a great deal more than piano lessons.

It took the doctor and her husband a year to conclude that Lisa would not fit into their lives. They phoned the adoption agency in Halifax and informed them they were returning her, like a pair of ill-fitting shoes. Her few belongings were packed into a bag and Lisa, for the second time in her life, boarded an airplane.

Lisa Goler, now twenty-one, is, in the words of one observer, "emotionally fragile." Though she was finally placed in a caring foster home after three years of temporary ones, she struggled through the remainder of her childhood and teen years. Donna didn't see her again for several years. When they were reunited with the help of Lisa's new foster parents, Donna was shocked to find that her sister didn't really remember her. The two girls seldom saw each other more than once a year thereafter, but the foster parents kindly sent Donna Lisa's book reports, sewing projects and art work. They were treasured possessions. "Even though I didn't see her, I still had something," Donna emphasizes. "I save everything—and I mean everything."

When Lisa left her foster home to live on her own, Donna tried to rekindle the relationship, sometimes paying her sister's rent or other bills when the social services cheque somehow evaporated. A few men have come and gone in Lisa's life, sometimes leaving their mark on her face or body. Donna, with plenty of her own hard experience, wasn't slow to give advice—advice that wasn't welcome. The two sisters, once so close, are now estranged. The separation and infrequent visits loosened the bond that once entwined them. Donna is waiting and hoping that Lisa will "pull herself up, take control. She's got to do it, you know, it's the only way. I just don't want her to be a victim all her life." When Donna speaks of Lisa, there is an uncompromising toughness in her voice but sadness and loss etched in her face.

Lisa's memories are as veiled as South Mountain when it is shrouded by a Maritime fog. She knows where she came from but none of the details. Still, she can't avoid the little flashes of remembrance that catch her unawares from time to time. And her foster parents can't help worrying what might happen if Lisa, willingly or not, ever comes face to face with her past.

SANDRA

Donna and Lisa haven't laid eyes on their older sister since the 1984 trials. Though she lives in the Valley, Sandra Goler, now twenty-eight, has gone back to the Mountain many times to visit the Clan—

it is for her, as it is for many of the children, an irresistible magnet. But her father's anger at her betrayal still simmers more than a decade later. Other family members say Sandra has tried to reconcile with William but he rejects her. "She's gotta live with what she done," William growls, when asked about it. Donna doesn't speak with Sandra either; she sees no reason to. They were never close as children and the tragedy of their early lives didn't change that. Sandra sees Hazel, her mother, occasionally, but the acrimony she grew up with still infects that relationship.

Unmarried, with two children of her own, one of whom spent most of its early life in hospital in Halifax for treatment of numerous health problems, Sandra is supported by social services. "She's here, there and everywhere," says one employee of Family and Children's Services. "You never know who Sandra is going to be hanging around with. I'd have to say she's one of the ones who didn't turn out so great." When asked if there is anything that could have been done, could still be done, to give Sandra and her children a chance, the woman shrugs. She doesn't quite say it but her eyes telegraph her thoughts: "She's from the Mountain—what can you do?"

MICHAEL AND ANNIE

The youngest child, Annie, five years old at the time of the trials, is blissfully unaware of who she was. Her adoptive parents, who don't live in Nova Scotia, pray she'll never find out. Her mother, Marjorie, one of two Goler sisters who was never charged, and her father, Curtis, whose charges were dropped, have tried for years to find her. She remains well hidden.

Michael, Annie's brother, now twenty-three, spent years in a series of foster homes, then returned to his mother. They live in the Valley but still visit the rest of the Clan on the Mountain. Michael's life has also been turbulent. Like all of the children, he faced a difficult time in school, but he fought back, carving out a reputation for bloody fist fights that his cousin Matt says, with no small measure of pride, are still talked about in the Valley.

But Michael's difficulties weren't limited to school. Twice he was accused of molesting a young girl—once by his foster parents and once by a neighbour. Nothing ever came of the accusations but they have scarred him. "It's like you're marked," his cousin Jennifer says. "I don't know what he done or what he didn't do, but it don't matter. It's like people are saying, you're a Goler, victim or criminal you're all the same."

Michael perseveres, striving to become only the second member of the White Rock branch to finish Grade 12. His cousin Matt was the first, graduating from Kings County Vocational School at the age of nineteen.

SALLY

Sally, Stella Goler's youngest daughter, nine when she was taken from her home, was adopted quickly and carefully shielded from her past by her new parents. She's had no contact with any member of the Clan, not even her brothers, Kenny and Doug, or her sister, Pam. Sally was so terrified during the preliminary hearings that her testimony was all but useless. At one point she and her mother Stella "accidentally" met in the court-house and a brief but terrible scene ensued with Stella screaming at her child. Officials quickly hustled the trembling, incoherent child out of the court-house. She had difficulty speaking for nearly six months and, according to her adoptive parents, appeared to have walled off the first years of her life in her memory. Her parents know that one day Sally, now twenty-two, may have to confront the facts of her past, but they hope the blight of the Mountain has been eradicated by geographical separation and love.

PAM

Pam, now twenty-six, is still Pam—wilful and mercurial, with a short fuse. She can be offhand, vague and uninterested in what is going on around her one minute and the next intensely curious and questioning, like a terrier with a rat. She bounced from one foster home to another, eventually returning to the Mountain. Pam had a child a few years ago and now lives a stone's throw from Stella, her mother, and her most recent stepfather, Gabriel Dodge, in much the same conditions as those she grew up in. Her apartment is in a bizarre structure that looks like an oversized house dropped into the middle of the bush by someone who changed his mind at the last moment and turned it into suites. Everywhere are the signs of failure and indecision. A giant deck starts out promisingly and then simply ends, half finished. There is no access to the front door, which sits five feet above the ground, waiting for stairs. There is no driveway, just a rough path and hard-packed grass where cars can pull over. The back yard is filled with abandoned projects and garbage. In the hallway a boy, about twelve years old, lolls on the stairs leading to the upper level. When asked if his mother is home, he shrugs. "Not since Friday." It is Wednesday. Of his father he says, "He's inside," meaning jail.

Pam's mother's house is less than a shack. The roof sags, the walls list, the floorboards give beneath your feet and a septic smell of rot and garbage pervades. There are no steps to the front door, and the entrance, through the attached woodshed, is guarded by a lake of mud. Decades of debris are strewn everywhere in the yard. Ducks and geese squawk angrily in the background. Even on a sunny day, the highest of spirits are flattened once inside the tiny dwelling.

Despite a lifetime of poor nutrition and poor circumstances, Pam has matured into a lovely woman. When it's washed, her hair is a thick, glossy mane and the animation in her eyes, whether it's from anger or joy, lights up her face. Her body is softening into puffiness but even draped by a soiled white blouse and ill-fitting, ripped pants with her feet clad in large rubber boots, her basic attractiveness is still abundant.

Pam fills up every room she's in with her voice, her movement, her activity. She commands, demands, pushes, prods. You can't ignore her, she won't let you. In one corner of her mother's kitchen her child, face smeared with dirt, perches on a stool scribbling on paper. "Ain't no one going to touch my kid, I'll tell you that right now." Pam punches the words out furiously. "Anyone tries an' I'll kill 'em, just kill 'em! I don't let no one get in my way, no one bothers me, you got that? I do what I want now. I had enough o' those people"—she cocks her head in the direction of the Valley—"telling me what to do. Putting me here and there. It didn't do no good. Tell me what good it done. Just screwed everything up. They shoulda left us alone."

Pam both denies and admits what happened to her as a child—sometimes in the same breath. "It was all lies, you know, lies!" she bellows at an unwelcome visitor asking about her past, angrily thrusting her head forward, daring the person to disagree. "Them police made us lie, they didn't care," she shouts. "Nobody cared about us. In the trials everything got twisted around." She pauses for a moment, tells the visitor to get lost, then drags a broken chair over to the open doorway and plants herself on it, legs spread on either side of the cracked seat. The chair tilts slightly as it sinks into a rotten floorboard.

In a sudden about-face Pam eagerly continues the conversation—setting the interloper straight. "You see, it's all over now," in quieter tones. "What's done is done. I forgave 'em. Didn't nobody worry about me when it was all happening. Didn't nobody help me out or give me nothing. We was like dogs, just passed around. Them welfare people weren't no different. They just wanted it over and done with, swept under the carpet. They all just wanted to forget about it."

Stella, her mother, is in the background, furiously stabbing at potatoes in the dim light over the kitchen sink. The potatoes are ancient and filled with scabs and brown spots. She pares away with a knife until they are not much larger than small plums. "They took my kids away," she snarls. "I didn't do nothing but they just come and took 'em away and said I couldn't see them ever again. Is that right? Those kids was confused. They was scared. Wouldn't you be if them police was yelling at you all the time? Things up here're same as they always was and them people don't give a damn. They shoulda just let us be. Least then we'd still be a family."

DOUG

Pam's brother Doug is now a muscular, compact twenty-seven-year-old. Unlike Pam he remains completely still when he talks. Outwardly he is calm and relaxed and shakes hands cordially with a firm grip. His eyes hold your gaze, they don't flicker and dart as his sister's do. But his body is coiled and ready. He stands with his legs slightly apart, his hands resting in the pockets of his oil-stained overalls. His stance seems neighbourly but it is a wary posture as he assesses, measures before making the decision to keep his fists where they are or drive them into the face of the person talking to him.

Doug ignores a pair of geese snuffling around a mud hole at his feet. He doesn't move an inch or flex a muscle and he manages to appear as immovable as a guard dog in front of his mother's house. Behind him a torn, dingy curtain is pulled back slightly from the single front window. A young woman's dark head dips hesitantly forward to peer out, then retreats again quickly. A naked child ducks under the curtain and gawks curiously before being yanked back by an unseen hand.

Doug's hair is close-cropped, almost shaved. In the centre of his forehead a small blue heart is tattooed, the mark of Dorchester penitentiary. "I been doing time since I was fifteen," he says quietly. "I'm gettin' married now." He flicks his head infinitesimally towards the window behind him. "I got kids, four of 'em. I want to look after them." He won't say whether they are his.

"I done put my life together but things keep coming up at me," he says matter-of-factly, but a flash of the fearful, insecure fourteen-year-old crosses his face. Jailed first for sexual assault as a teenager, shortly after the trials, and then for armed robbery as an adult, he estimates he has spent more than half his time since 1984 in one prison or another. And it isn't over yet. He had been out of jail only a few months in 1996 when he got into an argument with Pam and a male friend. "I just tried to protect my niece [Pam's daughter] and look what good it did me."

Doug refuses to detail exactly what danger he was protecting the little girl from, but in the scuffle a pellet gun went off, the police were called and once more Doug felt handcuffs around his wrists. "I'm representing myself," he says firmly. "I learned everything I need to know in jail. How to do the legal stuff. I can do it just as good as any lawyer. I don't trust 'em, any of them. Don't need 'em."

Doug knows that if he's convicted after two previous offences, he faces a long stretch in a federal jail. He is resigned to it. "I don't expect no one to give me a break. Why should they?" He realizes it may be years before he sees his children again, but then, such things have happened within the Goler Clan before. Still, he talks of marriage, of getting on with his life, as if the minor detail of hard time can be brushed away or at least ignored for the moment.

Oddly, though he is standing in front of his mother's house, sees his uncles, aunts and cousins regularly and even interceded on behalf of his niece, he says he's cut himself off from the Clan. "The past is past. I don't want to get involved with them and get it brung up and all that. I don't have nothing to do with my family, 'cept Kenny, my brother. He's a good guy. He don't have nothing to do with any of what happened. Pam's crazy, you can't talk to her. The rest of 'em are gone from me now. I just want to get out of all this and look after my family."

Doug reeks of missed opportunities, of raw ability bent and misused. For all his stillness and matter-of-fact acceptance of his fate, there is a deep sadness about him—for he knows what has been done to him, what he has lost and what it has all cost him.

"I forgive my uncles," he says as if reading your mind. "I forgive all of them for what they done to me. It's over. It shouldn't've happened but it did. I forgive them." And then he will say no more.

MATT

"Nothing happened to me. It was all lies. I was never abused," the young man maintains quietly but vehemently. Matt, now twenty-three, says when he was taken to the police station from school in February 1984, he told the police no one in the family had ever touched him. "I kept saying nothing happened, nothing happened. My cousin Jeff and Jennifer was there. Jeff said he saw stuff happening after I'd been saying nothing happened to me."

Though his testimony was instrumental in putting his mother Josephine, his stepfather and four other Clan members in jail and even though several other children saw him being assaulted, Matt is unwavering in his denial of being abused. He cites as evidence a medical examination conducted on him by a Valley physician that found "no evidence of anal penetration." The police counter that the medical exam was cursory, conducted by a practitioner without specialized training in such matters. "We didn't pay much attention to the medical aspects, because we had so much eyewitness testimony," points out Baxter Upshall.

Matt's explanation of what happened to him is eerily similar to that of the Goler adults then and now. He says he was bulldozed into testifying against the four Goler men by police pressure. He was a good witness, giving detailed and consistent evidence on the stand, but he says he carefully memorized it all with the help of his first foster parents from a script provided by the police. "They had a china cabinet and the testimony was sitting on top and every day they would take it down and we would go over what was in it, make sure I remembered what I had said and if I didn't, if I said something wasn't the thing they would correct me and tell me what it was and ask me questions over and over and over."

Matt maintains the police showed him a sheet of paper with statements by his cousins detailing sexual abuse by his mother. "They said, you sign the paper and you get to see your mother later on. So I signed the paper and I saw my mother as I was leaving the police station for the last time in eight or nine years."

Matt, like most of his cousins, suffered terribly as a teenager. The normal turmoil of the transformation from child to adult was complicated by guilt, fear, anger and self-loathing at what he'd done to his mother. "I didn't know [what I said] could put her away. When it came time for me to testify, I couldn't even look at my own mother because I knew it was lies and the times I did I would break down and cry and the court would have to stop and I would have to leave for a while." In retrospect, Matt feels his tears made it look as if he was upset about what had happened to him. "But it was because I knew what I was saying wasn't one hundred percent truthful."

The police say that Matt was one of the boys who volunteered information about the Goler women, his aunt and his mother, once he was away from his family—in his case, late in 1984, several months after he'd been adopted. He denies it politely, but very firmly.

Matt spent his first months away from home with a foster family—"the foster farm," he says scathingly—where a large number of children, some in their late teens, worked on the land when they weren't in school and all summer long. At night they slept five to a room. "Let's put it this way, it wasn't the most pleasant experience in my life. I was spanked on the bare bottom, I was hit with a belt for some of the weirdest reasons. There'd be a weed or two in the garden and you'd get the belt." One day Matt, his cousins Jennifer and Jeff and several other children were caught playing hide and seek instead of doing their chores. Matt was locked in his room for the day and not allowed to use the bathroom.

He recalls being injured badly when he fell off the back of the farm truck. He bruised his ribs, sprained his arm, skinned his legs and a long cut bled over one eye. "I should have been taken to the hospital. Instead I was taken back to the farmhouse and they patched me up there. I couldn't even move my arm. There wasn't much I could do. My arm was in a sling so I drove the tractor with my other arm." The lack of medical attention disturbs him more than the work he had to do while injured. "I was nine," he shrugs. "I could handle the tractor. It wasn't going that fast anyway."

One day during this period, his foster mother accused him of stealing twenty dollars. "I didn't even know what that looked like because I'd never had that much money. They said, 'We were thinking about adopting you but where you're stealing the money we're not going to.' They said that right to my face one day. I said, 'I didn't steal the money from you but if it means not getting adopted by you, I did it!'"

One of the social workers from the time dismisses his recollections as stories designed to gain him sympathy today. But she has no answer when asked why a child who was believed so implicitly in 1984 should be condemned as a liar in 1997. Nor has Matt ever asked for sympathy. He has kept his real identity secret for fourteen years. As for the stark difference between Matt's testimony in 1984 and his denial today, no one has an explanation, not even him. "I just don't want to hurt my family any more, even if they did wrong," he says softly.

A kindly Christian couple from the Valley adopted Matt shortly after the incident and a wall of new experiences began to shut him off from his past. Even so, he never felt he belonged. It was a familiar feeling. With his mother, Josephine, he had moved around constantly with a revolving door of new "fathers." One year, when the Clan was still together, he attended one school for a few months, was enrolled in a different one for a single day and then ended up back at his original school. But in the past, he'd always had the Clan to fall back on. "No matter what'd happen we'd go up on the Mountain, visit my grandparents and have a good time. There'd always be kids running around, someone to play with," he says, relishing the memory. "I was lucky to have such a big, close family," he adds, oblivious to the irony.

The Clan was the enduring influence on Matt's life; he had no outside friends and school was just a distraction. Like the rest of the Clan he learned, as a very young boy, that it was them against the rest of the world. "People from the Valley all stuck together, dressed a certain way and thought we were pretty much all scum. No matter who you are, if you came from the Mountain you were scum. I remember going to the Kentville school, I think I went for one or two days. I couldn't handle it. There was just me. I didn't dress the way they dressed, didn't talk the same. They all tormented me and on a kid that's in Grade 2 or 3 that's extremely hard to deal with."

Though slight and, on the surface of it, no match for boys who were determined to show him his place, Matt had two hundred years of Mountain survival in his blood. "All the Mountain kids turned out pretty rough, pretty bad. If you grew up on the Mountain you've had a fight. So when people know where you're from, they naturally associate you with fighting and you get a reputation." Today, Matt is as proud of having learned how to walk away from trouble as he is of standing up to it. By the end of his first year with his adoptive parents, he had stopped answering every taunt with his fists.

For the first few years, things went well with his adoptive parents. His father took him fishing and his mother doted on him. At school he worried about people finding out who he was and how they would react to him if they knew. And he had a special problem now that adoption had changed his name. "Every time I'd meet people I'd try and treat 'em like family 'cause you're not sure. Especially if I hear my [real] last name. There was a guy in my school and I treated him like a brother because I didn't know whether he was or not. There was another girl I never really met but she had the same last name and I'd wonder what she'd think if she knew. I'd be worried about her because I wasn't sure if she was related to me."

Then Matt's adoptive mother died and once more his life heaved and twisted in confusion. He loved her and was closer to her than he was to his adoptive father. When Matt's father met a woman and invited her to live with them, Matt grew bitter and resentful. It was bad enough losing first one mother, then another, but to have someone new dropped in as a poor replacement filled him with anger. He clashed with his adoptive father until a raw wound opened between them.

By then Matt's mother, Josephine, was long out of jail and he had already made contact with her, something his adoptive parents had encouraged, feeling it was inevitable. The first meeting after nine years of separation came in an arcade—it was a halting, awkward exchange, like that of two teenagers on a blind date. She came up behind him and hesitantly tapped him on the shoulder. "Are you Matt?" she asked. "I'm your mother." At first he couldn't believe his mother really wanted him back.

After reconciling with Josephine, Matt returned to the Mountain. "I was scared to death that my family would hate me, really hate me because of what I said. And I found out that when I went back home, my family welcomed me with open arms. They pretty much forgive what happened but they never forget. They bring it up every chance they get, especially my aunt Mary. She loves talking about it. We would appreciate it if she would stop bringing the past up. I mean, I love my aunt Mary and I try to spend as much time as possible with her. But when she brings that up..."

Some of the Clan want Matt to see a lawyer and confess that he lied on the stand. "We done talked about that," says his aunt Mary hopefully. "But I dunno if it would do any good. They didn't believe us then. If the whole thing were brung up again maybe they'd jus' put us all back in jail." While Matt would love to have his mother's conviction overturned, he's not sure he could live through what people would say if they knew who he was. "I'm still afraid of people finding out. I mean, people don't look too favourably on this, especially in the Valley."

Though he denies he was abused, Matt does allow that some of his cousins may have been victimized. "Pam might have been one of those because I noticed that most of the people that I think was abused are pretty strange now. Like Doug, he had a lot of anger and stuff like that and Donna, little Donna, she doesn't want nothing to do with the family at all. She always was different, tough, you know. Still, it coulda happened to her. And Sandra, well, there's Sandra! She's out there! She coulda been one. Stuff happened, but it was a very select group of people."

Matt's adoptive father is very religious, and Matt, now reconciled with him after several years of separation, has followed him into the church. He has a good life now, with a job, a girlfriend, prospects for the future, and a renewed attachment to the Mountain. He's taking a computer course and would like to be a detective. But Matt is never quite able to leave the shadow cast by South Mountain. His girlfriend, who was abused physically as a child, is still a teenager and he worries that if people discover he was part of the Goler Clan they will assume he is trying to take advantage of a young girl.

JENNIFER AND JEFF

Jennifer doesn't look at all like where she came from. She smiles shyly in agreement when you say that, as if it is something she has known and clung to for a long time. "Some of us look like the Mountain. Michael does. My brother Jeff does. Others of us don't." When she utters the words Jennifer remains motionless for a moment, fixing her beautiful blue-grey eyes on some distant point. She doesn't say it but the implication is clear: *I'm one of the lucky ones.* The distance between her and the hump of granite that sheltered the Goler Clan is as vital to her as air. With her boyish body, elfin face, translucent skin and air of knowing she could fit in anywhere—Kitsilano, Forest Hill, the Upper West Side. Only her twangy vowels and occasional double negatives betray her, but she could just as easily be a spoiled rich kid who's rebelled and adopted street argot as an ill-educated, abused child born into the Goler Clan.

"You'd never catch me on the Mountain," Jennifer states firmly. "Some of us got out because we didn't go back. I didn't. I won't." In February 1997, her life was starting to respond to her determination. She has a small child and she and her fiancé are building a house. She has a job that she doesn't pretend is high status, but it's decent, steady and has a future. Her employer praises her as a dependable, diligent and efficient worker. As a young adult, she started seeing her mother again but only in the Valley. She swore she would never tell her child about his grandparents but she wanted him to know them, to have a complete family. As for the Mountain, Jennifer was sure she'd exorcised it from her soul. But the Mountain has come to her—re-infecting her life with its poison.

One day in the middle of winter, she got a phone call that entangled her and her young child once more in the twisted world of the Clan. At the other end of the line was a social worker who told Jennifer that she knew who she was and knew that Mary, her mother—a convicted Goler—had been baby-sitting Jennifer's son. The social worker said it had to stop. "Somebody ratted my mother out," Jennifer sighs. "Somebody found out they were up on charges and ratted her out—but it's me and my child that pays the price." The social worker explained that Jennifer could not leave her son alone with her mother or stepfather Rick, who was also convicted. Even if Jennifer was in the house, the child could not be in the same room with Mary and Rick without supervision.

Normally Jennifer is almost supernaturally calm. She seems to be able to control her reactions to everything around her. But at the threat to her child and her carefully reconstructed life her face closes down, panic turns her eyes dark and her lips work against sobs or screams. "Over my dead body," she whispers. "They'll take him away over my dead body." The social worker threatened to put her son in a foster home if Jennifer continues to allow him to be cared for by convicted sex offenders. The only way out is for Mary to seek counselling and provide proof of that to the satisfaction of social services. No court order backs up the social worker's words, but Jennifer is a child of the system. She knows who has the power and believes that in any battle between her and the system over the fate of her child, she will lose. How can she not? She is of the Goler Clan. She carries that knowledge within her like a concentration camp tattoo.

When Jennifer was first taken away from her mother and stepfather, she was placed on the same "foster farm" that took Matt and her brother Jeff. It was a time of helplessness and hopelessness for her. In addition to the sexual assaults and the cruelty, Jennifer had been abruptly wrenched from the only family she knew. "I didn't care what they did to me. It didn't matter to me if we were together. I just didn't care about anything." She was eventually moved to a permanent foster home, where a compassionate family tried to make her care about something in life. "They treated me good," Jennifer acknowledges a little sadly, "but I didn't want to obey them. I physically slapped my foster mother, I've thrown her around, pushed her around. I'd scream at her, 'You're not my mother!' I was just crazy."

Jennifer's school years were filled with fear and loneliness. For years her five-foot three-inch frame carried less than eighty pounds as anorexia threatened to leave her with permanent physical problems. She prayed no one would ever find out who she was, but someone always did. "People knew, I don't know how but they'd know. I've had total humiliation. I even moved to Cape Breton once to get away. Even then they'd find out somehow. They thought it was cool. 'There's a Goler,' they'd yell it right out." Sometimes she'd walk down the hallways at school and hear the chant, "Easy, easy, easy," and worse, far worse, following her. Boys would tell her they knew she wasn't a virgin and expect her to "put out." The fact that her virginity had been violently taken from her when she was eight years old only seemed to heighten their disdain.

Like all the children, no professional help was given to her after a brief meeting or two with a child psychiatrist or psychologist during the trials. Once a permanent home had been found for her, her foster parents were left to deal with the trauma, which included far more than just sexual and psychological abuse. "Aside from everything else I'd had a lot of spankings in my [previous] life with everything you could think of, the metal end of a fly swatter, a belt—the buckle end, everything. I seen my stepdad whaling on my brother. I'd get spanked for getting home two seconds too late." She recalls the memories with a face devoid of emotion but she can't hold onto the blankness for long. "I went through it. It was hell."

Jennifer is not one who denies the "terrible things done to me," most of which never came out at trial—many of which are unknown to police even to this day.

Once out on her own, Jennifer navigated life as if she were walking through a minefield, never knowing when she'd be exposed. She has little contact with Jeff, whose life has veered and careened from one extreme to another. "He can't hold a job. It just doesn't interest him. I haven't talked to him in a long time. Just as well, he's always bumming money."

Jeff, like Matt, recanted his testimony. Egged on by his mother, Mary, who talks obsessively about the trials, he took a bold step and consulted a lawyer in the Valley. He spilled out a muddled tale of statements dragged out of him by the police and prosecutors that were not true. Nothing came of it, but the act itself was sufficient to keep the Clan talking, arguing and worrying over the possibility of a new trial and exoneration like dogs over a well-chewed bone.

Jennifer tries to march on with her life, ignoring it all. But the fact that she still has contact with her mother who, until recently, has been baby-sitting her only grandchild doesn't allow Jennifer to let go completely. She is terrified of losing her child and worries that one day a car will drive up and he'll be snatched away—just like that day in 1984 when the police and a social worker removed her and Jeff from their home. She is convinced that her mother and stepfather, regardless of what they did in the past, have not repeated it with her child. But when asked if her parents can resist taking him to the Mountain, she cannot say yes. She is not sure. She simply hopes and prays her mother would never take her child to visit his great-uncles on the Mountain. But the doubt is there. Her hands shake when she thinks of it. Her voice chokes with tears when she talks of the possibility. She could, and perhaps should, walk away from them. But half a lifetime spent without a family is a hard thing for anyone to bear.

Like all the children of the Clan, Jennifer has never emerged fully from the shadow cast by South Mountain. It took nearly four years after she met her fiancé before he could touch her without causing her to flinch. Today, he and their child are her family. Until the social worker called, they had been looking forward to a normal life, the kind of life she saw all around her once she was taken from the Clan. As distraught as she is about the appearance of social services in her life and her exposure, once again, as a Goler, an aura of survival haloes her.

"I got out," she repeats with finality. "I'm not going back."

Chapter Fifteen

Return to
South Mountain

◆ DONNA GOLER FOLLOWS IN THE footsteps of generations. She walks from the gravel parking lot, then stands in the middle of the small park, arms folded, and surveys the view. It is her first visit to the once famous Stile. Though she lived only a few miles away, her family weren't exactly given to sightseeing. Besides, her own tiny shack commanded one of the most breathtaking panoramas in the country. She finds it ironic that this little spot on the Ridge Road behind Wolfville was once a Mecca for university students, tourists and picnickers.

Donna Goler may never have visited the Stile, but she knew what the Ridge was all about—the point separating Mountain from Valley. Gazing over the gentle Gaspereau Valley and the forested slopes reaching back over the Mountain, she narrows her eyes. "It's all different," she says to her companion, "but it's all the same."

Donna Goler has come back to South Mountain.

It's been thirteen years since she was the star witness whose testimony convicted her father, uncles, two of her cousins and numerous family friends. Ever since then she's been in hiding, running constantly from her past, building up walls between herself and her family, bricking them over, reinforcing them with layers of cold, hard resolve. Donna has never erased the fear that her father, William Goler, would find her.

A wrong number on her telephone, a strange man in the neighbourhood, an unexpected knock on the door, and even one heart-stopping moment when her uncle Cranswick came to her foster parents' house by accident, all send shafts of terror into her soul. Not that she has let it show. Donna was tough at eleven and she got tougher—on herself, the people around her and her relatives. "I had to be that way; if I wasn't, I'd be back on the Mountain with fifteen kids and no brain."

Donna delivers the words flatly; they thud as stones against flesh—their harshness a strange contrast to the woman. In manner she is like a foal, at once forward and shy, warm and stand-offish, excitable and deadly calm. In body she seems too delicate for the weight of certainty and the bluntness of her words. She's no longer tiny but her five-foot five-inch frame carries less than a hundred pounds. A child could encircle her wrist with a single hand. Her oversized hazel eyes, fringed by long curving lashes and high broad cheekbones, give her a vulnerable, wondering look. But what really distinguishes Donna is her determination and how much she feels sure of at an age when so many are still fumbling around for the opinions that will solidify as they age. "I definitely grew up too fast," she sighs.

The child who wept and pleaded to be released from testifying against her father is still there. So too is the little girl who said the words that had to be said. It has taken her thirteen years to repair the life those words tore apart, years filled with all the normal mistakes of youth and early adulthood compounded by the desperation and depression of her broken world. Inch by inch, she has built a new foundation, not as solid as she would like, but for the first time in twenty-five years she has something she can call her own—a life. So it is only now that she can turn around and look back.

Watching Donna standing straight and defiant on the Stile, the demarcation between Mountain and Valley, one can't help thinking of another strong woman, Esther Clark Wright, who loved South

Mountain but sensed the evil and distress within. Wright spent a good part of her life plotting to fix the Mountain. She would have been profoundly sad at what was done to Donna Goler on her Mountain, but at the same time she would have liked what she saw standing on her Stile—the slender young woman just entering her mid-twenties, come back to face her nightmares.

As far as Donna is concerned, her life began at age twelve and she's spent most of the last thirteen years obliterating all traces of who she was. But she, like the rest of the children, has never been able to escape completely the shadow of South Mountain.

Donna's experience in the foster home was bitter. She disliked her controlling foster mother, often quarrelling with her and the numerous other foster children in the house. At fifteen she left. Her foster mother says she gave Donna an ultimatum—submit to counselling or find another place to live. Donna smiles at that. "Choice? There was no choice. She threw me out." And even if there had been one, the choice would have been easy for her to make. The memory of the police, lawyers, doctors, social workers, the court and their broken promises was still raw; nothing would persuade her to turn her life over to yet another professional for dissection.

"You have to remember that we'd all been told that everything was being done for our own good. From the moment we were taken away to every time we went to a new foster home. We should have been taken away, but it's pretty hard for a kid to believe that. And how was it supposed to be good for us to never see our sisters or brothers again? How could that be good for us? I loved Lisa, they took her away and didn't let me be with her again. Then this woman tells me to go get counselling because it would be good for me. What would you do? Who would you believe?"

Donna bounced around from one job to another, never landing in a place where she felt at home. Though her name was now different, there was always the fear that someone would identify her as a Goler—or worse, that a Goler would find her. Her first boyfriend beat her and her first sexual experience not at the hands of her family was a horror. "I thought he was going to rip me apart." Thereafter Donna went from one disastrous man to another.

She modelled for a while when she was nineteen until the photographer made unwelcome advances. "People might have said I just got what I was used to because I was a Goler, but I went to the police. I charged him with rape but it got thrown out. I guess it probably happened because that's the kind of people we attracted." There isn't a shred of self-pity in her words. It's an emotion she identifies with the Mountain and she won't tolerate it.

The child born of the incident is a boy. Donna appreciates the irony of his gender. "All those years my father kept saying he wanted a boy. There were times when I wanted to go to him and say, 'You couldn't produce one, but look, I did!'"

The birth of Donna's son brought both joy and pain. "I thought he was an elephant coming out." It was hard enough trying to find a life for herself, let alone make one for him. Any twenty-year-old single parent faces a formidable task, let alone one with no resources, no money, no profession, no parenting skills and no family to fall back on. The relationship between her and her son's father was tempestuous, filled with disagreements about how to raise the boy. He had behaviour problems, and she struggled with them, reluctantly turning to social services for advice and help. She even initiated contact with her foster mother to act as an intermediary between her and the father. Things didn't improve much. Between 1992 and 1995, there were six separate court orders regarding access to and custody of her son. It had all the earmarks of a classic battle between two parents warring over a child.

Without a high school education, her opportunities were limited but she enrolled in a government-sponsored health course and excelled in her class. She loved the work; it was a wonderful feeling, being able to help others. The people she cared for depended on her, needed her, just as Lisa once had. Slowly Donna put the pieces together: she met a man who became her fiancé, she found a good job in a nursing home, a house of her own and had another child, a daughter—she finally felt she'd shed her Goler skin.

In early 1997, a few months after her son started pre-school, Donna was stunned when his father applied for custody. His interest in the boy was curious. The father had rarely paid child support and when his son visited, he often turned him over to Donna's one-time foster mother, Roberta Lawrence. Yet he still wanted custody.

This time the boy's father had an arsenal of witnesses willing to testify to her unsuitability as a mother and willing to use her past as definitive proof that she could not, should not ever have a child in her care. The father had a powerful, well-off, ally, Roberta Lawrence. Though the child had been born four years after Donna had left her foster home, the woman, who adopted or fostered fifteen children over the years, became obsessed with wresting the child from Donna.

"She's not stable, you know," she said of Donna to a reporter. "She has to control everything in her life. She wants to dictate everything for him." The foster mother had been acting as a go-between, ferrying the child between Donna and the father, driving the forty miles from the Valley regularly to pick him up and deliver him on visitation days. "He's my grandson, whether she likes it or not," the woman stated. "She's not going to take him from me."

In retrospect Donna sees the mistake in it. "I didn't know how much she wanted the boy to be hers. I didn't have any family of my own to help. She was the only one I could turn to. Having her pick him up meant I didn't have to deal with the father. I didn't want to start arguments in front of my son. It was better to have an intermediary."

During the custody hearing it was revealed that her foster mother had once complained to social services that she thought Donna had burned her son with cigarettes, drank heavily and was generally a neglectful parent, though no evidence was ever presented to support the allegations. A home study expert, hired by the father and paid for by Lawrence, spent thirty-five minutes in Donna's house and, leaning heavily on Donna's supposed lack of parenting skills, recommended custody be awarded to the father. The report is filled with words like "allege" and "claim," when referring to Donna's comments about her son and the father. Virtually everything she said is countered in the report in such a way as to leave no doubt that she was lying. All Donna's concerns about her son's aggressive behaviour, for which she sought professional help, read like the neurotic worries of an unbalanced woman. And throughout the report there is a subtle but clearly evident inference that who she was, who she'd been and what had been done to her were insurmountable.

At one point during the custody case, the judge, Moira Legere, questioned Donna about the trials of 1984, and the 1986 "Fifth Estate" documentary of the "hillbilly sex ring," which Donna saw for the first time in 1997. The judge asked her about the film and how she felt when she saw the Clan again. "I told her I jumped up and grabbed a mirror, and when she asked why, I told her I needed to check to make sure I didn't look like any of them. I just studied that mirror and the TV. I went back and forth—me, them, me, them—if I saw any resemblance I'd cut my hair, dye it, have a nose job, anything so I didn't look like them."

For three days, witnesses detailed Donna's faults, bringing up time and again her background, her instability, her lack of parenting skills. "It wasn't what they were saying that bothered me so much, it was the fact that they were saying because of who I was, because of what happened to me I should not raise a child. That was not me they were talking about. That isn't me. They made up that person based on my past. I am not a victim any more."

The father's case was financed by Donna's foster mother, including the home assessment by psychologist Sharon Cruickshank. That information, plus the fact that the father had not paid child support, had no home of his own but lived with his mother and often turned the child over to Donna's foster mother on his visitation days, made it seem that Donna had a strong case. Her lawyer, Leonard McKay, felt confident, especially after the expert testified that she based part of her assessment on a report drawn up two years earlier by social services after Donna had sought help with her son's behavioural problems. Much had changed in her life since that report, and when McKay asked Cruickshank about it, she admitted she would have to re-assess her recommendation to grant custody to the father.

During the agonzing wait for the desicion, her foster mother peppered Donna with phone calls and prowled her neighbourhood, peering at her house like a detective. She contacted the place where Donna worked and revealed what she had taken pains to hide. Donna was a Goler, one of them, part of that disgusting, infamous

Clan and Lawrence suggested the nursing home was remiss in hiring such a person.

A week before Donna's wedding, the sixty-page decision by the judge arrived. Donna had twenty-four hours to turn her son over to his father.

She had never felt such pain. Hot blades stabbed her again and again. She felt she was bleeding to death, suffocating, drowning—all at once. She'd made mistakes, she hadn't been perfect, she had learned to be a mother the hardest way imaginable. But Donna thought—no, was sure—she was a loving, responsible mother. Now the judge told her, in sixty pages, that she wasn't and that the man who'd had very little to do with raising his son over the previous five years, and had little experience in the day-to-day business of being a father, would be better suited to take care of him.

"Once a Goler, always a Goler," she whispered hoarsely while reading the judge's words. In the absence of any evidence of physical or psychological abuse, the judge turned to Donna's past for a reason to take her child away. "As reluctant as I am to create a situation which makes her bear the consequences of a childhood fraught with physical and sexual abuse, the welfare of the child must take priority."

It was a classic Catch 22. The major reason the judge cited for awarding custody to the father was the fact Donna didn't seek out counselling to deal with what had happened to her as a child. But when she did get help early in her son's life because he was exhibiting fairly severe behavioural problems, it was held against her. Common sense suggests that any child at the centre of a tug-of-war among two parents and a foster mother will act up, but the blame was all laid at Donna's door. The home study report, paid for by Roberta Lawrence, was highly critical of Donna and a key factor in the judge's decision. But no similar assessment on her behalf was made of the father or the foster mother, at whose home the child would clearly be spending a great deal of time.

Money played an important role. Donna couldn't afford the type of costly expert who spoke against her. In a very real sense Roberta Lawrence bought Donna Goler's child. "She probably would have got custody herself, if she'd applied for it," confirms Donna's lawyer.

Flight was Donna's first thought. Take her daughter, take her son and hope her fiancé would follow. In the end, she chose to do what she had always done—fight. She attacked the phone, calling anyone she could think of to help her; nearly a dozen lawyers, a provincial women's rights organization, her member of the Legislature, a friend in the police department. Finally, she took the most extreme step, the one most costly to herself—she went public.

Talking to a newspaper reporter and posing for a picture, for Donna, was equivalent to someone with severe vertigo jumping out of an airplane. But she pushed aside the fears of exposure she had nurtured for thirteen years. She didn't tell her entire story, only a tiny fraction of it, the fraction revolving around the loss of her son, and she cloaked herself with a false name. But her face was splashed across the page and the words in the story connected her to the Clan.

Having spent every penny, and more, on her first lawyer, finding a new one to handle an appeal wasn't easy: the transcripts alone from the first case would cost close to $2,000. It would be a long battle and possibly a hopeless one, and doubtless the father would be financed by the deep pockets of the foster mother. The judge did allow for a review in four months' time. Donna would wait and try again. "I may lose him," she admitted, "but by God, I'll go down fighting. I have a real family for the first time and I won't let some judge destroy that without fighting. Everything I did to become a mother and try to put together a good life, she used against me. I'll show her she was wrong."

Living without her son left Donna with a hollow, grinding feeling, like an ulcer eating away inside her. On his twice monthly visits Roberta Lawrence, in control of the child as Donna had expected, delivered and picked him up at a nearby donut shop. One day Donna arrived early and stepped into the restaurant for a coffee. When she looked out the window Lawrence was rifling through her car. Donna marched out to confront her just as her former foster mother was walking away with a folder containing odds and ends.

"Excuse me!" Donna said, fighting to keep her temper. "Don't you have enough of my life already?"

Lawrence, not the slightest bit concerned about being caught red-handed, said she was searching for a letter she thought the boy had written to his father. She didn't bother to explain why she took the folder, not did she apologize for invading Donna's car. She didn't need to. The judge had protected Roberta Lawrence well by placing virtually all blame for any of the boy's problems on Donna's shoulders and by ordering that Lawrence remain a "significant person" in the child's life. Even more frightening, the judge had made it clear that should the child experience any difficulties or trauma in his visits to his mother, she would re-examine Donna's already limited access to her son. Donna didn't dare risk protesting Lawrence's behaviour.

Little pieces of Donna's armour had begun to flake away during the tug-of-war over her son. She didn't notice at first, but gradually she began to worry less and less about two things that had been central to her for more than half her life—her father and her last name. As the weeks went by, an idea began to germinate. The trial had stripped away much of her protective covering and she'd ripped the rest off herself by going to the newspaper. She couldn't live her life constantly hoping no one would discover her, shutting out the thoughts and memories. And between the lines, the judge seemed to be saying that the only way Donna was going to get her son back was by confronting her past. The judge wanted her to do it in the acceptable, safe, middle-class way with counselling and therapy, fifty-minute discussions with a professional. Donna, as always, chose to do it her own way. She would go back—back to South Mountain.

First she looked for her anonymous benefactor, the person who had become so dear to her heart through the gifts of clothing and the hot lunches at school. She found him, an elderly Baptist dedicated to what he called an "anonymous ministry" of charity and help. She called to thank him, told him how much his gifts had meant to her—how much hope for a better life they had kindled in her. At first there was no response on the other end of the telephone, but after a time she realized he was crying. "In all my years serving on the Mountain, no one has ever tracked me down and thanked me. That wasn't supposed to happen," he said, his voice cracking. "We will never know how much those children and their families suffered. I'm so happy what little I did helped in some small way."

The second thing Donna did was make contact with one of her cousins, something she'd sworn never to do. She chose Matt. Though they hadn't seen each other in thirteen years, there was an immediate affinity. "Matt's a neat guy, and the best part of being with him is that you don't have to explain things to him—he knows, he lived through it." Matt surreptitiously got pictures of her from the Clan. When he turned them over to her, Donna couldn't tear her eyes away from the first sight of herself as a child, a scrawny little girl with huge eyes, a jagged part in her lank brown hair, and crooked teeth, grinning and squinting into the camera for a Grade 1 school photo. Two hours later, she was still poring over the picture.

She also sought out her birth and medical records. One of the first things she saw was the chart of her weight gain as a newborn. It's an ordinary thing—every hospital does one—but as Donna held the evidence of her early life, a sense of wonder enveloped her. "I had no past, nothing, no family pictures, mementoes. Nothing to say I even existed but now I have a piece of it back." She gazed at the lines rising on the graph. "Hey, look at that! What a pig I was!"

But all this was just the preliminaries, her preparation for the main event—Donna Goler's return to South Mountain.

◆

Standing where the wooden Stile used to be, Donna raises her arm and points down into the Valley at a low brick building just above the village of Gaspereau. "That's my school. I loved school. It was the only place I felt safe." She strolls the borders of the Stile, ducking under the branches of the neglected apple trees beginning to colour with the flowers soon to suffuse the landscape with the sight and scent that make the Annapolis Valley famous. For sixty-five years, the renowned Apple Blossom Festival has filled the towns and villages with floats, festivities, fireworks and tourists celebrating the bounty of its orchards. As a child, Donna never went to the Apple Blossom Parade, the biggest single event in the Valley.

They drive down into Gaspereau, over the picturesque bridge

spanning the river, past a dairy farm, up the hill and into the school-yard. She hops out, businesslike, walking back and forth, looking at the buildings and grounds as if she were a real estate agent conducting a site inspection. But when her eyes shift to the school's upper floor, her face softens and she smiles. There is no time or place in her first eleven years on earth that isn't blighted by dark memories, like pervasive scabs on unsprayed apples. But here in the Gaspereau school some light shone—arithmetic, spelling, books with neat, clean pages and orderly words, pictures on the walls and maps that pulled down like blinds to display the world, and food, glorious food—lunches provided by her mysterious benefactor. Certainly there was cruel teasing about her tatty clothes and shoes, an unsympathetic teacher or two and the constant reminder that even here, among other children from the Mountain, her poverty stood out and marked her. But it was also her place, somewhere she felt comfortable.

Donna opens her arms wide as if to hug the building. "God, if only I could have lived here everything would have been okay." She takes a big breath and grins. She doesn't feel sad and it surprises her a little. She feels curious, as anyone would visiting a childhood haunt; it's almost normal, a concept that makes her laugh when applied to her past. After snapping a few pictures, she waves her companion on. "C'mon, let's go!" She's sailed over the first hurdle and landed intact.

The next stop is the house where one of Donna's aunts now lives. "I wonder who she's fucking now," she says matter-of-factly, as if pondering her aunt's shopping habits or some other mundane detail of daily life. "I never could keep all the men straight. I don't think she ever got married—then again she never really needed to." As the car slowly rolls past, Donna cranes her head for one last look. "Hard to believe a Goler lives there, it looks too clean." She's disappointed there is no car in the driveway, and with the curtains drawn the house clearly looks as if no one is home. Donna has discovered that her aunt works in a restaurant and she suddenly develops an overwhelming urge for coffee.

The car has hardly stopped before Donna is out the door and marching into the restaurant. There are several women behind the counter. Donna dismisses them one by one. "Too young, too pretty, too thin, too neat." This last is said with a chuckle. She's thoroughly enjoying herself. A beaten-down older woman emerges from the kitchen with over-dyed hair, a substantial belly hanging over chicken legs and a worn face marked by a black eye. "Maybe, maybe." A young waiter approaches as Donna, standing at the counter, slowly stirs her coffee and stares hard at the woman. "Can I help you?"

"Nope," she replies cheerfully. "Just being nosy." The man smiles at her. "No charge for that." Donna boldly asks him the woman's name—it's not her aunt. Then she asks when her aunt works and he tells her she comes in at night.

When Donna talks about her years as a Goler, she lends a painter's eye to the detail. She describes events with distance, sparely, but deftly coloured by emotion and splashes of surprising humour. "The first time I remember the whole thing happening to me was my birthday, the last day of school, grade primary [kindergarten]. I came home all excited because I got my report card and my little graduation cap. Him and Wanda had a fight, she left and he blamed us. Sandra stomped off and Lisa was sleeping. He beat me with a belt and then—I don't know how you would put it—then he came up to me. I think it stands out because I was beaten so bad. Then afterward he said he was sorry, after he made love to me."

Donna pauses, aware of how odd the word *love* sounds in relation to her father. "Or whatever you want to call it," she adds wryly. "He was always telling me he was making love, he loved me and all this crap and if I told anybody he said he'd kill me. He didn't care two hoots about us. All he wanted was a boy. That's all he cared about, he wanted somebody to take the name."

As Donna sips her coffee and speaks softly of the cruelty and degradation suffered at her father's hand, Madonna sings, "Don't Cry for Me, Argentina," in the background. Donna smiles and nods her head in agreement at the sentiment. Then a guffaw erupts. "Hey, you want a good laugh? Take a look at that." She gestures at a baseball-capped man who has entered the restaurant and is ogling her. She stares back. "Why do men always gawk?" she queries idly, then slides her eyes down to his crotch and breaks into giggles as she points out the gawker's wide-open zipper. He moves along quickly.

Donna has come back to South Mountain not to talk to her relatives, but to observe them, refresh the picture of the Clan in her mind, confront the memory. "Kinda like going to a farm to see what a pig looks like because you haven't seen one for a while," she says, savouring the image. "I don't have to get back at them. I don't have to get even. I'm past that. I can just sit on the sidelines waiting for the day they all die." Donna reads the newspaper avidly and her favourite section is the obituary column. "You want to see something funny? You watch me go down there with a bottle of champagne and watch my old man get buried. I'll be toasting the day."

Donna does admit that occasionally, when the mood strikes, revenge has a pleasant taste. "If I was giving out punishment," she muses, "the first thing I would do is chop off his little thingamajiggy. No, I wouldn't do that first. First I would tie him to a chair, take that belt that he hit *me* with and beat him as hard as I could, as many times as I could, before he passed out. Then I'd put salt in his wounds and cut his little thingy off. No, first I'd circumcise him and then cut his thingy off. Wanda—I'd just run her over." Revenge is simply something Donna toys with in her mind. It would require involvement. Observing the Clan and where they now live is one thing; retribution would re-connect her to them.

But this day a different kind of revenge is in the forefront of Donna's mind, thanks to her reading material on the long drive to the Mountain. She ignored the scenery as her companion drove through the stark, grey Halifax shale, past the white gypsum-rich cliffs of the Rawdon Hills and up the gentle slope leading out of Windsor offering the first panoramas of Minas Basin and Blomidon. As she read, she concluded there was a reckoning due, but not with the Goler Clan.

Each page she turned brought more colour into her alabaster skin. She shook her head in astonishment. "Will you look at this?" she muttered once. Another time, "I can't believe this!" She laughed sardonically now and then. Donna Goler held her medical records, the history of her life from birth to age four, then in sketchy detail until age ten. They document a dreadful litany of neglect by her parents that was known, noted and ignored by the medical profession.

At least seventeen hospital visits before she was two, constant high temperatures, bleeding rashes, nine instances of bronchitis in four years, anorexia, severe mouth sores, worms, fleas, pustules on her face and chin, malnutrition, seizures and a general failure to thrive.

Each time Donna was sent home to conditions described in her records as too wretched for any child, let alone a sick one. At eight months, "tiny child, does not sit, does appear bland with inappropriate crying. Does notice objects but other than this its development is markedly retarded" and "baby was discharged with no hope of improvement at home and probably necessity of readmission." At fourteen months, "Mother highly inadequate, father just as bad." One month later, "Extremely withdrawn and fearful child. Hides behind her hands. Initially refused to co-operate. Very irritable." Eighteen months after that, "Family situation is well known, being both mentally inadequate parents and a home situation which makes it impossible to care for sick child."

A harsh laugh explodes out of Donna as she flicks the page to another report. "Well, this is nice, this is perfect! Did you know I am mentally retarded? Says so right here. Well, that explains everything, doesn't it?"

One name appears over and over in her records—Dr. Paul Kinsman, respected physician, later a member of the Nova Scotia Legislature, an honoured, important Valley citizen. It is Kinsman who diagnoses her as developmentally and mentally retarded yet sends her back to the Goler Clan sixteen times in twenty-five months.

It is Saturday and Donna drives to Dr. Paul Kinsman's office in Wolfville, a small medical building tucked up against a long stretch of apple orchards and shaded by elegant old trees. The building is locked. Donna startles the cleaner inside by banging on the door. The doctor is not in. Next she checks the phone book for his address, which leads her to a tidy but modest old yellow house in the centre of town. Laundry dangles from a clothesline, the front porch sags slightly and there appears to be no driveway for a car—hardly what you'd expect for a rich Valley doctor. An elderly woman redirects her to the Ridge Road above Wolfville, just beyond the Stile.

It is a glorious day, one of those perfect mixes of clear, sweet, blossom-scented air, and a lush canvas of green that the Mountain serves up now and again. As the car climbs the hill leading towards South Mountain for the second time and crests the Ridge, it's a little hard to believe that the lovely stretch of road has been a dividing point between good and bad, moral and immoral, intelligence and stupidity, for more than two hundred years. Recently, the dividing line has been breached by Valley people who have come to realize that the Mountain possesses extraordinary views and inexpensive land. Since the Goler trials, large custom homes have begun to appear on plots commanding the choicest vistas. In places, splendid structures with generous garages, rose gardens, Mexican tile foyers and floor-to-ceiling native stone fireplaces sit uncomfortably close to homes where the family room, living room and kitchen are one.

Dr. Kinsman's house, well back from the Ridge Road, is framed by landscaping artfully placed so as not to disturb the 360-degree views. Though it is modern, it has a charming weathered look and blends tastefully into its surroundings. A short distance from the Stile, the Kinsman house, and its neighbour, have begun to redefine the tone of the area. "It's all gettin' some fancy," sniffs an old woman whose family has lived on the Ridge for seven generations. "Perfessors and doctors and all them, pretty soon the Queen'll be moving in." She points at Kinsman's house. "That one's got three bathrooms, leastaways that's what I hear!"

Donna knocks on the door, her normally pale face growing even whiter when she hears footsteps approaching. A small, slender man roughly dressed in gardening clothes answers—Dr. Paul Kinsman. Donna shakily asks for a few minutes of his time and he graciously ushers her and her companion inside to sit down in his spacious, dark wood–floored living room. "I'm not sure you'll want me to stay when you hear what I have to say," Donna warns, nerves quavering her voice. She perches on the edge of a love-seat and Kinsman sits beside her. He is the consummate professional with a well-honed bedside manner; he smiles encouragingly as if she is a reluctant patient raising a sensitive medical issue. There is an awkward pause as Donna fumbles for her first words.

Suddenly she smacks her hand on her medical records. "I want you to explain this!" Once launched she soars. Outrage, anger, disbelief pour from her. Kinsman briefly looks taken aback by the intensity of her emotion, but he is a smooth, practised man who quickly masks his feelings. "You wrote right here that my mother was incompetent, my father was incompetent. You said they couldn't look after me." She stabs her finger at the records. "I understand you're upset," Kinsman soothes, using the tone of voice perfected on thousands of patients. It's a mistake. "I'm not upset!" Donna explodes. "I'm angry!"

She begins reading phrases she has underlined. "Mental retardation! How'd you get that?" Kinsman explains he likely diagnosed her as such because of her appearance and her lack of response to normal stimulation. "I was probably starving to death," Donna shoots back. "Look at this: you admit me, fatten me up for a few days and send me back. Here, look here, I gain weight after my first meal. I'm in the medical field, I know what this means."

Seeing an opportunity, Kinsman unctuously tries to shift the focus of the conversation. "Ah, you're in the medical field. What do you do?" Donna brushes the question aside and bombards him with more of her own. "Why didn't you call someone, social services, someone? They could have taken me away, given me a good home, a good start on life. I could have had a family who cared about me. You knew how bad it was and you did nothing." Kinsman rakes his fingers through his hair and nods calmly, sympathetically. "The law was different then," he intones, emitting sincerity and concern from every pore. "We weren't required to report certain things as we are today."

"But you're a doctor, you're supposed to do more than stick a bandaid on," Donna emphasizes. Again Kinsman tries to move the subject away from the medical records. "I can understand that you feel your life would have been better, your current situation . . ." Donna blazes at him, "My life is fine! I made it what it is through my own sweat and blood, no thanks to people like you." Kinsman tries again: "I understand how you feel . . ." Another mistake.

"Pardon me," Donna roars, "you can't understand! You have no idea what we went through." Her voice drops. "But you could have changed things. You saw, you knew, you could have done something.

You kept sending me back to live where I wouldn't put pigs. Sixteen times in two years, you kept sending me back."

"Well, your mother wanted you. Your parents wanted to keep you," Kinsman replies weakly.

"Wanted! Wanted! I want a nice, big house like this. Should I get it just because I want it? I want fifty children. I can't care for them but I want fifty children. Does that mean I should get them?"

Under Donna's relentless attack, Kinsman rearranges himself constantly on the cushiony love-seat, inching infinitesimally away from her until he is wedged against the arm. It is the only sign of discomfort in the man. "Hindsight is a wonderful thing," he says, conceding nothing. A few tears of frustration and sadness dampen Donna's cheeks and she impatiently wipes them away. "It's not just that I was sick over and over again. High temperature, acute bronchitis, sores all over my mouth. But lots of times my mother brought me in and there was nothing wrong. She must have begged you to admit me and take care of me. I can see you were getting fed up, look here."

Donna reads his words, contempt chasing disbelief and outrage in her tone. "Listen to this," she says. "Same old story. In hospital in March, 2 months ago. Ill defined complaints on part of mother in the office but when mother gets it in her mind the child is sick, she will persist seeing doctor after doctor until she gets child in hospital. i.e. with a story that forces Dr. to admit to observe re the complaints of mother.' She was asking for help! They couldn't look after me! *You knew that!* You had a responsibility. How can you call yourself a doctor? You're a disgrace!"

Kinsman begins to show a hint of his aggravation; his hands scrub repeatedly through his hair. "What exactly do you want?" his voice rises slightly. Donna gives him a half-smile. "You know what I think? You thought I was retarded. You wrote that lots of times. You thought my parents were mental. So it didn't matter what happened to me." This strikes home. Kinsman sits up. "No!" he responds with the only emotion he has let show. "No, that's not true." Donna pauses for a moment and leans slightly towards him. "I wouldn't let my children anywhere near you." She taps the papers. "You call this medical care? You should never have been a doctor."

At that moment Donna realizes her words are bouncing off him like rubber balls. She stands up quickly, giving one last contemptuous look at the man who did not think it was his responsibility to report the hopelessly inadequate care and appalling neglect of "Baby Donna Goler." She marches from the room, leaving the beautiful house for the midday sunshine illuminating the red banks of Blomidon in the distance. The car backs out of the driveway and heads along the Ridge Road. Donna draws a deep breath. "I hope I ruined his day."

Strangely, returning to the Mountain has taken on the air of a celebration, akin to getting stitches out after a terrible wound has slowly healed. No matter how gruesome the scar left behind, taking out the stitches represents an end. Donna confesses she is nervous but eager; once she made the decision to come back, she couldn't wait.

Her next stop is the one she has been avoiding for thirteen years— White Rock, her father's house. The winding Deep Hollow Road looks exactly as she remembers it. For much of her childhood, the Golers had no car and she recalls the agony of her legs in the seemingly endless walk from the small store in White Rock up the huge hill to her home. At one bend in the road, she comes across the rubble of a home site; nothing much is left but a refrigerator, piles of garbage and the pieces of an old wood stove. Only the outhouse is still standing, leaning back towards the trees as if it would like to retreat from such a desolate place.

"There!" she shouts. "That's where he lived, Lawrence whatshisname, that bastard!" Her companion asks, "Which bastard?" Donna grins. "Right, there were a lot of them." As the car moves on, she twists around to look at the sad remnants of habitation. "I remember when Lawrence first came into the picture," she muses, "my father abused me right in front of him. He thought it was great."

Up past the White Rock crossroads, over the bridge and past the hydro dam. At the edges of the pond created by the dam, groups of people are fishing happily. Their presence is odd, so ordinary, in comparison with Donna's mission. As the road straightens and the fields widen near the top of White Rock Mountain, she sucks in her breath and holds it. Up ahead is a copse of trees and a white house, so small it seems miniature. A dog is chained up outside and a large dark red late-model car is parked in the driveway.

"Will you look at that! I grew up with a bucket to shit in, no running water, no electricity and got screwed or beaten any time those bunch of sickos felt like it. Now they've got a government house, water, everything. They still don't work. Look at that car. I wonder where that came from."

Donna's tone lightens. "There's the blueberry field," she says, pointing out a patch of rough grass. "At least that's where it was. My old house was there, Henry's broken-down wreck there and my grandparents' back there." When told that her home has been recently towed away for use as a garden shed she chortles, "I guess that's all it was good for. Gee, I wonder if the people who took it knew who it belonged to. If they did they might burn it."

Donna peers out the window and reaches for her camera. She snaps one picture and as she is refocusing for a second the front door swings open. A middle-aged man, short, stocky and powerful looking, steps out of the house. "What in hell are ya doin'? Dontcha got no respect!" he shouts angrily. "Get outta here, you assholes! Go on or you'll be sorry! Get outta here!"

William Goler. Donna's father. The creature of her nightmares strides forward ominously. Donna turns to her companion, as if for support, then shifts her body to face her father. She extends her arm out the open car window and thrusts her middle finger high in the air. As the car pulls away, she gives him the finger again as if recocking a rifle.

Eyes closed, breath coming in shallow puffs, Donna leans back against the seat. "Oh God! Oh God, that felt so good!" She repeats the phrase over and over all the way back down Deep Hollow Road.

Donna has one more stop before she leaves the Mountain—the graveyard where some of her relatives are buried. "I know they're dead, I just want to make sure." The cemetery is in West Brooklyn near the eastern point where the Mountain and the Valley tail out and blend into each other. The Baptist church, situated as most of them are at a crossroads, is typical of the area—tidy, white and modest. Behind it stretches a graveyard, less than one-third inhabited. She walks through the wrought-iron gates and winds her way past the stones. "Hey, don't step there!" she admonishes her companion. "Move! You're standing right on him."

"Whoever it is he's long dead," her friend replies. "Oh, I know, it's silly but I just hate the idea of walking over them. It's a bit of respect." Then she remembers her father shouting that same word at her less than an hour ago. "See, I do have some respect. Just none for him."

Donna searches the graves for familiar names. Many sites have no proper stones, just small, white wooden crosses, about eight inches high. They look like crossed popsicle sticks, only a little larger. Someone has written the plot number on each one and the dead person's name; 81—G. Pinch, 67—F. Kelly. No date of birth or death or details of next of kin. In several cases not even a first initial. Donna approaches one stone in the back row. It is incongruous among the severely utilitarian monuments that fill the cemetery, a large pink granite heart with etched flourishes and the names of three people inscribed across the bottom: GOLAR—Cranswick, his son Eric and his wife Ruth May. She's mildly curious about her grandfather's half-brother, Cranswick, and his family, but she doesn't remember meeting them.

Nearby is another gravestone, a rectangular chunk of grey, chipped rock tilting to one side. The letters on its face, the plastic, stick-on mailbox variety available in hardware stores, read: Charles Goler, 190 –1987. The last number of his birth date is missing. Behind the grave is a rusty metal post driven into the ground. On it hangs a gaudy plastic banner rimmed with a pink flowered border and across the middle, in red, is written in small plastic flowers the word DADDY. For a moment the terrible sadness of that single word hangs over the cemetery.

Not a flicker of sentiment crosses her face as she stands in front of her grandfather's headstone, staring. Suddenly Donna leaps into the air and lands on his grave. Up and down she jumps. Her statement is over as quickly as it began. "There." She dusts off her hands. "That's better. Let's go."

On the way back to the car, Donna stops abruptly and looks back over the gravestones and little crosses. "There were babies, you know," she says when her companion joins her. "The kids had babies.

I saw one of them buried." Several other Golers will hesitantly confirm that there were children born to the young girls of the Clan, some of them not more than ten or eleven years old. "I could hear her screaming," Donna whispers. "There was a doctor from the Valley there to help. He was one of the men my father rented us to." She smiles sadly at her friend's shock. "Hard to believe, isn't it? So many people knew. So many people did nothing."

She describes the baby's birth, her deformed limbs, the growth on her belly, even the name given to her by the child's mother. It was early evening and the light was just fading. The doctor had a bottle in his hand, soaked a rag with a sickly smelling liquid and placed it over the baby's mouth and nose. Donna recognizes now that the substance was ether. "We all got in the car and drove for quite a while. I don't know why they bothered to come so far. They dug a hole. I guess the ether was wearing off because she started crying again. She was wrapped in a striped blanket. They put her in a box and buried her—alive."

For the first time that day she is overwhelmed. The weight of the past appears to crush her and for a moment she looks as if she might collapse. It is the first time she has spoken to anybody, except her fiancé, about the unknown Clan babies.

With so many men, whose idea of birth control was "spilling my seed on the ground," forcing themselves so many times on so many female children, there had to be babies. Officially, various authorities all deny they knew anything. Privately it is a different story. "It's been going on in that area for so long, why should this generation be any different?" one social worker says. "Oh, yes, we knew the stories," a policeman agrees. "There were at least four children born to the adult members of the Clan in the same way—when they were just children and probably fathered by an uncle, a grandfather or a father. Two of them are apparently still alive in a home and two more are dead. One died after living part of his life tied to a tree at one of the homes."

Donna takes one last look. "I'd like to find them all and put up a stone or a cross, something, just to let them know they are remembered."

It's been a long day, exhilarating, draining, nerve-racking, cele-
bratory and sad. Donna settles in her seat for the drive back. The
car has barely left the Mountain when she turns to her companion.
"I want to go back. I need to see it one more time." There's no hatred
or bitterness in her voice, just an earnest desire to embed in her mind
what is left of the place where she spent the first half of her life, to
remind herself of what she escaped and, most of all, to leave a last-
ing imprint of the four walls that house the man the courts called
her father. What harm can it do?

The sun is casting long shadows by the time the car tops the Ridge
and once again heads up Deep Hollow Road towards White Rock.
Donna isn't nervous this time as the car stops on the shoulder of the
road. After years of worrying that he would find her, she has come
to him. She is the stalker this time, he the prey. She takes out her
camera again. "Am I violating his rights or anything? I hope so."

The door of William Goler's house swings open shortly after the
car stops and a shorter, stouter, balding man marches out quickly,
glances furtively at the onlookers and dives into the passenger side
of the car parked near the house. It's Donna's uncle, Cranswick. He
backs out from the car, his arm crooked as if he were carrying something long. Donna suddenly recalls that Cranswick was the hunter
in the family. "Time to go!" At the same instant, William comes running out of the house, also carrying something indistinguishable.

As they drive down the Mountain, Donna shakes her head.
"Whew! Probably wasn't a gun or anything. Right?" Then her companion looks in the rear-view mirror and sees the red car emerging
from William's driveway, spitting gravel. As it hits the pavement,
oily smoke pouring from its tires, the car accelerates so quickly its
body rocks violently from side to side. It comes over the rise directly
behind them at such speed it takes air. Only a battered blue van, a
few car lengths back, protects them. The red car barrels up behind
the van and pulls out to pass, swinging back in again as the road
twists sharply.

"Go! Go!" shouts Donna. What to do? Drop back and prevent
them from getting in front of the van or floor it and try to leave the
pursuers behind? Dropping back increases the risk that the Golers

will get in front of them and force them to stop. On the other hand, Donna's car is a subcompact, no match for her father's larger, faster vehicle. They choose distance and speed. The Valley is four miles away, the police station in Wolfville eight.

It takes every ounce of concentration to stay on the road—its treacherous bends and dips are built for fifty kilometres an hour, not eighty, touching on one hundred. The van pulls into a side road and William's car roars up behind, smashing into their rear bumper, once and then again. The Golers' faces are like horror-show caricatures. Enraged gargoyles, lips spread in snarls of fury, faces pressed as close to the windshield as they can get. Surely someone will notice two men chasing two women down the Mountain and intervene. But it is a quiet Saturday, late in the afternoon: the road is deserted.

The car smacks them again, jarring gasps of terror from Donna and her friend, forcing them onto the shoulder in a spray of gravel and dirt. It gives William an opening and he swings out to pass, nosing them over—the ditch and trees loom. Deep Hollow saves them with a whippy cutback that drives their pursuers wide, giving them the precious inches needed to pull ahead again.

As they reach the bridge near the crossroads, the speedometer tops one hundred. A bump, at the edge of the pavement, sends them sailing into the air, forcing them to brake sharply as the car slides on landing. Another opening. The Golers draw even with them again. It seems certain they will sideswipe the women. Donna ducks down into her sweatshirt. "He can't recognize me!"

"Which way? Which way?" demands her companion as the village intersection looms. Donna's head pops up. "Straight. Don't stop!" They roar through White Rock and pass the lumber mill. Chunks of mud from the trucks are strewn across the road. Time freezes. The road ahead is flat, its curves gentle. Donna and her friend can't outrun William and Cranswick now. In their plummet down the Mountain, they haven't seen a single car, except for the van. Then a glorious vision, a sedately moving old truck carefully driven by a wizened man. His eyes bug at the sight of the two cars, side by side, streaking towards him. He has nowhere to go and his horn honks out an alarm. William drops back. Just ahead is the highway overpass and people beyond, lots of them, wonderful, normal, everyday people.

As civilization looms, the Goler car abruptly pulls over. Donna and her friend can hardly believe their pursuers have given up. Shakily, they drive the last half mile into the Valley, hands damp, hearts thudding. At the first opportunity, they too stop. For a few seconds the only sounds are strangled, heaving breaths.

"I don't bleed well," Donna says inexplicably. "What? What are you talking about?" her friend gasps. "I don't bleed well. I get nicked and I just rain blood." It's funny—hysterically, ludicrously funny. The women scream with laughter until they are reduced to near sobs. "Wait a minute," Donna gasps out. "They might be coming back!" Her friend tromps on the accelerator and the car shoots into the traffic, nearly sending another driver into a head-on collision with an oncoming car. "Some adventure, huh?" Donna comments blandly as they drive soberly through Wolfville. This too is hilarious, convulsing them.

In Grand Pré the dying sun has warmed the dikeland into rosy fields broken by the rounded humps built by the Acadians two hundred and fifty years ago. Donna and her friend stop at a small store that once served the finest lobster roll in the province—an Atlantic specialty, chunks of seasoned lobster meat, mayonnaise and celery in a hot dog bun. People from away often think it sacrilege to pack such delicious morsels in a cheap, white, store-bought hot dog bun. But the flavour is uniquely Maritime and after a few months most people get over their aversion. Now the lobster rolls are long gone and the two women settle for drinks instead. "I don't drink," observes Donna after a long swig of chocolate milk. "But this might be the time to start."

They feel buoyant, elated as they drive away from the Valley. What a day, what an ending. "Gee," says Donna, thinking of how abruptly their pursuers gave up the chase. "Maybe Cran had another heart attack. That'd be nice." Two weeks later she will discover that is exactly what happened. "Didn't kill him though. I guess I'll have to keep reading the obits."

Suddenly Donna's hand reaches out and grabs her friend's arm, the car wobbles as she starts with the strength of Donna's grip. "Did you see them?" Her voice cracks with horror. Her friend's eyes shoot to the mirror, expecting the red car to be bearing down on them again. There is nothing, only a ribbon of highway in both directions. "See what?"

"Toys! There were toys in front of *his* house. Kids' toys!"

Epilogue

✦ FOUR WEEKS AFTER DONNA GOLER'S
return to South Mountain her father, William, and uncle, Cranswick, were charged with two counts each of sexual assault and sexual touching involving a three-year-old girl. She is the daughter of
one of the original victims.

Notes

The following notes reflect quotes taken from print, radio or television sources. All other quotes come from interviews by the authors.

Chapter One
4 "Over the brow": Wright, p. 170.
5 "remote, dull, stupid": Foster, p. 168.
5 "all the luxuries": Foster, p. 169.
6 "The weather co-operated": Wright, p. 172.
7 "It does not, we believe": Wright, p. 162.
7 "The pews in there": Wright, p. 163.
8 "And it was such good glass": Wright, p. 166.
8 "Wouldn't her mother": Wright, p. 167.

Chapter Two
18 "one of the greatest deeds": Clarke, p.26.
19 "lands and tenements": Ross and Deveau, p. 62.
23 "ignorant, indolent, bad managers": cited in Brebner, p. 139 and 142.
24 "scum of the colonies": Armstrong, p. 25.
25 "The Christians were sometimes": Eaton, p. 308.
26 "But just to be sure": Foster, p. 170–71.
28 "O Lord, when will": Untitled, Acadia Archives, Acadia Institute collection, file 6-2-2.
30 "he has had as much antagonism": Hillis, p. 14.
30 "While some of the people": Edith White thesis.
32 "In the schools": Wright, p. 152–54.

Chapter Three

41 "Now then, Ada": from Allen Robertson, family oral history.
43 "Thus were lost": Wright, p. 108.
43 "As a password": Wright, p. 109.
44 "What we owe": South Mountain Study, Acadia Archives, Acadia Institute collection, file 6-2-2.
47 "degenerate stock in the community": White thesis.
47 "be protected from the immigration": White thesis.
47 "Enough vitality remains": White thesis.
47 "Many of the girls": White thesis.

Chapter Four

50 "Early evening, with the sun": Wright, p. 41.
51 "There was a strange": Wright, p.188.
53 "A generation ago": Wright, p. 65.
54 "Two of the girls": Esther Wright to G.B. Hillis, Nov. 3, 1958. Acadia Institute collection, file 6-2-3.
54 "2 room shack": Gaspereau Study, field notes, Acadia Institute collection, file 6-3-2.
55 "over industrious, over-moraled": Gaspereau Study, field notes, Acadia Institute collection, file 6-3-2.
55 "deplorable social, moral": *Chronicle Herald*, October 2, 1950.
56 "shockingly inaccurate and irresponsible": *The Acadian*, October 19, 1950.
56 "It is a play ground": Wright, p. 46–47.
57 "The usual practice": Wright, p. 49.
57 "to expand the contribution": Hiltz and Morse, p. 1.
57 "The persistence and magnitude": Norman H. Morse to the Honourable Malcolm Leonard, Minister of Public Welfare, June 23, 1958.
58 "gain at first hand": Fraser, 1957.
59 "a group of 'ignorant": F. Clarke Fraser to Norman H. Morse, November 27, 1958. Acadia Institute collection.
59 "Like a pumpkin-blossom": F. Clarke Fraser to John A. DeCoste, November 11, 1989. Acadia Institute collection.
59 "In most of the families": Soltan, January 1962.
60 "contemplating a consanguineous": Soltan, January 1962.
61 "clubbing of the fingers": Hugh N.A. MacDonald, M.D. to Dr. Hubert Soltan, June 28, 1961. Acadia Institute collection.
61 "Any stealing in the valley": Hillis, p. 29.
62 "[T]he valley folk find": Hillis, p. 30.

62 "The valley people have been ardent": Hillis, p. 30

63 "mountain folk were born": Hillis, p. 16.

63 "There are some rather strong": Fred Hockey to G.C. Baker, Acadia Institute collection.

63 "On page 16 a minister": G.C. Baker to Fred Hockey, Acadia Institute collection.

Chapter Five

72 "We now wait for something": O'Leary, p. 53, King's County Vignettes.

78 "can't talk, has tantrums": Fundy Mental Health Clinic records, 1956.

78 "cannot talk plain": Hubert Soltan, research notes, Acadia Institute collection.

Chapter Six

88 "Presumably, the physical presence": Finkelhor, p. 24.

90 "She was 9 years old": Toronto Star, April 11, 1980.

90 "My mother was away": Toronto Star, April 16, 1984.

90 "This is not a nice conversation": Globe and Mail, August 30, 1980.

Chapter Seven

102 "That's an odd way": William Goler preliminary inquiry, July 10, 1984, Stella Goler cross examination.

102 "I have heard Willie": William Goler preliminary inquiry, July 10, 1984, Stella Goler cross examination.

110 "At the Goler residence": Cranswick Goler preliminary inquiry, May 24, 1984, Constable Craig direct examination.

111 "I might as well be truthful": Cranswick Goler preliminary inquiry, May 24, 1984, Constable Craig direct examination.

111 "If I knew you fellows": Cranswick Goler statement to police, February 24, 1984.

Chapter Eight

115 "I've had sex with them all": Ralph Kelly statement to police, February 24, 1984.

116 "Every time I tried": William Goler preliminary inquiry, July 10, 1984, Stella Goler direct examination.

118 "He has become open": William Goler trial, July 24, 25 and August 3, 1984, Rayburne McNeil direct examination.

119 "The Bible is not": "Fifth Estate," CBC documentary, March 1986.
119 "It's no longer something": The *Advertiser*, February 22, 1984.
124 "You had sexual intercourse": William Goler trial, July 24, 25 and August 3, 1984, Sandra Goler direct examination.
129 "All right, and what did your uncle William": William Goler trial, July 24, 25 and August 3, 1984, Pam direct examination.
131 "Now when was the last time": William Goler trial, July 24, 25 and August 3, 1984, Pam cross-examination.
135 "Your Honour, you're probably": William Goler trial, July 24, 25 and August 3, 1984, arguments.
136 "Now, at any time": William Goler preliminary inquiry, April 13, 1984, Doug direct examination.
138 "Do you know William": William Goler preliminary inquiry, April 13, 1984, Matt direct examination.
139 "Do you know William": William Goler preliminary inquiry, April 13, 1984, Donna direct examination.

Chapter Nine
148 "Did anybody go upstairs": Cranswick Goler preliminary inquiry, May 24, 1984, Donna direct examination.
150 "I might as well be": Cranswick Goler statement to police, February 24, 1984.
151 "I wouldn't hurt anybody": Cranswick Goler statement to police, February 24, 1984.
151 "What happened, Doug": Cranswick Goler preliminary inquiry, May 24, 1984, Doug direct examination.
153 "Now did Mr. Goler": Cranswick Goler preliminary inquiry, May 24, 1984, Sandra direct examination.
153 "When you make love to her": Cranswick Goler statement to police, February 24, 1984.
154 "The first time I was": Cranswick Goler statement to police, February 24, 1984.
154 "I don't like her anyway": Cranswick Goler statement to police, February 24, 1984.
155 "When was the last time": Cranswick Goler preliminary inquiry, May 24, 1984, Jeff direct examination.
157 "Pam, did you ever see": Cranswick Goler preliminary inquiry, May 24, 1984, Pam direct examination.
157 "He took his own pants": Cranswick Goler statement to police, February 24, 1984.

158 "Now at any time": Cranswick Goler preliminary inquiry, May 24, 1984, Matt direct examination.

159 "Do I have to say it": Wanda Whiston preliminary inquiry, June 13, 1984, Donna direct examination.

160 "at a mentally retarded level": Dr. L.R. Denton, psychological evaluation of Henry Goler, December 18, 1984.

161 "thrown in the cooler": Dr. L.R. Denton, psychological evaluation of Henry Goler, December 18, 1984.

161 "I put my finger": Henry Goler statement to police, February 14, 1984.

161 "his dink in Lisa's": Henry Goler preliminary inquiry, May 10, 1984.

162 "Who is Kenny": Cranswick Goler preliminary inquiry, May 24, 1984, Sandra direct examination.

Chapter Ten

167 "He left some wicked": William Goler trial, July 24, 25 and August 3, 1984, Stella Goler direct examination.

168 "Roy beat hell": William Goler trial, July 24, 25 and August 3, 1984, Stella Goler direct examination.

168 "to keep his damn hands": William Goler trial, July 24, 25 and August 3, 1984, Stella Goler direct examination.

168 "I hardly ever let": William Goler trial, July 24, 25 and August 3, 1984, Stella Goler direct examination.

168 "*She* put my cock": Roy Hiltz's statement, February 16, 1984.

169 "Now Donna, did you ever see": Cranswick Goler preliminary inquiry, May 24, 1984, Donna cross-examination.

170 "Did you think they would not": Cranswick Goler preliminary inquiry, May 24, 1984, Donna cross-examination.

171 "You're in a foster home": Cranswick Goler preliminary inquiry, May 24, 1984, Donna cross-examination.

172 "Insects?": CBC Television News interview, May 11, 1984.

172 "a good provider": Dr. L.R. Denton, psychological evaluation of Mary Goler, May 8, 1985.

173 "He was quite talkative": Earl Johnstone preliminary inquiry, May 17, 1984, Ted Corkum testimony.

174 "She was hinting around": Earl Johnstone statement to police, February 15, 1984.

174 "He's not that type of man": Earl Johnstone preliminary inquiry, May 17, 1984, Josephine Goler direct examination.

174 "Okay, and how many times": Earl Johnstone preliminary inquiry, May 17, 1984, Pam direct examination.

177 "I didn't come in her": Lawrence Kelly statement to police, February 16, 1984.

177 "Because I was horny": Lawrence Kelly statement to police, February 16, 1984.

179 "could have a piece": Gabriel Dodge statement to police, February 17, 1984.

179 "had sex with them all": Ralph Kelly statement to police, February 24, 1984.

179 "started playing with my": Ralph Kelly statement to police, February 24, 1984.

180 "She followed me over": Ralph Kelly statement to police, February 24, 1984.

180 "screw standing up in the water": Ralph Kelly statement to police, February 24, 1984.

Chapter Eleven

185 "You're coming in here": Wanda Whiston preliminary inquiry, May 10, 1984, Sandra direct examination.

186 "was basically like the": Wanda Whiston preliminary inquiry, May 10, 1984, Sandra direct examination.

186 "my cunt—she made": Wanda Whiston preliminary inquiry, May 10, 1984, Pam direct examination.

187 "Then Dad would come": Wanda Whiston preliminary inquiry, May 10, 1984, Donna re-direct.

188 "If you do I'm gonna": Wanda Whiston preliminary inquiry, May 10, 1984, Sandra direct examination.

188 "I was visiting Nannie and Papa": Wanda Whiston preliminary inquiry, May 10, 1984, Matt direct examination.

188 "She was putting her finger": Wanda Whiston preliminary inquiry, May 10, 1984, Donna re-direct.

189 "I only looked": Wanda Whiston preliminary inquiry, May 10, 1984, Donna direct examination.

189 "She pulled her pants down": Wanda Whiston preliminary inquiry, May 10, 1984, Jeff direct examination.

189 "She puts all the pressure": Wanda Whiston preliminary inquiry, May 10, 1984, Jeff direct examination.

190 "Well, she just wanted": Wanda Whiston preliminary inquiry, May 10, 1984, Jeff direct examination.

190 "started doing dirty stuff": Wanda Whiston preliminary inquiry, May 10, 1984, Jeff direct examination.

190 "kiss her and feel": Wanda Whiston preliminary inquiry, May 10, 1984, Doug direct examination.

191 "She told me she had": Lawrence Kelly statement to police, February 16, 1984.

191 "She told me about her": Ralph Kelly statement to police, February 24, 1984.

192 "Have you ever screwed": Cranswick Goler statement to police, February 14, 1984.

193 "Why would she make": William Goler trial, July 24, 25 and August 3, 1984, Stella Goler cross-examination.

193 "being bad": Cranswick Goler preliminary inquiry, May 24, 1984, Matt re-direct.

194 "put her finger up": Mary Goler preliminary inquiry, February 1, 1985, Matt direct examination.

195 "her boobies and stuff": Mary Goler preliminary inquiry, February 1, 1985, Jeff direct examination.

Chapter Twelve

196 "The mess consisted of": The *Advertiser*, May 23, 1984.

201 "he was never really loved": Fred Golar pre-sentence report, February 15, 1985.

203 "On the way, we started": Fred Golar preliminary inquiry, September 5, 1984, Wendy direct examination.

204 "God, I feel terrible!": Fred Golar statement to police, May 12, 1984.

205 "My mother is his": Fred Golar preliminary inquiry, September 5, 1984, Wendy direct examination.

205 "What happened in the": Fred Golar preliminary inquiry, September 5, 1984, Wendy direct examination.

207 "In my opinion": Fred Golar pre-sentence report, February 15, 1985.

208 "incestuous relationships": Fred Golar pre-sentence report, February 15, 1985.

Chapter Thirteen

212 "As far as I'm concerned": "Fifth Estate," CBC documentary, March 1986.

212 "Where the evidence of": Sentencing decision, August 3, 1984.

212 "I formed the opinion": Sentencing decision, August 3, 1984.

213 "After all it's just": *Toronto Star*, February 21, 1984.

214 "I'm a fellow inmate": prisoner to Claire Culhane, March 2, 1986.

215 "looking forward to your": Claire Culhane to Ron Taggart,
April 24, 1986.

215 "I am some worried": William Goler to Claire Culhane, undated,
1987.

219 "from which they will never": Sentencing decision, January 4,
1985.

220 "done with the full knowledge": Supreme Court of Nova Scotia,
Appeal Division, May 27, 1985.

221 "see any substantial difference": Sentencing decision, January 4,
1985.

221 "unreasonable and cannot be": Supreme Court of Nova Scotia,
Appeal Division, October 22, 1985.

222 "In view of that finding": Supreme Court of Nova Scotia, Appeal
Division, October 22, 1985.

222 "I rely on her evidence": Sentencing decision, January 4, 1985.

224 "As to the evidence of": Sentencing decision, January 4, 1985.

224 "no force was used by him": Supreme Court of Nova Scotia,
Appeal Division, September 12, 1985.

225 "spirit of the legislation": Director, Clemency and Pardons
Division, to Kentville County Court, April 28, 1993.

225 "dependable and a hard worker": Sentencing decision, January 4,
1985.

227 "There is no violence involved": Sentencing decision, January 4,
1985.

227 "It is significant": Sentencing decision, February 15, 1985.

Chapter Fifteen

255 "As reluctant as I am": Judge Moira Legere, June 26, 1997.

262 "tiny child, does not sit": Doctor's notes, Eastern Kings Memorial
Hospital, March 3, 1973.

262 "Baby was discharged": Doctor's notes, Eastern Kings Memorial
Hospital, March 3, 1973.

262 "Mother highly inadequate": Doctor's notes, Eastern Kings
Memorial Hospital, August 6 and 19, 1973.

262 "Extremely withdrawn and fearful": Doctor's notes, Eastern Kings
Memorial Hospital, September 23, 1973.

262 "Family situation is well known": Doctor's notes, Eastern Kings
Memorial Hospital, March 27, 1975.

265 "Same old story": Doctor's notes, Eastern Kings Memorial
Hospital, May 9, 1973.

Bibliography

BOOKS

A Natural History of Kings County. Wolfville, Nova Scotia: Blomidon
   Naturalists Society, 1992.

Armstrong, M.W. The Great Awakening in Nova Scotia, 1776–1809.
   Hartford, Connecticut: The American Society of Church, 1948.

Bell, D.G., and Muise, D.A., ed. The Newlight Baptist Journals of James
   Manning and James Innis. Hantsport, Nova Scotia: Lancelot Press, 1974.

Brebner, J.B. The Neutral Yankees of Nova Scotia. New York: Columbia
   University Press, 1937.

Buckler, Ernest. The Mountain and the Valley. Toronto: McClelland &
   Stewart, 1952.

Campbell, G.G. A History of Nova Scotia. Toronto: Ryerson, 1948.

Cann, Linda. A Bold Step Forward: The History of the Fundy Mental
   Health Centre, Wolfville, Nova Scotia. Wolfville, Nova Scotia: Fundy
   Mental Health Foundation, 1986.

Chute, A.C. The Religious Life of Acadia. Wolfville, Nova Scotia:
   Kentville Publishing for Acadia University, 1933.

Clarke, George Frederick. Expulsion of the Acadians. Fredericton, New
   Brunswick: Brunswick Press, 1955.

Collections of the Nova Scotia Historical Society. Halifax, Nova Scotia:
   Imperial Publishing Company, 1938.

Conrad, Margaret, ed. Intimate Relations: Family and Community in

Planter Nova Scotia 1759–1800. Fredericton, New Brunswick: Acadiensis Press, 1995.

——, ed. *Making Adjustments: Change and Continuity in Planter Nova Scotia 1759–1800.* Fredericton, New Brunswick: Acadiensis Press, 1991.

Davison, James Doyle. *Mud Creek: The Story of the Town of Wolfville, Nova Scotia.* Wolfville, Nova Scotia: Wolfville Historical Society, 1985.

Eagles, Douglas E. *The Churches and Cemeteries of Horton Township, Kings Co., Nova Scotia.* Sarnia, Ontario: the author, 1974.

Eaton, A.W.H. *The History of Kings County, Nova Scotia: 1604–1910.* Salem, Massachusetts: Salem Press, 1910.

Finkelhor, David. *Child Sexual Abuse.* New York: The Free Press, 1984.

Foster, Malcolm Cecil. *Annapolis Valley Saga.* Windsor, Nova Scotia: Lancelot Press, 1976.

Griffiths, Naomi E.S. *The Contexts of Acadian History 1686–1784.* Montreal: McGill-Queen's Press, 1992.

Haliburton, Thomas. *A General Description of Nova Scotia.* Halifax, Nova Scotia: Royal Acadian School, 1823.

Hergett, H. Douglas. *Visible Faith: The Wolfville Area Interchurch Council and the Interchurch Housing Society, 1970–1990.* Yarmouth, Nova Scotia: Stoneycroft Publishing, 1991.

Kings County Vignettes vol. 5–6. Kentville, Nova Scotia: Community History Committee, 1994.

MacKinnon, I.F. *Settlements and Churches in Nova Scotia 1749–1776.* Montreal: Walker Press, 1930.

Martell, J.S. *Pre-Loyalist Settlements around Minas Basin: 1755–1783.* Halifax, Nova Scotia: Dalhousie University, 1933.

Milner, W.C. *The Basin of Minas and Its Early Settlers.* Halifax, Nova Scotia: Province House, n.d.

Mosher, Edith. *White Rock: The Story of Gypsum in Hants County.* Hantsport, Nova Scotia: Lancelot Press, 1979.

Nieman, Alice Rogers [with Allen B. Robertson]. *Windham Hill Is Home: A Rogers Geneology.* Halifax, Nova Scotia: Halcraft Printers for the author, 1989.

Robertson, Allen B. *Tide & Timber: Hantsport, Nova Scotia 1795-1995.* Hantsport, Nova Scotia: Lancelot Press, 1996.

Ross, Sally, and Deveau, Alphonse. *The Acadians of Nova Scotia, Past and Present.* Halifax, Nova Scotia: Nimbus Publishing, 1992.

Wright, Esther Clark. *Blomidon Rose.* Toronto: Ryerson Press, 1957.

ARTICLES, UNPUBLISHED MANUSCRIPTS, THESES,
GOVERNMENT DOCUMENTS

A Ballad of South Mountain, produced by Rex Tasker and Shelagh MacKenzie, National Film Board of Canada, 1986.

Brinton, Ellen Starr. "The Rogerenes," *The New England Quarterly*, vol. 16 (March 1943): 3–19.

Civil Registration of Marriages: Kings County, 1864–1909, and Hants County, 1864-1916.

Civil Registration of Deaths: Kings County, 1864–1977.

County Court, Nova Scotia, Kings County, District Number Four, notes, transcripts, charges, pleadings.

Department of Attorney General, Nova Scotia, Correctional Services, pre-sentence reports, prosecutor's notes.

Duchemin, James William. "The Beauville Study, Evolution of Class Structure," The Acadia Institute, Acadia University Archives.

Federal Census of Canada: 1871, Nova Scotia: Kings County.

Federal Census of Canada: 1901, Nova Scotia: Kings County.

Fraser, Clarke F. "A Preliminary Survey of Allegedly Inbred and Degenerate Group of Families in the Vicinity of Wolfville, Nova Scotia," The Acadia Institute, Acadia University Archives.

Hillis, George Bernard. "Class and Culture in Development of a Rural Area," M.A. Thesis, Acadia University, 1960.

Hiltz, J.E., and Morse, N.H. "Acadia University Institute, 1955–61," Acadian University Institute, Wolfville, September 1961.

"Once More for Children," The Report of the Province-Wide Study of Psychiatric Mental Health and Related Services for Children and Adolescents, Nova Scotia, 1983.

Provincial Court of Nova Scotia, Kings County, preliminary inquiries.

Registry of Deeds: Kings County, Nova Scotia.

Robertson, Allen, "Atwell Family of Horton Township, Kings County, Nova Scotia," Public Archives of Nova Scotia.

——, "Bondage and Freedom: Apprentices, Servants and Slaves in Colonial Nova Scotia," Collections of the Royal Nova Scotia Historical Society, vol. 44 (1996): 57–69.

——, "Preliminary Sketch of the Welch Family of Kings County, Nova Scotia," (1982).

——, "Tenant Farmers, Black Labourers and Indentured Servants: Estate Management in Falmouth Township, Nova Scotia," presented at the Third Planter Studies Conference, Acadia University, October 1993.

——, "The Family of Rolen Rogers, A New England Planter in Kings County," *The Nova Scotia Historical Quarterly* 9, no. 2 (June 1979): 177–87.

———, "To Declare and Affirm: Quaker Contributions to Planter Nova Scotia" in *Making Adjustments: Change and Continuity in Planter Nova Scotia 1759–1800*. Fredericton, New Brunswick: Acadiensis Press, 1991: 129–39.

Soltan, Hubert C. "Hereditary Factors Influencing Deaf Mutism and Its Incidence in a Localized Community," The Acadia Institute, 1961, Acadia University Archives.

———, "Genetic Studies on an Isolated Population in Nova Scotia: A Preliminary Report on the Inheritance of Congenital Deafness," The Acadia Institute, January 1962, Acadia University Archives.

Supreme Court of Nova Scotia, Appeal Division, notes, decisions.

Supreme Court of Nova Scotia, Trial Division, notes, transcripts.

Tucker, Sara Jones. "An Ethnic History of Early Canada: An Outline," The Acadia Institute, 1961, Acadia University Archives.

Way, Hedley. "A Study of the Prevalence of Mental Retardation of a Selected Sample of Elementary School Children in Kings County," The Acadia Institute, 1960, Acadia University Archives.

Welsh, James E. "A Nova Scotia Family [Welch]," *The Fountain*, July–September 1996, p. 50.

White, Edith M. "The Lack Family," *Social Welfare*, vol. 12 (1923): 249–54.

ARCHIVAL COLLECTIONS

Acadia Institute papers, Acadia University Archives.

Baptist Collection, Acadia University Archives.

Chipman Collection, Public Archives of Nova Scotia.

Diary/Account Book of David H. Welch: formerly in possession of Morley Welch, Wolfville, Nova Scotia.

Randall House Museum, photo collection and papers relating to early life in Wolfville and Kings County.

MAGAZINES
Chatelaine
Homemaker's
New Maritimes
Nova Scotia Law Reports

NEWSPAPERS
Halifax *Chronicle Herald*
Halifax *Daily News*
Kentville *Advertiser*
Toronto *Star*
Toronto *Globe and Mail*
Wolfville *Acadian*

Acknowledgments

✦ SO MANY PEOPLE HELPED, SO MANY GAVE us their time, so many opened their lives and told us things that were difficult to express to family and friends, let alone to strangers. Most of all we are grateful to the children of the Clan. Not all wanted to talk to us, understandably, but the many who did spoke from the heart. Their stories were difficult to tell and difficult to hear. We thank all of you.

Dr. Allen Robertson's vast knowledge about the Rogers clan he himself is part of was invaluable. His insight, astonishing recall and detailed research on many aspects of Nova Scotia helped us tremendously. Without his information parts of this book would be much less than they are.

Pat Townsend at the Acadia Archives was also wonderful in tracking down documents and collections and she was free with her assistance and advice. She found many interesting and obscure sources for us that lent depth to the historical sections of the book. Heather Davidson of Randall House Museum kindly dug through her files for us and provided the cover photo. Sadly, Scott Milsom's *New Maritimes* magazine is no more but we thank him for allowing us to use the late Claire Culhane's correspondence.

In Kentville many people within the court system helped us gain access to records: Blanche Hendy, Ken Pineo, Susan Campbell Baltzer, Sandra Trefry, Lisa Taylor Farris and Verna Sampson. Many thanks. Also within the legal system Judge Don Hall, former prosecutor Jack Buntain and current prosecutor Darrel Carmichael were generous with their time. There were also many lawyers who gave us their impressions of the trials; Curt Palmer, Eric Sturk, Steve Mattson, Judge Bob Levy and Don Fraser. In Halifax Susan Potts, administrator of the Freedom of Information and Protection of Privacy Act, was also very helpful.

There were many within the church who offered us valuable information about South Mountain past and present including Henry Sharam, Harold Beaumont, David Long, Gary Manthorne and Freeman Fenerty.

Wendy Elliott, columnist with the *Advertiser*, shared a few cups of coffee with us and freely gave us the benefit of her experience and understanding of the Valley. She also allowed us access to local newspaper archives. Sarah Gray, also of the *Advertiser*, kept us of abreast of late-breaking developments. And we are grateful to Sherri Aikenhead of the Halifax *Daily News* for sending us documents in her possession.

An old friend from the Valley, Richard Collicutt, offered encouragement and provided many initial contacts.

We appreciate the books and reports loaned to us by Drs. Brian Garvey and Rhoderick Evans and also their perspectives about health care and sexual abuse as they relate to South Mountain.

There were several people within various police departments who spoke to us, often grudgingly, about this case, which is still a tender subject in some quarters. Sergeant Baxter Upshall was a key individual then and was to us in the past year. Many of the victims still remember him with fondness and gratitude. Similarly Dale Germaine was very helpful and her recall of events provided important detail to a complicated picture.

As with any non-fiction book, particularly one dealing with sensitive issues, there were many people who were sources of information but would prefer not to be identified. Thank you all. And a special thanks to Secret Squirrel.

Our children Claudia and Quinn suffered through the agonies of yet another book, all the while wondering if there wasn't a better way for their parents to make a living. Fiona, Pat and Peter listened willingly to our recitation of woes as our deadline drew near then passed. We thank you.

A grant from the Canada Council came when we needed it most. We are enormously grateful to the jury for believing in this story and our ability to tell it.

A very special thanks goes to Cynthia Good, publisher and vice-president of Penguin Books Canada. We have wanted to write this book since 1984 and Cynthia encouraged us and gave us the opportunity. We are also grateful to long-time supporter Brad Martin, Penguin president.

There are many others at Penguin who deal with our books at the very end when we are forgetful and grouchy. You drag the book to completion, often under terrific pressure and, I'm sorry to say, without sufficient back pats from us. Jem Bates—production master, Wendy Thomas—copy wizard, Molly Brass—cartographer extraordinaire, and Karen Cossar and Scott Sellers—publicity geniuses—a terrific team. Last, but defiantly not least, are all the representatives across the country who persuade book stores to put our latest on their shelves.

And, of course, top of the heap stands, sits or lies David Kilgour, an editor, a legend and a great friend who worked his magic despite a serious illness in the family and a leg badly broken after slipping on a manuscript in the shower.

Finally Donna. You gave us a unique insight into not only your life but the lives of all the Goler victims. We know that telling your story to us was often extremely difficult.